Adirondack Country

York State
BOOKS

Adirondack Country

✒ *William Chapman White*

Introduction by L. FRED AYVAZIAN, M.D.

Afterword by RUTH M. WHITE

Drawings by WALTER RICHARDS

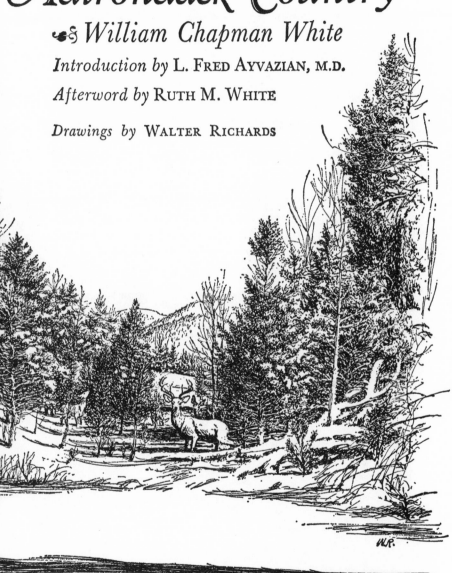

SYRACUSE UNIVERSITY PRESS

First paperback edition, 1985, published by Syracuse University Press.
Syracuse, New York 13244, by arrangement with Alfred A. Knopf, Inc., New York.
93 94 95 96 97 98 99   9 8 7 6 5 4

The paper used in this publication meets the minimum requirements of American National
Standard for Information Sciences—Permanence of Paper for Printed Library Materials,
ANSI Z39.48-1984. ∞™

This book is published with the assistance of a grant from the John Ben Snow Foundation.

Library of Congress Cataloging in Publication Data

White, William Chapman, 1903–1955.
  Adirondack country.

  Reprint. Originally published: New York : Knopf, 1967.
  Bibliography: p.
  Includes index.
  1. Adirondack Mountains (N.Y.)   I. Title.
F127.A2W5   1985   974.7′53   85-2592
ISBN 0-8156-0193-X (pbk.)

Manufactured in the United States of America

William Morris was a New York theatrical agent who came to the Adirondacks for his health. He regained it and lived for another thirty years.

In his gratitude he did much for the region, particularly for the village of Saranac Lake. Although he died more than thirty years ago he is still beloved in memory.

It is an Adirondack tradition that if a man needs help, whether when lost in the woods or for any other purpose, he need only shout. People of good will drop their work and come running.

William Morris lived by that tradition in many a civic and regional project. He was not alone. His story of finding new strength in the hills, then sharing it, is the story of many another man who has come at one time or other to the Adirondacks and remained. The Adirondack country is the better for them.

To William Morris, and to the many like him, this book is dedicated.

☙ Contents

◄§ *Introduction*

How can one introduce a work that speaks eloquently for itself, or update a book that has not in any important way aged? For in the thirteen years since its original publication, *Adirondack Country,* like the mountains themselves, has suffered no need for retouching, and its nature-clean prose has not staled with a fashion in writing. As Carl Carmer, the eminent historian of the Hudson Valley, noted in his *New York Times* review of 1954, William Chapman White's work "deserves to be ranked with the very best of American writing about nature—with Thoreau and Burroughs, with Joseph Wood Krutch and Edwin Way Teale. It is wise and simple and at the same time so crowded with the observations of a true poet that time and again the mind of the reader wanders off into contemplations of its own."

Here, then, is the enduring essence of this classic: it accompanies the reader through his own personal adventures. Those with the capacity to find beauty and fulfillment in the mountains and the lakes and the animal-tracked snows of this unspoiled haven will share this empathy time and again, and will treasure this book on some companionable shelf easily within reach. For one returns to *Adirondack Country* repeatedly—as one does to a favorite sanctuary—never tiring of its imagery or of the vicarious sensory gratifications.

All this is achieved in an economical and unadorned style which yet manages to evoke the fragrance of balsam and the taste of fresh sap as it runs from the maples. To enter these pages is to realize the calm of the wilderness, to feel underfoot the soft crush of pine needles, to sense against the skin the sub-zero touch of February. And in the book's final section, as the author guides one, month by month, through the entire Adirondack year, even the native of many seasons is startled with recognition and discovery, and he is awakened to the distinction between simple perception and true appreciation.

The author, Mr. Carmer further observes, "obviously believes that a writer of integrity has a duty toward his opinions." And indeed, Bill White had a second mission: to add his plea to those dedicated to protect and preserve "one of the wildest and best loved people's parks on earth." And this timeless mission remains undiminished at this critical interval in Adirondack history, when millions who own the forest preserve are being asked to decide the fate of their rich heritage. Bill White recognized the issues that the constitutional delegates will be weighing when they reassess Article XIV of the New York State Constitution—the so-called "Forever Wild" amendment—that since 1894 has guarded the Adirondack Wilderness. He appreciated the problems involved and knew them to be without easy answer, and he extrapolated them with such foresight that his writings of over a dozen years ago apply without change today. Indeed, these issues have grown and intensified as the advocates of ski runs and four-lane highways, the lumber profiteers, and the commercial interests behind high-powered motor boats and amphibious planes and helicopters and snowmobiles (already a thirty-million-dollar industry) have become the most strident voices in the wilderness, calling for repeal of Article XIV. Unless checked, such exploitation could for all time destroy this unparalleled North Country area of New York State, leaving only such written renderings as these of William Chapman White, and their counterparts on canvas, the paintings of Winslow Homer.

"As a man tramps the woods to the lake," wrote Bill White, "he knows he will find pines and lilies, blue heron and golden shiners, shadows on the rocks and the glint of light on the wavelets, just as they were in the summer of 1354, as they will be in 2054 and beyond. He can stand on a rock by the shore and be in a past he could not have known, in a future he will never see. He can be a part of time that was and time yet to come." Yet, recognizing the threats to this cherished retreat, he added, "So long as the forest preserve is in the constitution, safe against the vagaries and ambitions of local politicians, any change will have to be voted on by all the citizens of the state. It is their woods. It should remain so."

But *Adirondack Country* is not a polemic; its sole purpose is not to crusade for a natural phenomenon in danger of extinction. It is a document of many textures: historical, affectionate, humorous, humanistic. It involves its unique people in the context of its unique country with a diverting interplay of fact and anecdote. "Perhaps no one in recent years loved the Adirondacks more than he," wrote Paul F. Jamieson of William Chapman White, "certainly no one in our time has written better about them. His *Adirondack Country* is the most comprehensive book on the region since Donaldson's *History*."

L. FRED AYVAZIAN, M.D.
Medical Director
Will Rogers Hospital
Saranac Lake, New York

April 1967

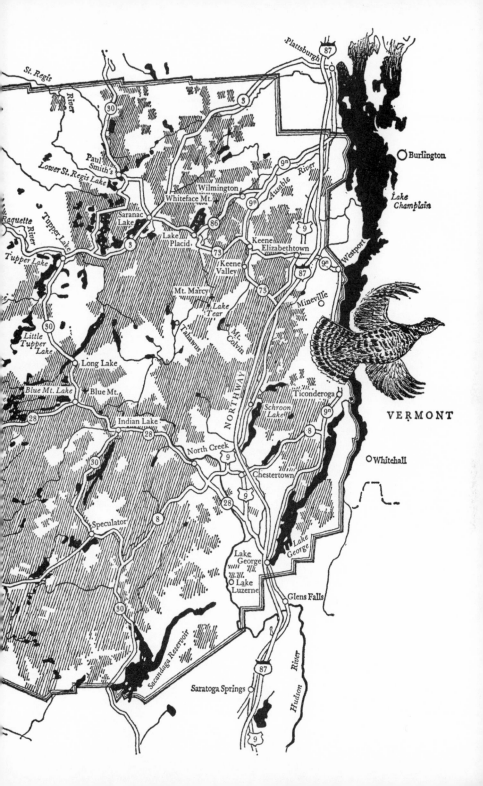

‹§ I ›ø
Adirondack
Land

To Begin With

It depends on what sort of day October 2, 1536, was. It may have been one of those high autumn days, so common in the northland, with infinite blue sky above, with clear air that brings distant horizons near. If so, the first white man ever to see the Adirondack Mountains of northern New York was the French explorer Jacques Cartier.

On that day, in the full flaming of autumn, he came to the Indian village that was to be the site of Montreal. The Indians led him up the high hills behind the mud flats. He saw the river below and the level woods that stretched away unbroken to the south. On the horizon, seventy miles off, were mountains, not one solid range but a broad sea of hills, intensely blue under the October sun. Cartier may have asked questions about them, for at some time he learned that to the south was "an unexplored region of lakes, of mountains, and delightful plains."

Three generations of Indians lived and died by the Saint Lawrence before another white man looked on those hills. In July, 1609, Samuel de Champlain, who had been in Canada for a year trying to revive the French settlement, explored that land to the south. With a small group of Europeans and Indians he moved slowly down the Sorel River to the mouth of a lake and saw "a number of beautiful islands filled with fine woods and prairies." He named the lake after himself. As he continued down its west side he noticed high mountains on the east and to the south.

He saw no people, although his guides told him that the country was inhabited by Indians. Champlain found that out for himself a few days later as his group came near the head of the lake. Here they met a band of Iroquois; when Iroquois and Canadian Indian met a fight always followed. In this fight Champlain used his arquebus loaded with four balls. His one shot instantly killed two Iroquois. That shot, in the shadow of the Adirondacks, changed American history. The Iroquois never forgot it. Forever after, they hated the French with the special hatred usually reserved for the Canadian Indians.

By odd coincidence, less than two months after Champlain first saw the Adirondacks at close range, another European, Henry Hudson, came near them. In September, 1609, he sailed up the Hudson to stop above Albany where the rolling country hints at the blue hills to the north.

After Champlain's passage, the waters of Lake Champlain and Lake George just below it, which set the eastern boundary of the Adirondack country, were red with blood for the next one hundred and seventy years. Blood of red men and white stained the pine duff on the forest floor by those lakes. A few Jesuit missionaries trod the Lake Champlain–Lake George route to constant torture from their Indian captors. Trappers from Montreal and from Fort Orange, later Albany, traveled the region. While a few men did settle on the fringes of the region in the middle of the eighteenth century, most of the history of that period is military history, of fighting between French and British and later British and American rebels for control of the lake route north and south.

Although the southern boundary of the Adirondack country is only two hundred miles north of Manhattan and less than fifty north of Albany, it was not explored in any detail until the

1830's. Explorers had gone into the Northwest Territory as far as the Pacific before anyone even climbed Mount Marcy, the highest of the Adirondack peaks. The sources of the Columbia River were known sixty years before the northernmost source of the Hudson was finally located. The mountains were not named "the Adirondacks" until 1837. Less than forty years later men were saying sadly that the Adirondack country, bristling with newly built summer hotels, was hunted out, timbered out, overrun with people, and ruined. When the country did develop, between 1840 and 1880, it developed fast.

Today almost every part has been trodden at one time or another by hikers, hunters, and visitors. Instead of being impassable no spot today is more than ten miles from a road of some sort. The Adirondack country can be crossed by car, north to south or east to west, in three hours. Approximately a rectangle, it contains five thousand square miles, which is roughly the size of Connecticut.

No one, with the exception of state surveyors and the Conservation Department pilots, knows all of it. Its geography is so varied that any over-all description gives no clear picture. It has four distinct quarters. The southeast quarter, with low hills and a few lovely lakes, its center at Lake George, is largely resort country. The roads that Revolutionary armies trod are lined today with motels, cabins, outdoor movies, and other tourist facilities. The northeast quarter contains the high peaks, all within a few square miles. Near Lake Champlain are Westport, Elizabethtown, Keeseville, and Ausable Forks, century-old small villages. This quarter has the unique Adirondack villages of Lake Placid and Saranac Lake, busy all year round.

The northwest quarter, least known and least settled, has little for tourists except in its southernmost part. It does have the busy woodworking village of Tupper Lake, many ponds, and the large Cranberry Lake. Its hills are not high, but it is the quarter of rivers which tumble or meander on their way to the Saint Lawrence. The southwest quarter has only low hills but it is the area of lakes, many interconnected, so that from the air the region in places seems more water than land. Here are the tourist centers at Blue Mountain Lake, Long Lake, and Old Forge, alive in summer, dormant or sporting new ski tows in winter.

Famous as the Adirondack country may be for its mountains and lakes, to many it is infamous for its climate. To those who know little of the area the idea of living through a winter in what used to be called "the Siberia of America" seems unthinkable. Certainly the winters are long and sometimes cold, but "they ain't the kind of winters our grandfathers used to have." Records on Adirondack weather over recent years prove just one thing, its unpredictability. The region has registered a high of 105 on a summer day, three degrees higher than anything ever experienced in New York City, and a low of 52 degrees below zero on one day in 1934 at one Adirondack village. The records also show that the annual mean temperature runs only ten degrees lower than in Manhattan. Adirondack cold is a dry cold and usually with little wind.

Fewer than one hundred thousand people live the year around in the Adirondack country; most of these are in its score of villages. In summer, visitors swell the population by the half million. The Adirondacks are within one day's easy drive for thirty million people on the Eastern seaboard. On a July Sunday afternoon it sometimes seems that all of them are on the Adirondack highways at once. The Adirondack country is the place where many city boys and girls first learned something about outdoor life at summer camps; the mountains and lakes are remembered fondly even if they have never been revisited. Some city people return every summer to a beloved spot, just as their fathers did for fifty years before them. Although they never see the region between September and July, they call it, in part, home. As if to echo the Psalmist's, "I will lift up mine eyes unto the hills," thousands of sick people have turned to the Adirondacks in the past century to find new health and strength.

Few people think of New York as a mining state or of the Adirondack region as mining country, yet it has iron mines, a garnet mine that has been worked for the past fifty years, and, just beyond the western edge of the area, talc and lead mines. Lumbering in the Adirondacks might seem to belong to the past, but each year thousands of feet are cut on private holdings and trucked to mills. New York no longer leads the nation in the production of lumber as it did in 1860, nor in the production of paper as it did in 1900, but some paper mills still use Adirondack wood.

Several themes run through Adirondack history. First is the continuous coming of people who hoped to make their fortunes. Over the years the descendants of settlers who came from New England, hoping for an easier life, have tried to make a living by farming the rocky soil. Others have sought fortunes in the abundant iron ore; until 1870 much of the iron used in the Eastern states came from Adirondack mines. Others have tried to get rich from the great supply of lumber once available. The timber industry goes back far into history; the earliest written record of exploration in the eighteenth century is that of a French timber cruiser searching for marine timbers.

The second theme is the happy one of discovery and ever widening use of the region as a vacation area. Sixty years ago it was in part the playground of the rich. An Adirondack hunting lodge was once as much a part of fashionable America as a villa at Newport. Today the Adirondacks are no longer "fashionable," but many more thousands enjoy them. That prime use provides the region's chief industry, summer and winter. It is the site of many a well-known hotel, pretentious camp, private preserve, and ski tow. For other thousands it is the ideal place to pitch a tent and spend a vacation at little cost, deep in the woods or close by the woods and lakes.

This points to the fundamental fact about the Adirondack country: The whole area has been a state park since 1892. Half of its five million acres is privately owned; the owners may do with their land as they like, with restrictions only on renting space for billboards and on outdoor fires. The other half is owned by the state as a forest preserve and is managed by the state's Department of Conservation. The state lands are not in one piece but in many parcels, from a few acres to many thousands; on a map they look like a flaming case of measles. Those who live or visit in the Adirondacks have 2,179,556 acres of state land where they may go as they wish, camp where they please; they have for their pleasure a huge estate which is owned by the people and subject to the fewest possible number of rules.

The other 902 state forests and 1186 state parks in the United States are smaller than the Adirondacks. No national park is as large. None has the unique development that is Adirondack history. Few have thriving villages right next to the state woods and a permanent population that lives the year around with the woods at the back door, setting a pattern of life unique in America. It is that inseparable connection between the Adirondack woods, open on all sides, and the Adirondack people that makes the area what it is.

That, and one other fact — perhaps the most important: The public ownership of the Adirondack Forest Preserve and the provision that it cannot "be leased, sold, or exchanged, nor shall the timber thereon be sold, removed, or destroyed," were written into the state constitution in 1894, along with the provision that "the Forest Preserve shall be forever kept as wild forest lands." From that sentence comes the handy phrase "forever wild," common in any discussion of Adirondack problems. It sums up the constitutional provision and means that not one tree can be cut or cleared from state land, that no sort of "managed forestry" is to be permitted. To many this seems a shameful waste of salable timber; to others, keeping the woods wild and as wilderness is what gives the Adirondacks their greatest appeal.

The constitutional provisions can be altered only by amendment voted on by all citizens of the state. They were put in the constitution to protect the woods against pliable legislators and pliant governors, from whom the Adirondack woods suffered many an injury before 1894.

That is the third theme of the Adirondack story — of saving the woods for generations to come and of the acute problems that have arisen in considering the future of those woods.

This book, therefore, is the story of the Adirondack woods, of the life in them, of the people who have walked them or dwelt by them, and the story of how those woods have been used.

Mountains Lakes Rivers

When the Adirondack State Park was set up in 1892, the official map used a blue line to mark the boundaries of the area. Thereafter, "inside the Blue Line" and "outside the Blue Line" became common Adirondack phrases. The line was redrawn in 1929 to include lands on the west shore of Lake Champlain and the area on both sides of Lake George.

The Blue Line marks the boundaries of the state park. Since only half the area enclosed is state-owned, it obviously does not mark the forest preserve. When first drawn it surrounded not only the main and scattered pieces of forest preserve but also the land (outside of village and city limits) which the state hoped some day to acquire in entirety so that the park would be solidly forest preserve. That hope has long been abandoned; private land and state land lie side by side. The Blue Line today is a historical relic, but it is also a most convenient phrase. New

York State owns other blocks of forest-preserve land outside the Adirondack area; the largest is in the Catskills. In his basic history of the Adirondacks, Alfred L. Donaldson limited himself to the area within the Blue Line. So does this book. Little that is Adirondack in spirit lies outside the Blue Line. The "North Country," a picturesque name, has come into use in the past fifty years. It was probably introduced by the novelist Irving Bachellor. The name refers, however, not merely to the land within the Blue Line but to all of northern New York above the Mohawk.

With many a jog and turn, the Blue Line surrounds a rough rectangle 120 miles on each side. Inside the Blue Line are all or part of ten of the state's sixty-two counties, about one eighth of the state's area. Included are all of Hamilton County, the least populous county in the state, most of Essex, half of Franklin, a large part of Saint Lawrence, Herkimer, and Warren, and small parts of Lewis, Fulton, Saratoga, Clinton, and Washington counties. The counties are divided into "townships," but that word is not common locally. These subdivisions are called "towns." The word in the Adirondacks for what is a town elsewhere in the world is "village." The result can be quite a pile-up of language, as in one legal phrase, "The Village of Saranac Lake in the Town of Harrietstown."

The Adirondack country is a varied land. Seen from the air, a series of high peaks at the center, most irregularly placed, run off almost to sea level on all sides. In forty miles the land drops from 5344 feet above sea level on Mount Marcy to 100 feet at the shores of Lake Champlain. Not all the region is mountain and lake. As the land slopes down from the higher altitudes in the northeast and the northwest, it levels off for a time into rolling country and broad plateaus.

To people who know the Alps or the Rockies the idea of calling the Adirondacks "mountains" may seem ridiculous; the city of Denver is higher than any Adirondack peak. They are not jagged brute rocks piercing the sky, with summits almost always cloud-wrapped. On clear days the round top of Marcy can be seen from thirty miles away. Almost all the Adirondack peaks have these rounded tops, worn by storm and time.

Of the hundreds of hills and mountains in the Adirondack country, some are famous, others little known, but each is as beloved in its own neighborhood as any famous peak. When one sees them from an airplane or while driving through, disorder seems their only order, yet five ranges do run from northeast to southwest. The ranges are nearly parallel, with axes about eight miles apart. Cross spurs and eccentric ridges sometimes connect the various ranges, making it almost impossible to shepherd them into neat order. The five ranges do rise successively higher, with the most northerly the highest.

While more than one hundred peaks are higher than thirty-five hundred feet above sea level, many seem only like giant bumps, for they take off from a plateau of fifteen hundred feet or more. The forty-six that are more than four thousand feet high represent the "high peaks." Almost all are crowded together in an area of fifty square miles, and topped by the summit of Marcy.

The many mountains have some things in common. Some have abrupt rocky slides, often rising out of lakes; these precipices may not be thousands of feet high, but even one five hundred feet high, rising sheer, is quite a sight. As a group the mountains have little topsoil on them. Trees grow, but little farming has ever been done on their flanks. Another feature is the number of lakes found close to the mountains. The belief that between two mountains there must be a valley is not always true in the Adirondacks; likely as not, a lake is there instead. Finally, the interconnections of the various ranges are such that a man can climb up and down many peaks, one after the other, without coming down to the twenty-five hundred foot level.

The lower hills, perhaps not impressive except en masse, are unknown to visitors and scarcely known to natives who do not live in their shadow. No one ever mentions Bearpen Peak, or Elephant, Puffer, Siamese, Ice Cave, or Devil's Ear mountains. They too are the Adirondacks. Many Adirondack peaks were named by unimaginative people, the first surveyors who went through the area in the eighteenth century. A few have been named for assorted worthies, some of whom never set foot in the region. At least a half dozen are still nameless.

The Adirondack people use their lakes, rivers, and woods, but, except for small boys on small peaks, they do not go in much for scaling the hills. No arrowheads or other relics have ever been found on mountaintops to show that the Indians climbed the peaks. Few pioneers did any mountain climbing; life was tough enough without that. Climbing as sport began after the announcement in 1837 that Marcy was the highest point in the state. Today it is the outsiders and the vacationists who do most of it. Thanks to the magnificent system of trails built by the Department of Conservation working with the Adirondack Mountain Club, climbing is more popular than ever today. Trails lead up most of the better-known peaks; along many of the paths are state-built lean-tos where hikers can spend the night. One favorite mountain hike is along the one hundred and thirty-five mile trail from Lake Placid to Northville.

The existence of a marked trail does not mean therefore that the way is easy going. Climbing can be arduous, particularly on the more than twenty peaks over four thousand feet that are still without trails. Those skilled enough to try unmarked ascents find exciting climbing on the many steep cliffs and precipices. The more daring, using regular Alpine equipment, try them each summer. In many places the rocks have been worn so smooth by slides that they offer few cracks for the *pitons,* the metal points which climbers use. In recent years winter climbing on snowshoes or skis has become popular.

Two ambitions have marked Adirondack climbing. The first was to climb every one of the forty-six peaks over four thousand feet. A second ambition, popular twenty years ago, was to start as early in the morning as a man could wake, and by going in marathon fashion see how many peaks, what total elevation, and what mileage could be made in one day. By starting at 12:01 A.M. on October 7, 1933, and keeping on the go until 11:52 P.M., H. L. Malcolm of Florida, a forty-nine year old member of the Adirondack Mountain Club, set the record for all time. On that day he started up Giant and Noonmark, then covered Little, Lower, and Upper Wolf Jaws, Armstrong, Gothics, Saddleback, Basin, Little and Big Haystack, Little Haystack for a second time, Marcy, Skylight, Colden, and Algonquin, then Mount Jo by the shelter of Heart Lake. That totaled 19,352 feet of ascent and it was only 11:06 P.M., fifty-four minutes until midnight. He climbed Mount Jo for a second time to set the record at total ascent of 20,067 feet, for a hiking distance of 40⅛ miles up and down eighteen peaks. There is no report on what Mr. Malcolm did the next day or, in fact, when he got on his feet again.

For those who cannot or do not like to climb, the automobile road up Whiteface, built in 1927 and fought vigorously by most conservation groups, offers a chance to see what the world looks like from an Adirondack peak. On a clear autumn day, the hills at Montreal are on the distant blue horizon.

Men have tried to describe mountain scenery and mountain views. It is futile. Older Adirondack literature is full of such descriptions. Some are flowery:

> A horizon of peaks, each peak a gigantic violet or a vision of rose purple. Ah, there is Hurricane Peak, seeming as soft and peaceful as an infant's eye!

Or:

> Onward, onward! Past colonnades of lordly trunks, where the sunlight lay in speckles; past vistas opening denser shades and looking as if only the rabbit or partridge had ever left

a print: past hemlocks dripping with moss as old towers with ivy; delicate white birches glittering as if of silver: past delicious dingles where diamond runlets danced!

One description does stand out in Adirondack literature for its simplicity and beauty. It is that of the view from Marcy, as John Cheney, one of the first of the Adirondack guides, saw it in 1837:

> It makes a man feel what it is to have all creation under his feet. There are woods there which it would take a lifetime to hunt over, mountains that seem shouldering each other to boost the one whereon you stand up and away, heaven knows where. Thousands of little lakes among them so light and clean. Old Champlain, though fifty miles away, glistens below you like a strip of white birch when slicked up by the moon on a frosty night and the Green Mountains of Vermont beyond it fade and fade away until they disappear as gradually as a cold scent when the dew rises.

A view from any Adirondack height, even a lowly hill, or the view from an airplane over the region shows the second distinctive feature of the landscape, the tremendous number of lakes. The Adirondack country has more than 1345 of them named, and more nameless. In the southwest quarter many are connected by inlets and outlets so that canoe trips of one hundred miles can be made at will, broken only by a few portages of less than two miles each; at these carries today the Conservation Department thoughtfully provides wheeled boat carriers. In the famous Fulton Chain, known to many children who have been summer campers and made a long canoe trip on these waters as the high spot of the summer, eight lakes are strung together like beads on a necklace.

Elsewhere the lakes are beside mountains, between mountains, and, in some cases, on mountains. The highest lake is Tear-of-the-Clouds, forty-four hundred feet high on the side of

Marcy and the most northerly source of the Hudson. Many lakes are dotted with small tree-clad islands. Lake George has more than two hundred. Lower Saranac Lake has fifty. Some few lakes have white sandy beaches but most are tree-girt to the waterline.

While the Blue Line runs along the west shore of Lake Champlain at three places, for a total of more than a hundred miles, Lake Champlain is not usually counted as an Adirondack lake. If it were it would far surpass all of them in size and depth, for it is 107 miles long and 12 miles wide at its widest, with a depth of four hundred feet at one place. The largest lake fully within the Blue Line is Lake George, thirty miles long. Next in order are Long Lake and Indian Lake.

The Adirondack lakes are of various sorts. Most have clear, clean water, spring-fed, with rocky shores. Because of their springs the water of the lakes is cold in summer although it may sometimes be 70 degrees in a few places. In winter the lakes are covered with ice, sometimes twenty inches deep. At the bottom their winter temperature is a uniform 38 degrees. Some of the smaller lakes are surrounded by swamp and mud and almost impossible to get at on foot in summer. Some were scooped out by glaciers and are small, neat ponds. Many, such as Long Lake, are the result of glacial widening of river beds, and are often long with narrow places; at some points Long Lake, in length 15 miles, is only 100 yards wide. Some of the lakes, like Cranberry and Flower in Saranac Lake village, are the result of damming a river or have been increased in size by such damming.

The naming of the lakes was as haphazard and unimaginative as the naming of the mountains. In a few cases Indian names were abandoned, as when some settler gave the name of Long Lake to what the Indians had called "Linden Sea." Early surveyors and settlers tagged on the first and handiest name which came to mind, with the result that there were many duplications, since so many of the lakes look round, muddy, or clear, and have duck and otter on them. The word "pond" is used quite as often as "lake." No one knows at what point of decreasing size a lake becomes a pond.

In the long list of Adirondack lakes, in addition to the well-known ones, are Single Shanty, Terror, Goose, Wild Goose, Whortleberry, Hog, Artist, Squaw, Poor, Big Slim, Little Slim, and three just plain Slim ponds. To confound visitors and natives, there are two Antediluvian Ponds, twenty Long Ponds, ten East Ponds, sixteen Clear Ponds, twenty Mud Ponds, six Mud Lakes, seven Spring Ponds, ten Round Ponds, ten Duck Ponds, twelve Otter Ponds, along with one Pepper Box Pond and one Queer Lake.

Even the most casual nomenclature ran dry by some lake shores. The best the early settlers could do for the lakes of the Fulton Chain was to name them First to Eighth Lake. Naming a chain of three lakes Upper, Middle, and Lower, as with the Saranacs, with the village of Saranac Lake not on any one of them, is sometimes confusing. Lake Placid is a lovely lake but the village of Lake Placid is on Mirror Lake.

When private owners bought Adirondack land in the early days the presence of lakes on the land was of little concern unless they were connected with rivers and could serve as highways for timber floating. In later years lake shore property became the most desirable and remains so today. As much as twenty thousand dollars was paid for just five acres of lake shore on fashionable Upper Saint Regis in the 1880's. Frontage on Lake Placid and Lake George has brought equally high prices. Today lake-shore property is eagerly sought, tightly held. Little is available, at least on the more accessible lakes. The question of the ownership of the lakes is complex. If so much as a foot of state forest land touches the lake, it belongs to the state and anyone may enjoy access and fishing. Private ownership stops at the low watermark unless the deed to the land specifically mentions riparian rights. If private land completely surrounds the lake, it is considered part of the estate. The great majority of Adirondack lakes belong to the state and are open to all.

Seen casually, one Adirondack lake may look like another. No one man knows them all. To pick out the loveliest is impossible. From the highway on a hill at the south, Lake George is a magnificent sight. Blue Mountain Lake, with its many islands, the deep forest by its shore, its clear blue water reflecting the mountains nearby, is often called the loveliest lake of the lot — an opinion immediately challenged and hooted at by anyone who knows some other lake a little better.

Any Adirondack native will defend the right to call eminences of fifty-four hundred feet "mountains," no matter what Colorado or Alpine people may say. He is not quite so sure that some of the streams deserve the name of "river." He has no doubt about the Hudson, rising on the side of Marcy, or the Raquette, the Saranac, the Oswegatchie, the Grass, and the Black, but he is uncertain about the other twenty and more "rivers," the Cold, the Bog, the Chazy, the Jordan, the Opalescent, the Chub, or the Cedar. At their mouths some of these streams may approach the common idea of river. Elsewhere they may often be only small mountain streams easily jumped by a deer and even by a hunter in pursuit.

These rivers carry much less water than in years past. Many a nineteenth-century story of adventure in the Adirondacks tells of pleasant boat trips down a number of the rivers; few people would try them today. The larger rivers and many of the small ones carried log runs in the spring that would be impossible on most of them today. That steadily decreasing volume of water has been noted in all Adirondack history. It is not a recent phenomenon but appeared after the first heavy lumbering.

The Hudson is the best known of the Adirondack rivers. Its northernmost source is more than four thousand feet up on

Marcy, in Lake Tear-of-the-Clouds. By the time the Hudson reaches Manhattan it is a sophisticated river, changing its mood many times. Below Luzerne, where the Adirondack foothills yield to rolling fields, it is broad and placid. At Glens Falls, out of the Adirondacks, it is a turbulent rapids and waterfall. At Troy it is dirty and bedraggled, showing no sign of the clear, green, mountain-water source whence it came. At Haverstraw it is a broad inland sea.

But up in the Adirondacks where it comes tumbling out of the mountains it is a gracious little stream that races over rounded pebbles and is all of ten feet wide. The children of the miners who work at Tahawus below Marcy cross back and forth, first carefully rolling up their jeans. The river that flows so majestically by the Palisades and on to its deep sea gorge may be the weary river of the poet at its mouth but it is fresh and young up where it begins. There it reflects the tamarack and the pine, and bears the little toy boats of the children. Far south it will reflect skyscrapers and carry ocean liners. It is still the same water, some of it, that has come gushing out of the ancient rocks of the Adirondacks.

More than any other stream, the Hudson helped to move the forest riches out to the mills. It carried lumber drives as early as 1813. During the mid-century most of the rivers of the Adirondacks were declared "public highways" for log driving by the state and log drivers were at work along them. Where rivers ran into lakes and then out into river again, the logs had to be floated through the lake in large booms to prevent them from piling up on shores. Today, shortage of water and scarcity of trained labor has made log driving forever a part of the Adirondack past. Trucks move the logs out of the woods faster, if less picturesquely.

The Adirondacks mark the water divide of the state. The same meadow on the shoulder of Marcy sends water south to the Hudson and north in the Ausable, which flows on to Lake

Champlain and so to the Saint Lawrence. This favorite two-pronged river of fishermen drops some four thousand feet in covering its fifty miles. Near its mouth it runs through a chasm advertised sixty years ago as one of the natural wonders of the world, a miniature Grand Canyon, one hundred and fifty feet high at some places and two miles long. Set conveniently by one of the main Adirondack highways, Ausable Chasm is still a tourist objective of the region.

Because the passage of most Adirondack rivers is frequently marked by falls, they have always interested private power companies. They have made various attempts to secure permission to use these Adirondack rivers, but conservationists and others who believe the region should be kept "forever wild" have successfully blocked most of them.

Each river has its own charms, although little traffic of any sort, even canoes, passes over them these days. The Raquette is the most meandering of rivers, coming out of Blue Mountain Lake through Long Lake. It flows one hundred and seventy-two miles on to the Saint Lawrence to cover a distance of perhaps eighty miles as the crow flies, and was once a favorite route for trips into the wilderness. Flowing south from Fulton chain, the Moose connects more than one hundred bodies of water, large and small. The Black River, flowing west out of the woods, has provided power and riches for the area around Watertown. The Oswegatchie, the Saint Regis, and the Schroon were all lumbermen's rivers in their day. Trout fishermen wade them in spring. The rest of the year the only sound along them is the rush of their own water, south to the Atlantic, north to the Saint Lawrence.

These are the mountains, lakes, and rivers of the region. Nowhere else in America but in this Adirondack country are so many varied features crammed into such a small space, with such a variety of jagged cliff, rolling hill, lonesome pond, upland meadow, placid farm-land stream, roaring mountain brook, fog-wrapped peak, and quiet lake, and all within a few miles of one another.

The Woods

Mountains and lakes may mark the region as unusual, but it is the woods, above all, that make the Adirondacks. They bring the summer people. They provide all or part of the income of many a family. For years it was believed that odors and chemicals borne on the air from the woods played an important part in curing the sick who came and found their health restored.

The Adirondack woods are not isolated patches but the ever present covering of the country. Now and then roads may run through a stretch of open country, but woods soon come to their sides, even on main roads. Driving them in spring and summer is like driving through green canyons. In many places, particularly on state land where the underbrush is never cleared, the woods seem impenetrable even a few feet back from the road. Woods frame almost every lake shore.

No fossil remains have been found to show what made up the woods in prehistoric times. The first white people to come saw the heaviness and density of the woods and marked the two great trees that towered over all others, the giant white pine and the huge spruce. Maples, birches, and other hardwood were not timbered for many years for they could not be floated out to sawmills as could the softwood evergreens.

The woods that the first white man saw are largely gone. Early settlers cleared some; intensive commercial lumbering during the nineteenth century and the great fires of 1903 and 1908 took more of them. By 1920 less than 4 per cent of the forest preserve was virgin timber. It is less today, because of the destructive windstorm of November 25, 1950, which took down some particularly fine stands of big trees. Thick as the woods may be in various parts today, they are mostly second growth, some a century old, and in many places third and fourth growth.

With a variation in altitude from almost sea level at Lake Champlain to more than five thousand feet on the high peaks, the Adirondack country has distinct forest zones. Red oak will grow in the lowland but not in the higher country. Balsam, tamarack, ash, cedar, and yellow birch are trees of the fifteen-hundred- to two thousand-foot plateau. Spruce and hemlock grow on the sides of the higher peaks where hardwoods disappear and the evergreens are eventually stunted. The top of Marcy is slightly above timber line; just below it dwarf balsams grow short and crooked but with as many as a hundred rings of growth, while on the peak is a genuine arctic or Alpine zone and many a rare plant. The southern border of the park also marks a dividing line in plant life. Poison ivy does not grow above it. The dogwood, so common to the south, dies in the Adirondack winter. The white pine does not do well below that line.

The trees in the Adirondack woods seem beyond count, but they have been counted on a rough guess basis. Sixty years ago a state forester once estimated that a typical Adirondack acre had on it one hundred and ninety-three trees over eight inches in diameter — which would put the total number of trees in the forest preserve somewhere above a quarter of a billion. He gave up trying to count the scrub growth of alder, ash, shad-bush, and a pesky hindrance in the woods, a whippy growth of a species of viburnum, called locally by the fitting name of "witchhobble."

Two characteristics mark the Adirondack woods. The first is the change in tree species. Because of changes in climate or for some other reason, in recent years the second growth has been largely hardwood, thus reducing the percentage of evergreens.

After fires, inferior trees such as cherry and poplar are the first to come back and thrive; birches appear next, and beech, but other trees may not show for decades. While most of the woods seem thick and heavily grown, a large part, perhaps as much as 50 per cent, has little or no timber worth the name. Except on the highest peaks, little is completely bare, but much is scrub growth, with many a meadow or sparsely grown clearing appearing in unexpected places. On the other hand, where lumbermen have worked on their own land or on leased land, fair second growth may show from "mamma trees," maples and spruces which have reseeded themselves. Parts of the Adirondacks that were cleared land seventy years ago are heavily and usefully wooded today. Such reforested farm land explains why, in places where trees are sixty years old and more, a hiker comes on a lone gnarly apple tree or even a lilac bush in the middle of deep woods. Nearby, usually, are the traces of the foundations of a house. But many parts of the woods still show in slash and vanished water resources where the nineteenth-century lumberman passed.

The second distinctive characteristic is the rich growth on the floor of the woods. Where no fires have destroyed the deposits of centuries, spring flowers are abundant, beginning with trilliums and lady-slippers. Ground pine is plentiful, along with partridge berry. Two years after storm damage or lumbering make a clearing, the open place can be a thick raspberry bramble. Ferns and mosses are abundant: forty-three of the sixty varieties of ferns found in the state grow in the Adirondacks.

Of the various trees of the Adirondack woods, the tall white pine stands out as best loved and most prized. The Adirondack woods have other native pines, red and pitch, but the white pines tower over them as the symbol of the North Woods. Once they stood seven feet through at the base. Eight oxen had to be hitched up to budge one thirteen-foot log. A few old white pines still stand, either saved miraculously on state land or overlooked by the lumbermen.

The white pine often appears in early Adirondack history. In the eighteenth century the French cut suitable trees for ships' masts and spars. They were floated to Montreal, then shipped to France for the royal navy. The British were just as busy in the woods around Ticonderoga. Both the British and French ships that fought at Trafalgar may have had masts, spars, and planking from the Adirondack hills. The British continued to buy Adirondack pine after the Revolution and had it shipped to them down the Hudson, then by sailing vessel from New York. White-pine boards, sledded from the Lake George region to Albany and down the Hudson, were shipped to Europe and even to the West Indies in the early part of the nineteenth century. Adirondack white pine helped to build many an early American building in the seaboard cities.

By 1800 much of the great white pine along the shores of Lake Champlain was gone. By 1850 the great trees had been cut throughout the region and the amount of white pine taken from the woods fell off sharply. The thousands of feet timbered later came from second- and even third-growth trees. Today the state sets out millions of white-pine seedlings in an effort to return to the Adirondack country the glory of the dignified tree. Most of the seeds are hand picked from parent trees, but some are collected from hoards gathered by squirrels. Wherever the white pine grows in the woods, it is liable to a blight called Blister Rust. This mysterious spore disease, which must have wild currants or gooseberries nearby for part of its development, is kept under control. Many a taxpayer's dollar goes to pay for men to tramp the woods and weed out the wild currant.

As the white pine disappeared the red spruce took its place as the backbone of the woods and of the lumber industry. Some were giants in the early days. The average tree was eighty feet tall, with a diameter of eighteen inches and a ring count of one hundred and seventy-five to two hundred years. Sixty years ago one spruce was found near Lake Meacham in the northwest quarter that was forty-one inches in diameter and overtowered the forest. It was later cut down for pulpwood.

The spruce entered into politics as the white pine never did. It was the decision of a pliant governor to let all spruce above a certain size on the forest preserve be lumbered that dramatized the need to protect the preserve, and brought about the "forever wild" amendment to the state constitution in 1894.

The most serious attack on the spruce was not the work of men who wanted it for lumber; it was, in fact, lightly timbered until the thick pine was gone, and even then only the largest trees were taken. The real attack came after 1867, when it was found that the long spruce fibers were by far the best raw material for paper pulp. Thereafter, the take was merciless and heavy.

In addition to fine lumber and the best of pulp, the Adirondack spruce had unique uses. The first log in the shaft, the "butt log," was eagerly sought from the virgin spruce of the southern Adirondacks by piano manufacturers for making the best piano sounding boards. The principal roots of the trees were sawed into the knees for boats. Some ancient uses for the spruce have been forgotten. Spruce gum gatherers went after its resin in winter to provide an early predecessor to chewing gum. No one these days collects the young branches of the spruce and boils them with sugar to make "spruce beer." Today, with spruce of decent size scarce on private lands the paper makers will take other trees, but they prefer spruce and pay a higher price for it; if a few parent trees and some of intermediate growth are left, it can be cut again in twenty-five years.

The spruces darken as winter comes and give the hills their black-green look, but two other trees add their coloring at other times. Maples fire the hills in autumn, birches set them shining in summer or winter. Of the four kinds of maples the hard maple is the most useful for lumber and sugar. The favorite birch of the woods is the canoe or paper birch, a dead-white chalky tree with black streaks on its bark which punctuates the lake shores and stands on the distant hills like an exclamation mark. The yellow birch, no less striking with its golden bark, is the favorite tree for furniture making and other commerical uses.

These and another score of species, from ash to ironwood and balsam, make up the Adirondack woods as they stretch from Poke O'Moonshine in the northeast to the shores of West Canada Creek in the southwest. They clothe the valleys, hills, and swamps. They give the land its color, through the greens of spring, the fire reds of autumn, and the blackness of winter.

Fish Fauna Fowl

Written Adirondack history begins with a fish story. In Champlain's journal of his travels down Lake Champlain he wrote:

> There is also a great abundance of fish, of many varieties: among others, one called by the savages of the country Cha-ousarou, which varies in length, the longest being as some people told me, eight to ten feet long. I saw some five feet long which were as large as my thigh. The extremity of its snout is like that of a swine. The fish makes war upon all others in the lakes and rivers. It also possesses remarkable dexterity, as these people informed me, which is exhibited in the following manner: when it wants to capture birds it swims among the rushes or reeds, where it puts its snout out of water and keeps perfectly still: so that when the birds come and light on its snout, supposing it to be only the stump of a tree, it adroitly closes it, which it had kept ajar and pulls the birds by the feet down under the water.

While little like the Chaousarou has been seen in any Adirondack waters since, some of today's anglers might welcome it. It would be a change from the pesky yellow perch and the sunfish.

The woods and their riches helped attract the first settlers to the Adirondack country. The animals in those woods and the fish in the lakes and streams were just as responsible for bringing many a later visitor who became a settler.

All Adirondack history affirms the truth of the warning about waste that conservationists have preached for a century. No area in America has had a more miserable story of ruthless squandering of natural resources, and of carelessness based on the supposition that the stock of fish and game, as well as trees, was infinite. The chief species of fish that the first settlers found were the speckled or brook trout and the monster lake trout. Some of the rivers were full of salmon. The fish were there for the taking, without much concern over bait or tackle. If a fish was not big enough, another larger one would be along imminently.

The salmon went fast, as did the trout. Today only a few of the fourteen hundred Adirondack lakes have any native speckled trout in them; only a few remote brooks have any native "wild" brook trout. "Fished out" has been a common cry almost from the first years of Adirondack history; it was said first, and rightly, of Saratoga Lake, where the last trout were gone by 1820. After 1840, the stories of fine fishing spread in an era when people were beginning to pay more and more attention to life outdoors. They came to see for themselves. Trout fishing became fashionable in the middle of the nineteenth century, and the city fellers joined the Adirondack people along the banks of the streams. As trout fishing was practiced the goal was big fish, but that quickly degenerated to fish of any size. One sportsman wrote in 1873 that on an Adirondack trip he had caught one hundred and thirty-five trout for a total weight of nine pounds, and added, "I return from the woods refreshed in spirit." He must have had quite a spirit, that he could be refreshed by a mess of fish of average weight less than an ounce, but he was not the only one.

Species of fish inimical to trout were put into Adirondack waters by design or accident. Horatio Seymour, governor in 1862, ordered bass put into Adirondack waters as the trout fishing waned. After his order was carried out it waned faster. Another introduction into Adirondack waters in the early part of this century took care of any trout the greedy fishermen, the pickerel, and the bass might have overlooked. This was the yellow perch, probably first brought by fishermen as live bait "minnows" and either dumped into the waters or allowed to escape into them. The perch is not particular about his diet; he eats baby bass as well as trout. This most nondiscriminating appetite with fins will turn out eight thousand eggs at a clip, sometimes twice a year. The trout spawns two hundred to two thousand eggs annually, the bass about as many. With four times as many perch as trout to grab available food, the trout just haven't a chance, particularly since the baby perch would as lief grab the baby trout.

Today fishing in the Adirondacks depends on stocking by the state. Brook trout, lake trout, and pike perch are put out by the millions, along with non-native brown trout and rainbows. Baby fish are dropped from airplanes in the remote lakes. Salmon have been put in a few lakes where the water runs deep and cold. A few bass are planted each year, although raising bass artificially is not easy.

The Conservation Department has been making a study in recent years of ways to clean out the undesirable fish by using rotenone, a poison. When everything finny is dead, the lake is then planted with trout. The scheme is too costly to try on any of the larger lakes or those with large inlets or outlets. As for the smaller ones, where the cost may be a thousand dollars or more, every brook and inlet has to be covered for if just one pair of perch should be missed, a fishy chorus of eight thousand new perch will scoff at the sprayers a few months later.

No better example of the problem of perch exists than in Cranberry Lake in the northwest quarter, a fine body of water which had the unusual distinction, and not so long ago, of providing good brook trout fishing. State stocking added to the native supply. In spite of all precautions, however, perch appeared a few years ago. The Conservation Department now has some interesting statistics. By questioning fishermen about the hours spent and the number of trout caught, they were able to produce a bale of statistics headed, "Hours Necessary to Catch a Trout in Cranberry Lake." The figures are sad: 3.3 hours in 1948; 3.2 in 1949; 5.6 in 1950; and 7.8 in 1951.

Those figures just about sum up all Adirondack fishing. Fish can be had and sometimes big ones, but as an old guide said, "Fishing for fish used to be fun. Now it's work." Many fishermen have their favorite "Lost Pond" or "Mystery Brook" where they have better than average luck, but it is hard to get the day's limit and harder to get any impressive fish. But if the fun is the fishing and not the fish, things are not too bad on Adirondack waters. The Ausable, the Saranac, and other rivers and brooks always provide a fine day outdoors.

Even though a law dated 1705 forbade killing deer except between August 1 to January 1, the early settlers had fresh meat in plenty. A 1793 geography said, "In the northern and unsettled parts of the State are a plenty of moose, deer, bears, some beavers, martens, and most other inhabitants of the forest." It did not take men long to wreck this zoological paradise. Beavers were so heavily trapped, even before the first permanent settlements, that by 1843 a naturalist could report: "I doubt if there is more than one pair left and they in Franklin county." Elk, never common, were probably gone by 1840. One last panther survived until after the 1870's. The last moose was shot sometime in the 1860's, except for one stray shot near Lake Placid a few years ago and another seen in the 1930's.

The deer of the Adirondacks, the common whitetail deer, have not only survived the heavy hunting of the past one hundred and fifty years but are presumed today to be more plentiful than ever. Their ability to find out of the way places and sufficient food has carried them through the periods of the heaviest slaughter. Continual lumbering, producing new clearings, probably helped them survive. Their number did drop heavily between 1870 and 1910 but increasingly stiff game laws gave them a break and they have multiplied. In each hunting season today about six thousand deer are killed legally. Some few thousand go to illegal hunters or are does killed by hunters in error and left in the woods to rot. On the basis of these figures the deer population has been estimated at about fifty thousand, but only one hunter in eighty ever gets one. Deer may be common and roam where they will, but in his ordinary rounds on the roads and in the woods an Adirondack native is lucky to see two or three a year.

The moose are gone and the panthers, but many of the animals reported in the early days remain. The wildcat, a little larger than a house cat, can wreck the quiet of an Adirondack lake with his night scream. Foxes bark at the edge of the deep woods. Whether or not wolves live in the remoter northern parts of the Adirondacks is a moot point; something like a wolf is seen now and then and a bounty is occasionally paid on one. The Conservation Department is inclined to call them wild dogs, but the local faith that they are wolves remains unshaken. Coyotes have turned up in recent years. Skunks, raccoons, and porcupines are common. The woodchuck sits on his haunches and looks over the quiet Adirondack country of a summer evening. Rabbits, ordinary and snowshoe, make winter hunting a rewarding sport. The red squirrel runs the woods along with the chipmunk. The strange "birdcall" sometimes heard in the woods is only the squeally protest of an angered chipmunk.

The largest Adirondack animal is the common American black bear. They weigh as much as three hundred pounds, although one taken in 1938 was a giant of five hundred and thirty-two pounds. While one hundred are killed each year, many Adirondack people have never seen a live one. The babies are born in January and weigh only a few ounces. When the bears are with cubs they may be mean if discovered. The rest of the year they run away fast. One Adirondack researcher has discovered that a bear runs twenty miles an hour, a fact established by chasing one down a highway at that speed in an automobile. He concluded, "The bear's speed looks faster because it's all rear end."

No better mink skins come on the American market than from Adirondack wild minks. They are scarce, but now and then they can be seen swimming in the back bay of a remote lake. On the slopes of the hills are the rare marten, fisher, and ermine. The first two often range over a hundred miles of woods for food. The story of the Adirondack beaver is one of the triumphs of conservation. A few pairs were settled in secluded places in 1902. They did so well that by 1940 an open season on beaver was permitted. In open seasons now most trappers get the limit of four to eight skins. Furriers find no finer beaver anywhere. Beaver dams stand on many a stream today, partly a nuisance for the trees they may kill by flooding, partly prized for the trout that thrive in the deepened water behind them.

With its many rocky ledges and sunbaked meadows, the Adirondack country might seem a perfect place for snakes, particularly rattlers of the kind found downstate. Early settlers in the southeast quarter did tell of them. Some have since been found on Tongue Mountain on the west shore of Lake George and in the hills along the southwest shore of Lake Champlain. They seem to be nowhere else. Any other snakes that show up in spring are harmless.

The chief nuisance of the Adirondacks is not reptile or beast but the notorious black fly, shaped like a housefly and one tenth the size. He is the flying form of the nymph which is hatched in running water and is a favorite food for trout. Black flies appear about the middle of May and stay around for six weeks. They are at their worst on a hot windless afternoon. Some people are immune to their bite; others get welts that swell to the size of a baseball. The punkies, mosquitoes, and "no-see-ums" that follow are a nuisance that stay around all summer, but the black fly, enemy of any warm-blooded animal, is supreme in its persistence and viciousness. In recent years attempts to spray whole areas with DDT from planes have been fairly successful; those flies left in the unsprayed areas, however, seem more numerous and hungrier.

The first person to report in detail on the birds of the Adirondacks was Theodore Roosevelt. As a boy, in the 1870's he spent three summers at Paul Smith's, one of the most popular and fashionable resorts. During that time he prepared a catalog of ninety-seven separate species. Later observers have listed about one hundred and fifty. No birds exist which are not found elsewhere in the state, but a few seem very much a part of the Adirondacks — loons and gulls on the lakes, jays and woodpeckers, and evening grosbeaks at a feeding station on a winter morning. The Adirondack region is no main flyway, but ducks and wild geese sometimes rest in mid-passage on Adirondack lakes and a few black ducks or sheldrakes may stay around the larger lakes most of the summer. Now and then, in most remote parts, an eagle may climb the sky.

The game birds of the Adirondacks, the woodcock, called locally the timberdoodle, the partridge, and the pheasant exist in no great number. Once there were more, but the insatiable appetite of the nineteenth-century American for game cost the

Adirondacks much. Today hunters go out after the game birds on a frosty October morning. Sometimes they put a few up. At times they may even bag a few. But the game-bird hunter, like the hunter after deer and the fisherman along the trout stream, all know what the old guide meant when he was asked about hunting and fishing in the Adirondacks. He had one stock answer. It was, "It's okey if you take along a Bible and read Hebrews 11:1." A curious visitor looked up the verse. It sums up most of today's hunting and fishing: "Now faith is the substance of things hoped for, the evidence of things not seen."

And People

"There's two kinds of Adirondack natives," Les Hathaway, an old guide, used to say. "There's them as was born here and stayed on. Then there's them as come here when they're growed up; it takes them usually about six months to become natives."

It is not easy to name one person and say, "There is the typical Adirondack man." He could be Harold McCasland, a fine small-town cabinetmaker, cigar always in his mouth, fishing flies in his ancient hatband. He is in demand for the sort of work he does, yet, no matter how imploringly housewives call, he has never been known to let an urgent job interfere with a good day for fishing or a fine autumn day for hunting.

He might be Fred Ransom, a farm-to-farm salesman on the back roads by day after his farm chores are done, a man as tough as any of the ancient rocks around, proud of his fine potato crop, sure with his rifle, able to do any of a hundred jobs, from peeling poplar logs, farrowing hogs, cooking flapjacks, or guiding hunters, to keeping school-board minutes. He might be Jerry LaBarge, grandson of a French-Canadian lumberjack, who swings his big truck into the woods in deepest winter and highballs the log cut out. His massive arms hold his truck and its ten-ton load down slopes where a mistake means an upset and probably a dead driver.

He might be Ed Smith, who made his millions in cottonseed oil and built a winterized camp back in the woods. There he lives the year around, entertaining his guests in summer, rarely seeing anyone in winter except when he comes out to buy supplies in town. It might be Joe Herder, a Lake George boy, who runs his tourist cabins on Highway 9 in the summer and heads for an almost identical set of cabins in Florida in winter. "More and more Adirondack people go to Florida in the winter," Joe says. "Florida's only Tupper Lake on Saturday night." Or it might be Dr. Edgar Mayer, a New York tuberculosis specialist who recovered his own health in the Adirondacks and now returns on every possible vacation to a camp deep in the woods or whenever he can help with medical problems in the area.

One thing these men have in common. They all know the woods of the Adirondack country and they love them.

The Adirondack native-born are tough people, slow to make friends, slower to lose them. For them, life in the outdoors is part of a long tradition. The weather and its variety, the wildlife in the woods and waters, the change of seasons, are as much a part of their daily lives as the meals they eat and the place they rest at night. The Adirondacks are not the wilderness today that they once were, yet the love of the woods remains. By sharing that and life in them, the nonnative newcomer quickly becomes an Adirondack "native," even though he may have grown up on big-city sidewalks or in the capitals of a dozen European countries and probably did not know a white pine from a white birch until he was a grown man. Not one of the newcomers has made much of an impression on the Adirondack people and their ways — whether he came as health seeker, vacationer, or camper and settled down for good, or stayed six months in the north and six months elsewhere. It is the men of the Adirondacks and their ways that have made their impression on the newcomers.

The Adirondack native-born are a mountain people, but the "hillbilly" types found in other mountain regions are rare. Few families have stayed beyond the flow of whatever civilization was passing by and remained unchanged or become ingrown over the years. The Adirondack area was settled late; except on the fringes, few settlements are more than a century old. State ownership of large blocks of land, forever undeveloped, was a barrier to isolated and inaccessible settlements. The development of road building, with a few main roads and fewer side roads leading to dead ends, kept the settlers on open lines of communication.

Finally, through almost all this history these native people have had contact with outsiders. The continuous flow of summer people, providing jobs, opportunities, and endless jokes, has had a profound influence on the region. For a hundred years backwoods farmers have been guides for wealthy tourists, caretakers or workmen on wealthy camps, or hosts and servants for vacationers. They may have envied these outsiders their wealth and learned much from them but they were never menial. When outsiders failed to recognize that in the woods the Adirondack men were at least their equals there was trouble. Adirondack independence bowed to no one. Twenty years ago a city lady hired one Adirondack native to help in her garden. She found him setting a border of whitewashed stones around the plot one morning and said, "I don't believe they're in good taste, Aden." He tipped his hat and said, "In my good taste they are." He walked off and has not been back since.

Those natives whose roots go back farthest into Adirondack history are, for the most part, descendants of Vermonters who came after the Revolution. Settlers from a few other New England states joined them. The old names of the Adirondacks show the New England origin — Moody, Fairbanks, Porter,

Locke, Miller, Hunt, and similar ones, still in the majority to-day. Few of the immigrants who came to America after 1880 settled in the Adirondacks, except for some Polish miners at Mineville. The only other European emigrants were the Irish who entered Canada after 1800 and came over the border.

The early Adirondack people did not strike everyone as exemplary individuals devoted to the love of nature and high thinking. A Pennsylvania clergyman who spent a few months in Saranac Lake in 1877 wrote of the Adirondack character: *

He could not migrate to better regions because of excessive poverty of purse and poverty of spirit. Shorn of manly pluck and ambition he was content to be a mere dawdler. Too dull, slow and stupid to learn anything for his improvement, he was also too obstinate to have any greatness thrust upon him. He had cunning and courage enough to club deer to death in the water or slaughter them in their yards when the deep crusted snow prevented their escape. He trapped a little and too often sold the pelts for whiskey and tobacco instead of procuring food for his hungry wife and child. Brag, bluster, drunken brawl, and bloody fight, licentious revel and dance, rape, incest, and bastardy were about the only pastimes and enjoyments of which he was capable.

The writer did not publish that until he had left the Adirondacks behind. He never returned. He never dared.

In the middle of the nineteenth century French-Canadian lumbermen and lumberjacks came into the region and later brought their families. There are many French-Canadian descendants among the Adirondack people in the northern part of the region. Some changed their names. Saboran became both Swinyer and Sweeney, le Mieux became Betters. Some spellings were simplified, to produce Patnode, Duso, Passino, and Mulflur, even as Saint Jean Baptiste was changed to Sabattis. Some families still speak French, particularly in Tupper Lake, where

* Reverend John P. Lundy, quoted on p. 168.

the lumber industry is still alive and where a Saturday night, when the lumberjacks are in from the camps, can have a fresh backwoods spirit all its own, with much of the roistering in straight French. Here the Gagniers, Levasseurs, Frechettes, and Lemesieurs take pride in their French names and customs. For years the French in the Adirondack country stayed apart, their language and religion both formidable barriers. Only in the past fifty years, as the influence of parents disappeared, have the French Canadians mixed with the New England descendants to produce strains that today are homogeneous and resist any analysis.

Among the Adirondack people today must be counted the great number who are Adirondack residents for three or four months each year, as they may have been for the past half century. Because of their affection for the region and their help to it they deserve to be counted. They come to their camps, large and small, or live in one of the villages. Among them are some few of great wealth; on a summer's day Saranac Lake and Lake Placid may have in their vicinity almost as many millionaires to the square mile of woods as Southampton, Long Island, and Newport. They are the best hope of the charitable benefit and a delight to the shopkeepers. One automobile dealer still remembers the lady who dropped in by chance and bought five convertibles at once and secured them for the dealer by telephoning her close friend, the president of the automobile company. These people may take little part in Adirondack life but their contribution to the economic welfare of the region is enormous.

The Adirondack native-born, with so much of Vermont in them, can be just as smart with their dollars as their neighbors across Lake Champlain. They vote a solid Republican ticket in the national elections. It was not always that way. A century ago a town meeting in Franklin County voted twenty Democrats to one Whig. Pliny Miller, first settler and village boss, rose to declare at once that there must have been some mistake. A second ballot was taken. That one came out twenty-one Democrats to none and Pliny sat down, contented.

Like Vermonters, the Adirondack people stick close to the localities where they live. If a man could not make a go where he was he saw no point in moving to another part of the region. He moved out of the mountains entirely. Today people who live by the Saranacs rarely know or visit the Lake Pleasant country to the south, just as the people of Lake George know little of Lake Bonaparte far out on the west. Visitors to the area who come to a different place each summer are likely to know more about Adirondack geography as a whole than most natives.

In many ways, however, the Adirondack people differ widely from Vermonters. Their long and close contact with outsiders has continuously added new blood, set new patterns, and hindered the creation of any one set type. Another Adirondack quality, often overlooked, is a real binationalism. Much of the Adirondack country is only a short drive from the Canadian border. Adirondack people will drive to Montreal for concert, theater, shopping or church. Many Adirondack families have Canadian relatives, English as well as French, and visit back and forth.

The Adirondack people have produced no writers, no painters, no sculptors. Outsiders have done the painting, the writing and even the pottery making. The native people have produced wood carvings and other craft work. One poem, author unknown, has come out of the Adirondacks and was once quoted in many a vaudeville skit on many a stage far from the hills. It is the epic "Allen's Bear Fight up in Keene," with the immortal stanzas:

> The bear with threatening aspect stood,
> To prove her title to the wood.
> This Allen saw with darkening frown,
> He reached and pulled a young tree down,

Then on his guard, with cautious care,
He watched the movements of the bear.

Against the rock with giant strength,
He held her out at his arm's length,
"Oh, God," he cried in deep despair,
"If you don't help me, don't help the bear."

The Adirondack country has many hunting and fishing stories, but too often they turn out to be only the hunting and fishing stories of all America, adapted to the Adirondacks. There are folklore tales for those with patience to dig them out. Once there was a wealth of anecdotage about lumber camps and lumberjacks; Paul Bunyan got his start, so the stories go, in an Adirondack lumber camp. There are many old guide stories, but as the old guides go they are being slowly forgotten.

As in Vermont, vivid phrases often color Adirondack speech. Not all are necessarily indigenous. Out in the woods men will say, "The deer are working in the balsam," meaning "feeding," or comment, "The snow is craunchy." They speak of an "outlaw," one who gets game illegally, "having a lick out," meaning that he has baited some spot with salt to attract deer. They will talk about having to hunt "in the swale," using an old English word for lowland.

A trapper will speak of catching "mushrats" and will tell how he "skins out a raccoon." The deer in late summer are "in fresh meat." In the deep winter they "yard up" in the swamps. An old guide will tell of days when he did "a heck of fishing." His phrase to describe an absolute ignoramus of a city visitor is: "He didn't know two." One old guide, boasting of his skill in mountain climbing, said, "There ain't a mountain been weaned I ain't been atop of." "You want I should do this?" one woodsman asked. "I'll do it all to once," he agreed. One of the commonest phrases is "over to" rather than "over at" — "He lives over to Lake Clear." A native will speak of "going to the village to do a little trading" when he means "shopping." A list of similar phrases could be much longer. It would close with the statement that "parsley" is often "pussley" and that when a wife in a village starts running around with another's husband people will say, "Well, she's traveling!"

As of today, people have few occupations to choose from in the Adirondacks. Like other rural regions it is losing its young people to better jobs and better opportunities in the cities. They go regretfully, with one foot always in the woods, hoping that somehow jobs will open back home and that someday they can return. Those who farm do not have it easy. The growing season is short. The choice of crops is limited largely to hay, oats, and potatoes. Field corn will grow for silage but will not mature its ears. The fields are rocky and in most places none too fertile. The commonest Adirondack farm picture is that of the elderly couple trying to keep a farm going with all the children off to Utica or Schenectady; when the old couple dies, no one wants the farm. Brush soon reclaims it.

Some few farmers have done very well. Some have discovered that the soil on the plateau north of Saranac Lake is superb for seed potatoes. They grow large crops that plant the fields of Long Island and bring more per bushel than table potatoes. Others have found that truck farming, even with the short growing season, is profitable. Adirondack spinach, lettuce, and cauliflower move down to Manhattan markets — that is, the part of the crop that the deer do not get. A few do well with dairy farming for local sale, even when the cows must be stabled from October until May.

The village businessmen live by the seasons. If the summer tourist trade is good, then the bleak months when no new customer comes into the stores, when no strange face ever shows on the village streets, will be bearable. The people who run the tourist facilities also live in famine and plenty. Some of these facilities are owned by "outside" people who may even manage similar quarters in Florida in winter. They furnish summer employment to local people and are welcome. The new popularity of winter sports has lengthened the season for these businesses, but the Adirondack axiom is still valid — "If you don't make it in four months you don't eat for eight."

In the Adirondack tradition hunting and fishing are still the popular sports. There are few Adirondack homes without rifles and fewer without fishing tackle. At one time the Adirondack people felt that the deer in the woods and the fish in the stream were theirs, given for the getting by a wise Creator; man-made game laws were of no importance. The story of the battle of the Conservation Department to teach people otherwise, to point out that deer and fish, wisely used, can be capital for the region, is a long but in general a happy one. Game is still killed out of season and a doe may be dragged out of the woods at night to be cut up quickly and put in the freezer — hoping a warden won't call and ask to look in it. "Lamb without horns" or "Adirondack goat" turns up at Sunday dinner in back country homes now and then, but the penalty, when infraction is discovered, is steep. A few "outlaws" try to get away with all they can; sometimes some of the most respected people in a community are among them. Once they used to be applauded for their courage. Today, if they are known, they are liable to be scoffed at — which is, in a way, another victory for the Conservation Department.

For those who live by the Adirondack woods, the woods are very real. There are few people who are not in them at some time during the year, if only for a picnic. The tradition of the woods as an inseparable part of everyday life lives on. That explains many things in the Adirondacks. It explains why the story of some big fish caught spreads around town in no time. It explains why, in time of forest fire, the one great fear in the Adirondacks, the rangers can command any passer-by to stop and fight the fire for small recompense and why men will give up their own work for days at a time to stand by and get that fire out. It explains why Gus Masur, a village barber, takes pride in knowing a place where arbutus grows which no one else has found, and why Maurice Chagnot, a hairdresser with a European background, brings yesterday's catch of bass or trout down to his beauty salon and shows it proudly to his customers. It explains a man's eagerness to help plow out his neighbor's driveway, and why a hundred men will stop their work and answer the rangers' call for help in searching the woods for a lost person.

In the Adirondack country the woods, miles of them, are the people's. For some they are a living. For others they are recreation. For all they are a way of life; that may not lead to riches for most of them, but they would not have it otherwise.

W.R.

❧ II ❧

Adirondack
Beginnings

Eons Ago

ONE thing about Adirondack geology is certain: The mountains that a tourist sees today as he drives through the region look much the same as they would have appeared to some prehistoric tourist ten thousand years ago.

Another fact is also certain: Adirondack geology is as complex a subject as any nongeologist may ever happen on. The basic problems of origin and age are still unsettled. Because they feel that present information is insufficient, some leading geologists are still unwilling to compile a geological map of the region. This is no place for an amateur to come along with breezy generalizations and conclusions. He is wiser, if less courageous, if he ducks behind "It seems . . ."

It seems that the Adirondack mountains are the oldest mountains in the United States and among the oldest in the world. Today's peaks are only stubs of the mountains that were. Part of them are of the bedrock on which the continent is built. In the beginning they rose from a nameless sea. The snows of winter covered them, the winds of ages wore them down, younger rock pushed up from below into them, glacier ice changed their lines, remolded their valleys, and covered them even to the highest peak. Never again, once the high peaks of the Adirondacks rose to the sun, was the sea to cover them.

Geologically, it seems, the central core of the Adirondack country is a region apart from the rest of New York State and even from the rest of the United States. It is part of Canadian geology, of the Laurentian system, and not of the White Mountains or the Alleghenies. The finding of small crystals of a uranium ore in a quarry west of the Adirondacks dates the rock there as one billion one hundred million years old; the Adirondack rock next to it is even older.

The oldest Adirondack rocks are the "Grenville rocks," so named from a Canadian town where they were first discovered fifty years ago. They form a thick section and have been much altered over the centuries, with sedimentary strata piled on strata. To say that only raises more questions; geologists still puzzle over the source of these rocks and the nature of the floor on which the sediment was laid down. In any case, they were formed in the days when there was little life on the planet. What did exist was small and insignificant — seaweed or minute sea animals, as the flecks of graphite in the Grenville rocks show. No coal or oil, formed in later ages, have ever been found anywhere in the region. To the regret of small boys from summer camps who search the woods with Geiger counters, there seems to be no uranium, in spite of slight findings west of the hills.

The geological story of the regions where the hills abut on Lake Champlain and where they run down to the flatlands on the south and west is a different one. These lands were younger lands, and were buried at times under prehistoric seas. Here marine shells and even the bones of walruses have been uncovered.

Following the shadowy Grenville period igneous intrusive activity occurred on a large scale. Other rocks were pushed up into the Grenville strata. That molten rock, cooled these millions of years into a tough coarse-grained bluish or gray stone, is "anorthosite." It is the heavy and enduring rock that makes up most of the high peaks. Other rock material appeared later. Pressures, heat and erosion have tangled the various rocks of different ages into a complex structure.

Somewhere in geological time great quantities of iron were deposited in many places in the Adirondack area. Some of it was a nuisance for early surveyors, working with compass needles that went awry. Hikers today often find that deposits will deflect their compasses. Various forms of iron are found, including magnetite, hematite, and bog ore. In some places it is closely bound with titanium — the curse of the early iron workers. The magnetite deposits at Mineville, southeast of Elizabethtown, near Lake Champlain, are second only to Swedish deposits in the richness of their ore.

The Adirondacks hold other valuable minerals. A garnet mine west of Lake George has been one of the chief sources of material for garnet paper, gems, and abrasives in America for fifty years. Very slight traces of gold have been found at North Creek. Adirondack history has many stories of men who came on lead or silver deposits in the deep woods and returned home to tell of them and get out their shovels, only to find that they could never again locate the spot where they thought they saw a clue to fortune at their feet.

Eons of erosion changed the lofty peaks. Ice age glaciers worked more changes. Scattered boulders on the mountaintops or signs of ice-borne rock scratched on the summits show that the mountains were once solidly ice-covered. The glaciers rounded the peaks into their present shapes, especially the solitary peaks like Whiteface. With the glaciers came rock and rubble that dammed up the valleys as the ice receded and formed some Adirondack lakes. Others were gouged out. In each ice age the location of lakes changed. Some Adirondack farms today have a sand bed, often of the purest white sand, in the middle of a field, marking the site of a lake of another age.

The rocks that the glaciers deposited on the land make the farmer's job of rock-picking his stony acres in the spring a tough one. The rocks that push up with each new spring may be millions of years old; they may have come from the bottoms of uncharted seas, or from a distant northland and were brought south by the ice, or were worn from the top of some considerably diminished mountain peak. These mysterious and even romantic sources do not make the annual rock-picking job any more attractive.

Solid as it may look, the Adirondack country has an occasional small earthquake, which is promptly and slanderously blamed on the more unstable states of Vermont and New Hampshire. In fact, the earth's crust is still rebounding in fits and starts from the overloading of glacial ice centuries ago.

The long and complicated history of geological changes is more than a geologist's delight. It has meaning for the casual visitor. The geological history has given to the Adirondack mountains their friendly "old shoe" look. They may lack the fresh stark drama of the mountains of the Far West but they do look as if they had been there since the world began. What's more, they practically have been.

Or so it seems.

Red Men

The Adirondack land lay under deep forest for ages before men ever entered. The known history of men in the area starts less than four hundred years ago. It is easier to read in the rocks the story of the first million years of the Adirondack country than to piece together the traces of the men of the seventeenth century who paddled the lakes, tramped the woods, and saw the rounded peaks against the sky.

Two stories sum up the history of the Indians in the Adiron-

dacks. The first is Champlain's own account of a chance encounter with the Iroquois:

> Now we travelled only by night and rested by day . . .
> At nightfall we embarked in our canoes to continue our jour-
> ney and as we advanced very softly and noiselessly, we encoun-
> tered a war party of Iroquois, about 10 o'clock at night at a
> point west of a cape which juts into the lake on the west
> side . . .
> Our savages killed several of them and took ten or twelve
> prisoners. The rest carried off the wounded. Fifteen or sixteen
> of ours were wounded by arrows . . .
> Having feasted, danced, and sung, we returned three hours
> afterward, with the prisoners.

The second story happened a few years ago on an island in
Lower Saranac Lake where a camper expected as his guest a
lady who was interested in Indian lore. He made a few preparations for her visit, to be sure she would find it interesting, then
went to town to meet her. In his absence a couple of boys from
the mainland happened on the island. They saw one arrowhead
right by the landing place, practically hanging from a tree, another two feet away, and a whole pile within ten feet. They
raced back home for shovels, told their friends, and collected
quite a crowd. When camper and guest arrived they found much
of the island well dug up, with people busily sifting the soil.
Since this was a state island, the camper had to explain to a
ranger the damage done. Later he had to explain to many people and particularly one lady how Idaho and Nebraska arrowheads turned up on an Adirondack island.

The facts about the Indians in the Adirondacks are few: two
hostile groups who claimed the area visited it from time to time
for hunting and trapping. Whenever they met by chance in the
area bloodshed followed. They had their trodden trails and
their favorite camping places but no permanent settlement has

ever been found. Except for a few relics found by chance, they left no traces.

The chief claimants to the region were the Mohawks, one of the Five Nations in central New York, called Iroquois by the French, and the Algonquins, a Canadian tribe. In spite of these conflicting claims neither group ever settled in the region; lands more easily tilled were available on the flatlands on all sides for the relatively small number of Indians in the country. The total number as estimated by careful historians always surprises anyone raised on the legend that the wilderness was knee-deep in red men. Some Indian authorities have estimated that the entire strength of the Iroquois at the end of the seventeenth century, over their thousands of square miles, was only a few thousand, because of losses by disease and war; the number of Algonquins was even smaller. The raiding parties that hacked away at each other in later years, often at the white man's instigation or under his leadership, rarely had more than forty or fifty Indians in them. The largest Indian force on record was one of eighteen hundred led by Montcalm from Canada to Ticonderoga in 1758.

The Adirondacks did provide one place for the Indians where meat for the winter could always be had. Just as important, the Adirondacks served as a hidden way south or north for any groups going out on some hellish mission. The easy way was through Lake George and Lake Champlain, either by canoe in summer or on snowshoes in winter, but any who passed by could be seen from the shores.

In addition to the Lake Champlain–Lake George route, other known trails ran north and south. One came up the Hudson, cut through the pass between the high peaks now known as Indian Pass, and came to the flatland below Lake Placid. Trails then led east to Lake Champlain or north over the hills to the Saint Lawrence. Another trail went up the Fulton Lakes, through the Raquette River, then, after a short carry at a spot still called Indian Carry, west of Saranac Lake, came onto the Saranac lakes and overland to Lake Champlain. Except for the remembrance in "Indian" Pass and "Indian" Carry and small relics found at the latter place, no trace of the trails remains today.

Those trails were used often in the seventeenth and eighteenth centuries. With reason could Frenchmen dwelling in the Saint Lawrence settlements write, "There is no ink black enough to describe the fury of the Iroquois." In 1690 some of the white men around Albany joined the Indians for an attack on the French settlements and followed the Lake Champlain route. "These Christians and Indians," the contemporary report says, "took the scalps of four women folks." In the winter of 1690 a group of Canadian Indians marched twenty-two days "along the course of West Canada Creek," in the southwest quarter, to descend on Schenectady. They killed most of the people and burned everything but two houses. Eighty-five years later a British governor, fleeing the rebels, left Johnstown and cut north into the Adirondack woods for Canada, following some trail that he and his Indian friends knew well.

Jesuit missionary work among the Indians brought men into the Adirondack region or along its fringes. Between 1657 and 1769 twenty-four missionaries worked with the Mohawks. One Jesuit, Father Jogues, who had been with the Canadian Indians, even made the same journey south that Champlain made, but he lay in the bottom of a canoe, tied with ropes, a prisoner of the Iroquois taken on one of their forays in August, 1642, his hair torn out by handfuls, his hands gnawed by human teeth. The priest and his captors went south for eight days; he may have been the first European to see Lake George. The following year he managed to escape and return to France, but in 1646 he was again in Canada. This time, in the hope of making peace, he traveled south to visit the Mohawks. As he passed Lake George he named it Lake Saint Sacrament. His efforts for peace seemed hopeful, but the Mohawk hatred broke out again. A few months later they murdered the patient and gentle Jesuit father with an ax.

Another less dedicated and far more profitable mission, the search for beaver, sent French, Dutch, and Indians into the Adirondack region. A hundred years ago a wheelwright at Malone, working an old Adirondack log, found a bullet in it which, as the ring count showed, had been fired two hundred years before, or about 1650. In another Adirondack log worked a little later a foreign dagger was found that had been there for several centuries. The demand for beaver for hats for the gentry of Europe was huge. Skins went to Europe by the thousand in the seventeenth century; in 1635, 14,891 skins were shipped from Albany. Trapping was a particularly attractive occupation for the Indians. Beaver skins could be changed at Montreal or Albany, at a standard rate. In 1689 three beavers bought one gun; four beavers, eight pounds of powder or forty pounds of lead. Six beavers bought six quarts of rum, probably the most desirable commodity of all. Of the men who may have perished by their trap lines from hostile arrows or Adirondack cold we know nothing.

A few places where Indians were accustomed to camp in passing have been found — three in Essex County, one in Franklin, eight in Hamilton, and seven in Warren. Legends were handed down of a great battle once fought on the plains of Elba and of a tribe of friendly Indians that lived back of Elizabethtown at the end of the eighteenth century.

The Adirondacks have their share of the legend of the leaping Indian. "At this point," guides on Lower Saranac Lake used to say, "an Indian maid jumped from that rock, sixty feet above the water, and killed herself, all because her father would not let her marry the brave she had chosen." As in many places in America, similar stories are told about other rocks on other Adirondack lakes.

With an Indian history that is so scanty, the study of authentic Indian names in the Adirondack country is understandably complex. Not even the names which the various Indian groups called the region are known for sure. A map printed in 1756 has written across the Adirondack area the words "Couchsachrage, an Indian Beaver Hunting Country." It adds, "This country, by reason of mountains, swamps, and drowned lands is impassable and uninhabited." "Couchsachrage," or something like it (for the map makers were never very accurate in writing down Indian names), may have been the Iroquois name for the area, but no one is quite sure what it meant. It has been translated aptly as "the Place of Winter," "the Dismal Wilderness," "the Beaver Hunting Grounds," and "the Place of the Beaver Dams." Certainly the Algonquins never used an Iroquois word for the region; what they did call it is unknown.

Until the state geologist Ebenezer Emmons came along in 1837, the Adirondack country had various names. The first map, in 1570, labels all of northern New York "Avocal," a word the meaning of which has been lost over the centuries. An English map of 1761 calls it "Deer Hunting Country" and lets it go at that. A number of maps down to 1800 call it "Irocoisia," which was applied as well at times to the land east of Lake Champlain. Early writers used various names, not all of which later historians can explain. These included "the Mountains of Saint Marthe," "the Mohegan Mountains," "the Black Mountains," "Clinton's Mountains," after De Witt Clinton, "MacComb's Mountains," after a large land speculator, "Corlear's Mountains," after a private citizen of Schenectady who tried to make peace between French and Iroquois and drowned in Lake Champlain en route to a truce talk, and "the Aganushioni Range," after the Iroquois word for long house. Some of the early French spoke of the mountains or at least one range as "the Peru Mountains," sure it contained the same sort of fabulous mineral wealth. A town near Lake Champlain and a bay on the lake still bear that name, which the Adirondack people pronounce "P'ru."

Downstate the area was called "the Great Northern Wilderness," a name that hung on until late in the nineteenth century. In the 1880's people continued to speak of "going for a vacation to the Wilderness," even when that meant two weeks at an up-to-date hotel, with croquet grounds, tea dances, and compulsory dressing for dinner.

While working on the first geological survey of the region in 1837, Professor Emmons named the main range "the Adirondacks." He explained his choice:

> The cluster of mountains in the neighborhood of the Upper Hudson and Ausable Rivers I proposed to call the Adirondack group, a name by which a well-known tribe of Indians who once hunted here may be commemorated. It appears from historical records that the Adirondacks or Algonquins in early times held all the country north of the Mohawk, west of Champlain, south of Lower Canada, and east of the St. Lawrence, as their beaver hunting grounds but were finally expelled by superior force of the Agoneseah, of Five Nations. Whether this is literally true or not, it is well known that the Adirondacks resided in and occupied a northern section of the State and undoubtedly used a portion at least of the territory thus counted as their beaver hunting grounds. The name is not as smooth as the Aganushioni, which has also been proposed as a name for this group, but the above historical fact has induced me to propose the one given above.

In a short time the name Emmons applied was used to describe the whole area. His history might not have been accurate, for "Adirondack" was not the name of one tribe but an insult applied to various groups, but it is fitting that the region did receive an authentic Indian name. When the Algonquins held the area is uncertain, as is the date when the Iroquois chased them out and called them trespassers. In the long run the trespassers have won; in nomenclature they possess the land forever.

The word "Adirondacks" is authentic Iroquois and is supposed to have been a term of derision spat at the Algonquins, who were forced to live on tree buds and bark during severe winters But this usually accepted meaning was disputed a few years ago by J. B. Hewitt of the Smithsonian Institution. He believed that "Adirondacks" was derived from the language of a tribe of Indians who lived on the lower Saint Lawrence in the early 1500's and meant "They of the Great Rocks." It passed eventually into the Iroquois language and was mistranslated as "They Who Eat Trees." To confound things to the ultimate, the word first appeared in print as "Aderondacke," in a vocabulary of Mohawk words compiled in 1634 by Dutch traders who were in contact with the Indians. There the word means "Frenchmen and Englishmen."

If the various Indians had names for the mountains they passed and the lakes they paddled, few are known for sure today, or, at least, few have survived. Among the few that would seem to be authentic are "Oswegatchie," meaning "Black Water"; "Kayederosseras," for the mountains southwest of Lake George, and meaning "Lake Country"; "Ticonderoga," usually translated as "Where the Waters Meet," although eleven other meanings are given; "Poke O'Moonshine," a mountain in the northeast section, meaning unknown; "Schroon" River or Lake, meaning "Large Lake," from the Indian word "Scaniadaroon." Too often, imaginative people have taken words the derivation of which may be clouded and have given them fanciful meanings. The word "Saranac" is the best example. Guidebooks translate "Saranac" as an Indian word meaning "the Lake of Fallen Stars." This is fitting, pretty, and bogus. In truth, a search for the derivation and meaning of the word crosses many trails and produces no absolute answer.

The name was first applied to the river that comes out of the

Adirondacks at Plattsburgh and empties into Lake Champlain. The earliest record of any name for it is in a report of a French timber surveyor made in 1745, preserved in the Public Archives of Canada, in which the writer speaks of the "Senaranac Rivière." That was probably the way he thought he heard his Indian guides pronounce their name for it. A map dated 1752 calls it "the Sataranac River." By 1775, to judge from a map of that year, French settlers by the river had renamed it the Saint Amant, which may be what the Indian name sounded like to them. The first Englishman to report on the area, in 1767, calls it the "Salasanac River." And a map printed in London in 1775 gives it two names, the French "Saint Armand," and the Indian "Salasanac." Some writers have assumed that "Saranac" is a misprinting of "Saint Amant." More likely the word comes from an Indian term "S'nhalo'nek," meaning "the Entrance of a River into a Lake"—a description of the Saranac at Platts-burgh.

In spite of the patent scarcity of authentic Indian names in the area, many a row has flared up over the use or abuse of Indian names. A chronic argument over the naming of "the High Peak of Essex" as "Mount Marcy," an argument that even breaks out now and then today, is the best example and the most ridiculous. The state geologist Emmons is the villain, because he named the highest peak after an Albany politician. Marcy was the New York governor who had appointed Emmons. When Emmons first climbed it the guide with him knew no name for the peak. It was Emmons's right to name it and he named it Marcy.

The first visitor to the mountain a few weeks later was a New York magazine editor, Charles Fenno Hoffman. Hoffman was familiar with the Indian language of central and western New York. While he said that Marcy had been christened "not improperly, after the public functionary who first suggested the survey of this interesting region," he added, "the poetic

Indian epithet of Tahawus ('he splits the sky') is hardly too extravagant to characterize its peculiar grandeur." On the basis of that generous comment, or on misreading it, later writers insisted that Emmons had brushed aside an "old" Indian name for the peak in favor of a little politicking. The first "Indian" to bring "Tahawus" into the Adirondacks was Charles Fenno Hoffman.

It mattered little which Indian tribe claimed the region, once the white men decided they wanted it. Iroquois claims conflicted with Algonquin claims until the end of the French and Indian War. With the British the victors, the Iroquois claims were recognized, but that satisfaction did not last long. The Iroquois generally sided with the British in the Revolution. When the Americans triumphed, the Indian land claims shifted to shaky foundations. In treaties with New York State, in 1787 and in 1795, the Iroquois "ceded and released to the people of New York forever all the right or title of said nation to lands within the State and claim thereto wholly and finally extinguished." For this the Indians received sixteen hundred dollars.

Some of the Indians were settled on reservations in western New York. One small group, the Saint Regis Indians, a small branch of the Iroquois, had settled near the Saint Lawrence, north of the Adirondacks, as early as 1760. Their claim to their small tract of land was recognized by the state and conceded to them by the treaty of 1796. Eventually their land was reduced to 14,030 acres. Today there are less than two thousand Saint Regis. Most gave up hunting and trapping as their sole work long ago. They work today as agricultural laborers and help in the harvest of hops in the hopyards near Malone.

Only a few scattered Indians and a few who claim to be Indians are left in the Adirondacks now. Some can be found along the roadsides trying to lure tourists into buying their birchbark souvenirs and their sweet-grass baskets.

White Men

When the British took Fort Orange from the Dutch in 1664 they set the course of history in the Adirondack country for the next century. Less than three hundred miles separated Fort Orange from the French at Montreal; a struggle for the sole possession of the Lake Champlain–Lake George route was inevitable. Until that level route was in firm hands once and for all, neither side could feel secure. The wilderness country of northern New York with its rich fur trade echoed the continuing quarrels between London and Paris.

Over and over again, as has been told, the French and their Indian allies moved down on the British. Again and again the British and their Indian allies moved up on the French. The only way to stop these continual raids was to seize strategic points on the route and fortify them. As early as 1690 the British had some sort of trading center at Crown Point but soon abandoned it. In 1730 the French seized the site and began to build a fort at a place where the lake is so narrow that the fort's guns could fire across it. As a small town and trading post grew up around it, Crown Point became the first settlement in the Adirondack area. The French made large land grants on the Champlain shore to French citizens. The eastern fringe of the Adirondack area was on its way to becoming French.

From Fort Edward, north of Albany, the British pushed up a little farther and built Fort William Henry at the south end of Lake George in 1755. The French countered that by coming all the way down Lake Champlain in 1755 to a most strategic spot at Ticonderoga, and began to build Fort Carillon just thirty miles from the seventeen cannon and four mortars at Fort William Henry. A situation was building up that could not last long. It exploded in 1757, as part of the French and Indian War. The issue was decided in the summer of 1759 when Lord

Geoffrey Amherst took Ticonderoga. In the course of those two years the Adirondack hills saw many horrible sights — Indian massacre, retreat, artillery attack. From under the pines came the skirl of bagpipes as the Black Watch regiment led five frontal assaults in one afternoon on the Ticonderoga fort, only to be thrown back. Amherst then turned all his artillery on the fort. That finished the French. They blew up the fort's magazine and fled north.

In the middle of the twentieth century the men who lived those desperate days seem far removed. Yet the weapons they used, the bullets they fired, and even some of the contents of their purses and pockets have been found in the fields around the fort. The fort itself has been superbly restored. The relics of bygone battle are in its exhibits so that people of today can have an afternoon in 1758 revived for them in startling reality.

At the end of the war Canada became British. The French were now out of the Champlain Valley forever. Amherst rebuilt the fort at once. He sent explorers out to make the first accurate maps of the region. The French land grants along the lake were wiped out. The country was ready for settlement, and there were some men who were ready to settle it. Many a soldier in the wars, passing by the fertile shores of the lake, had mentally marked the land as a pleasant place to settle if ever peace came. Since the royal government at Albany was eager to attract settlers to this open frontier, it granted bonus warrants for land to all who had fought in the war. Each field officer received five thousand acres; each private a hundred. A few New England veterans did come and start to clear land. Others, officers and men alike, sold their warrants to speculators in Boston and New York; speculation in wild lands even at this time was a thriving business.

At the same time James de Lancey, His Majesty's lieutenant governor at Albany, proclaimed that "the whole country along Hudson's River down to Albany will for the future be so effectively covered and secured from the Ravages of the Enemy that the Inhabitants may return to their settlements. Those who choose to go and settle between Lake George and Fort Edward will find there Several spots of cleared ground." This first real-estate advertisement in Adirondack history started no immediate land rush.

Among the first families who did settle on the Lake Champlain shores were two unusual men, Phillip Skene and William Gilliland. Both came to the area with dreams of great riches.

Skene, a Scotchman who had served with Amherst, knew well the land around the head of Lake Champlain. Either in the West Indies, where he had been a soldier, or after observing the large Dutch manors along the Hudson, he dreamed of building his own huge estate. First he needed land; he secured most of what was to be a twenty-nine thousand acre estate at the place that is the railroad town of Whitehall today. He settled thirty families from downstate as tenants. Then he needed slaves. He brought twelve from the West Indies, as strange an importation as was ever made into the Adirondack country. He called his settlement Skenesborough. In later years the Adirondack region was to see elaborate layouts built by men of wealth, but none ever surpassed Skene's dream as he put it into reality with a manor house one hundred and thirty feet long. No trace of it or other relic of Skene has lasted to this day.

He knew of the iron deposits in the hills just west of the lower end of Lake Champlain and bought title to six hundred acres of those lands. He built boats for trade with Canada. He built roads to get his lumber from the woods. He became lieutenant governor of Ticonderoga and Crown Point and he was the greatest man for miles around. But in the Revolution he sided with the British. His ships were confiscated, his property seized by the Colonies. Skene was jailed as an important British official. He could only return to England, with no part of his dream left, there to die.

The second settler of consequence was an Irishman, William Gilliland. He too had dreams of life in manorial style. He had served in His Majesty's forces, perhaps in the Ticonderoga campaign. He did have a land warrant for just one hundred acres. Settling in New York City, he became a successful businessman, but his dreams were to the north, "a howling wilderness," as he called it. To his own hundred acres he added thousands more, bought with the warrants of other veterans. In 1765 he went north and settled on the west shore of Lake Champlain at the mouth of the Boquet River, forty miles northwest of Skenesborough. With him he brought thirteen men, three women, and assorted cattle. Within ten years his colony had increased to several hundred families, but, as many another land subdivider was to find out in the Adirondack country, "it was necessary to use extraordinary discretion and liberality to induce people to emigrate so far from their friends and home into a strange and distant wilderness." He soon had a smithy and a sawmill operating and his little village of Willsboro prospered.

He explored some of the Adirondack country to the west of his holdings and left a most readable and valuable diary. Begun in May, 1765, and continued for two years, it gives a clear picture of life on the Northern Frontier, of clearing the giant pines from the land, making maple syrup, planting wheat, of March cold, spring sowing, and beef slaughtering.

In his eagerness to find new sites for water power Gilliland explored for a short distance west of Plattsburg along the Saranac River, which he called the "Savianiac." Nearer home he went up the Ausable until he reached the eye-catching chasm. "It is a most admirable sight," he wrote, "appearing on each side like a regular built wall, somewhat ruinated. One would think this pridigious cleft was occasioned by an earthquake, their height on each side is from 40 to 100 feet in the different places." (No boat, as was pointed out when this diary was first published in 1852, could have made that trip then; none can do it now.)

All the while he prospered, but sometimes the price of being lord of the manor is the jealousy of the tenants. Gilliland acted as landlord, employer and judge. As the quarrels that were to produce the Revolution grew hotter, Gilliland became known as a leading "rebel" in the region. The government in Canada set a reward on his head; some of his employees, disgruntled, tried to kidnap him and get him to Canada for that reward.

At Ticonderoga Gilliland tried to put down quarrels between two hotheads, Ethan Allen and Benedict Arnold. When an expedition from Ticonderoga into Canada had to retreat in disaster, Gilliland helped to care for the miserable men who came back. He entertained them, as he later wrote, "from the general down to the sentinel — three and four thousand men at his own expense" — which gives some idea of Gilliland's resources. Whatever he did was to little avail. Benedict Arnold took a great dislike to him and accused him of treason. The lord of the manor was jailed.

He never recovered from the enmity and the false accusation of Arnold, an odd man to call anyone else traitor. Even as Gilliland was protesting his loyalty from a jail cell, the British were destroying his farms and buildings on the lovely lake shore. After the war was over a flaw was found in his patent and the state confiscated the property. A bad business deal threw him into a debtor's prison. In time he returned to the lake shore he loved. On a bitter cold night in the Adirondack winter of 1796 he went walking. He was found in the morning, frozen to death in the woods, a tragic and bitter end for the first man to report in any detail on the Adirondack country. Nothing is left today but the names Willsboro and Elizabethtown, the latter named after his daughter, and a grave in a North Country cemetery.

In the 1760's, as Gilliland and Skene dreamed their dreams and saw them come to pass, other men had their own plans for great fortune. These men were the land speculators in Boston and New York, an aggressive and numerous breed. Their number included some of the best families of the time. Out of such a speculator's plan came the first of the several huge land purchases in the Adirondack country and the first private land ownership.

Two Connecticut Yankees, Edward and Ebenezer Jessup, came to Albany in 1764 and dabbled in land. By 1770 they had not only done well in business but they had won the friendship of the important Sir William Johnson, known for his great influence with the Indians. The Jessups were interested in the fertile land along the Hudson, near Luzerne, where the river leaves the state park. In the wilderness Ebenezer built for himself a house of logs near Luzerne that sounds like a forerunner of some of the luxurious Adirondack camps: "His commodious and comfortable dwelling, however rude may have been its exterior, was the frequent theatre of hospitable entertainments, its rooms garnished with elegant furniture, its walls embellished with costly paintings and choice engravings, its spacious tables covered in spotless linen and imported covers and loaded with massive silver plate." In that pleasant place they made their plans to buy more wilderness land.

The unclaimed lands of the state belonged to the Indians; to buy them white men had to deal with them. The shrewd Crown saw to it, however, that Indian title had first to pass to the Crown and then to the white man, thus giving the Crown a chance to collect large fees for its services.

In 1771 two hitherto unknown Manhattan shipwrights, Joseph Totten and Stephen Crossfield, asked for the right to buy a huge triangle of land that is now the central Adirondack region. Its northern line ran from Keene Valley to the west and south of Cranberry Lake and included Raquette Lake, Blue Mountain Lake, Indian Lake, Lake Pleasant, and many other lakes. The tract was estimated to contain 800,000 acres; in fact, it was 1,115,000 acres.

The two shipwrights had never seen the land they asked for and knew nothing about it. They were front men for the Jessups and various distinguished Manhattanites, including one Alexander Macomb who was to buy an even larger tract later on. The use of front men, a pattern followed later in other Adirondack land purchases, was probably decided on to keep political enemies from blocking any deal. At the last conference ever held by the Mohawks, they agreed to sell the land for £1,135, about four acres for a penny. The Crown asked forty thousand for acting as middleman in the transfer of title — eight times as much as the Indians wanted.

In addition to setting a pattern for later land deals, the Totten and Crossfield purchase, while aborted by the Revolution, had other importance in Adirondack history. The new purchasers, planning to subdivide the land into fifty townships and to sell it at a profit, ordered a survey at once. This was the first survey of the area, and the first exploration of a large part of it.

The chief surveyor was one Archibald Campbell. Coming through unexplored land from west to east he reached a point just south of present-day Tupper Lake. There he and his party of eight Indians climbed a low hill. The work must have tired him, for he then wrote in his notes:

> The within work was done by me the subscriber in the presents of Sum of the Indians who was Deputed by the Original Proprietors to Goe and attend the within said Survey. From the end of the Aforesaid Line I showed the Indians the courses of the Line to the East of a high hill which gave a full View of the East and they all agreed and was fully satisfied with the course to be continued and So Chose to Return home without going any further along said line.

Campbell made another note at the same hill, "At this point the rum gave out." This survey, by long-distance sighting from a hilltop to provide part of the upper line of the purchase, generated many a lawsuit for the next one hundred and fifty years.

When the Revolution began, the entire tract reverted to the People of New York. Once the war was over the land speculators were right back again, busy and hopeful as ever. Among them was Crossfield; the state approved his earlier purchase. Although most of the land went quickly to other people, Totten and Crossfield put their names in Adirondack history forever. The Jessups received less. Both joined with the Tories; their property was seized and they fled to Canada.

The same geographic and strategic facts that determined the course of the French and Indian War in the Champlain Valley set the course of the Revolution in the region. The British were in Canada, the Colonists in Albany. Either side could raid and harass the other until the Lake George–Lake Champlain route was firmly in one hand or the other.

In the years since the British had taken the lake forts they had been allowed to deteriorate. A sergeant and nine soldiers were in charge of Crown Point in 1775. At Ticonderoga a captain, a lieutentant, forty-three men, forty-five sheep, eleven cows, one wife, and two children held the fort. At Fort William Henry on Lake George, the British had only a half-dozen men. Ethan Allen took Ticonderoga with little difficulty on May 10, 1775. The symbol of the capture of one of His Majesty's forts was thrilling to all the colonies; to the attackers the capture of ninety gallons of His Majesty's rum was more exhilarating. Crown Point fell. Then, like many Indian expeditions in earlier years, the Colonials under Ethan Allen headed up the lake to besiege Montreal. They ran into winter and smallpox.

A short time later they retreated in tatters. They came down the lake shore, as miserable a group as ever the peaks of the Adirondacks looked down upon. Worse than the news of the retreat was the rumor that the British were bringing over crack troops who soon would follow down the lake, to sweep on to Albany, New York City, and end the rebellion. The disgruntled and miserable Colonials at Crown Point, many with the sickly stamp of smallpox on them, were in no shape to stop them. The few settlers on farms along the lake-shore land debated the wisdom of staying.

Crown Point was abandoned. All energy was concentrated on strengthening Ticonderoga. A chain, perhaps made of Adirondack iron, was strung across the lake, near the fort, to block the passage of any British ships, for those ships were abuilding up north. Everything that could be done with limited means was done — that is, almost everything. Sugar Loaf Mountain, a small Adirondack peak five hundred and seventy-two feet high, overlooked the fort. Any artillery on it could command the fort below. Some American officers urged that it be fortified, but Gates, the commanding general, insisted it was too steep for any artillery to scale. One officer, John Trumbull, later to become a famous artist, tried to convince him that he was wrong, but Gates left Sugar Loaf unarmed.

At Skenesborough, from whence Phillip Skene had fled forever, New England shipbuilders were fashioning the giant pine and spruce of the Adirondacks into one- and two-masted gondolas and galleys that could venture on the lake with sails and oars and be the first Colonial navy. The news that the British were building sixteen- and eighteen-gun ships did not stop them. Benedict Arnold made himself commander of this fleet, manning it with anyone who knew which end of a boat was the bow. In September, 1776, he moved up the lake. The British came down in October. In a fight off Valcour Island the American fleet was smashed. To this day men still find the remnants of sunken ships on the bottom of the lake. The British, ill-advisedly, did not follow up their victory but remained at Crown Point and then returned to Canada. The Colonists to the south had yet another year to prepare against any British invasion.

Many men died at Ticonderoga in the hard winter of 1776–1777, waiting for the British to come south and attack. The snow lay deep on the summit of Sugar Loaf, so blandly overlooking the fort. The British arrived in the spring, with seven thousand men under Burgoyne. The settlers fled their lands for good. The smoke of burning cabins hung heavy over the Adirondack peaks. Behind the walls of Ticonderoga three thousand men waited. The British had excellent maps. They came close to the fort, headed for Sugar Loaf, and promptly installed a heavy battery on its summit. The Americans fled the fort. The British took over, then set out for the south, not by the easier route that ran west of Lake George but east of the lake, through typically tough Adirondack woods. Thanks to the alder, the witchhobble, and the thick underbrush of the Adirondack terrain, they were three weeks reaching Fort Edward. The Americans had time to move north, and blocked Burgoyne. In September he surrendered at Saratoga.

The British held Ticonderoga until the fall of Yorktown. Small campaigns and forays along the lake shore continued until the Revolution's end. In time the fort was abandoned. Not until the twentieth century did the Pell family, who inherited the site, begin the startling work of restoration. Today, Ticonderoga, its standards flying, its cannon bright, is in better shape than when either French, British, or Colonials possessed it. It is one of the most thrilling and satisfying historical landmarks in all America and draws thousands of visitors each year.

When the Revolution ended scarcely one settlement was left anywhere on the west shore of Champlain. Hundreds of Americans, particularly men from New England, had seen the fringes of the Adirondack area during the war. They had vivid memories of the great trees and the empty land.

The wilderness was waiting for them.

~§ III §~

Adirondack
Century

New York Fever

DURING the Revolution the government at Albany made an unhappy discovery about the lands of the Adirondack country; nobody wanted them as a gift. To attract soldiers to guard the northern border, land that included what are now Lake Placid and Keene Valley was set aside to be given away to any men who would serve. No one hurried to claim any of it. When soldiers were offered better land in central New York they took that.

At the end of the Revolution all unclaimed lands were the property of the state. Albany did nothing for several years about disposing of them. At the same time some people who had settled by Lake Champlain before the Revolution now returned. Where they had once cleared the giant pine and girdled the huge spruce, they now had to chop away the new overgrowth of brush and rebuild their cabins on the ashes of the old ones. Once again a few former settlers turned north from Albany to land south of Lake George and along the Hudson where it comes out of the hills.

But most of those who were interested in Lake Champlain lands and trod the trace of roads, often clearing out fallen trees as they pushed ahead, were newcomers, taken with a strange disease called "New York fever." It hit all New England, but particularly Vermont. It was spread by returned soldiers who had fought on the shores of Lake Champlain and fired by occasional trappers who had ventured into the woods beyond those shores. One man told another that there, to the west, was fine land free for the settling; to New England people in 1783 and particularly to Vermont people, the Adirondack country across Lake Champlain was "the West." The New York fever struck especially at younger sons of large families or at men who had no luck and saw no future on the New England land. That western land by the shores of Lake Champlain looked better, and no one seemed to own it. It was there for the taking.

One story, typical of hundreds, is that of Stephen Spaulding, a simple farmer from Salisbury, Vermont. He had a wife and three children and had not done well. He listened to returned soldiers talking in the little general store. He made a decision and persuaded two friends to join him. Together they went to Crown Point. Their plan was to climb every hill and every eminence until they looked down at last on land that pleased them. On the third day they saw from one summit the land which Spaulding described as "splendid to behold." Then, like many another Vermonter, they returned home to get their meager harvest in. The following summer they were back on their chosen land and worked hard to clear a little of it and to build three cabins. With the cold weather they returned to Vermont. The following spring they moved families, oxen, and axes, to the clearing and the cabins. That was the fever at work.

In retrospect it is surprising that any settlers came. Much of the land they moved to, except for that immediately by the lake, was little better than the land they were leaving and even rockier. It did seem free and without owners, but only for the moment. After 1785 titles to thousands of Adirondack acres were sold in Albany. In time the new owners or their agents were at the settler's door, demanding high prices for the land he had cleared, or even the land itself.

Nothing deterred those smitten with the fever, not even the knowledge that more fertile land in the Mohawk Valley and in western New York was open for settlement. The Vermonters came singly and in small groups. Between 1783 and 1820 they settled the west shore of Lake Champlain, spread west on the lowlands north of the Adirondacks, then turned south to the flatlands of the Saint Lawrence country. The more affluent came with their possessions pulled by an ox — "As we went through the trackless country we prayed, not for ourselves but for the ox." The less fortunate made a "jumper" of two poles, strapped their belongings to it, and pulled it with their own strength.

Not all who came were "fever" victims. As soon as some of the land passed into downstate speculators' hands, land agents, representing the owners, toured New England as salesmen. As one contemporary said:

They trumpet these New York lands to be the finest in the world, and being Yankees, they have turned most of the emigration that way. At a very low price they induce vast numbers to stop at them. But it is a fact that nine-tenths of the first emigrants enquire for cheap lands and their reason for doing so is because they expect to sell their improvements and jog further.

Others found the winters tough and the farming tougher; after a year or so they moved down to the Mohawk and on west, or around the hills to the fertile flatlands west of the Adirondacks.

No matter how they came or with what motive, these settlers on the Champlain shores, only three hundred miles from Manhattan, less than one hundred and fifty from Albany, knew the same hardships that others were to meet years later in the Far West. The only one lacking was the Indian menace. These settlers came into a land without roads, a land heavy with forests. As they cleared space for their fields they were the first lumbermen. With grub hoes they dug the ground between blackened stumps and put in their crops. They hollowed out a stump and hung a rock from a nearby sapling to make a crude mortar and pestle for grinding their rye to flour. The most highly prized possession were the oxen, for they were better than horses at removing stumps and roots; they cost fifty dollars a team.

Until the first water-driven lumber mills were built the settlers built their houses of logs. When a location was found the straightest trees were cut, the logs sized, notched, and shaped, and the walls raised. A real fancy cabin might be twenty-four feet long and eighteen feet wide. Rough poles served for rafters to hold the strips of bark for the roofs. A door, made of tough hand-split planks, was a fancy touch. More often an opening hung with a blanket served as doorway. Greased paper covered the one or two window openings. The floor was of earth. The bedstead was built of poles. A slab of wood with holes bored for rude legs made the chairs. The fire was not built in a fireplace but on the ground at the end of the cabin. Smoke wandered up to a hole in the roof. Chinks between the logs were closed by cedar wedges from the inside and moss and clay from the outside. It was important to keep the fire going: matches were not invented until 1827. Animal fat or pine knots served for light at night.

While few families pushed deeper into the Adirondack country, for land was plentiful on the edges, some settlers, out hunting and trapping, must have followed the various rivers inland. Those at Plattsburgh before 1785 must have pushed up the Saranac River to its source in a chain of lakes, for those lakes appear on maps of that date. A few people did move inland, either because they were dispossessed by those who had bought titles from the state or because they were restless. Some families came into Keene Valley, thirty miles west of Lake Champlain, as early as 1797. When people settled in the interior they usually chose land on the hillsides rather than in the valleys, from fear of spring floods.

One woman who lived in the Adirondack country before

1800 told the story of her early days. She was a Mrs. Adolphus Sheldon, who came to Ticonderoga in 1797:

We came through from the head of Lake George on an awful cold day on the ice. No stages, no mail, hardly any travel so we had to track. The whole length of the lake the great pines stood all around on the mountains, one unbroken wilderness. On neither side was there any settlement except at Sabbath Day Point. Not an axe had been heard and hardly a gun to scare the deer. When we got to Ti it was all bushes. We had one cow and a yoke of cattle. We all went to cutting logs and when we got four walls locked together, half a roof and the chamber floor, we moved in. When we wanted groceries we had to cross the lake for them but oftener went without them. I remember once going to a mill and dusting up flour from behind the bolt that had worms in it, picking them out and so making bread. We had brown bread and wheat cracked in milk.

Father had to work over the lake in Vermont to get hay for his critters. Mother and I, when he was gone, used to take the axe and bush hook and go out to our clearing at the back of the barn and work all day. We used to cut out all the underbrush and staddles and then when Father came home, he cut the big timber. No sheep; Land! You could have no sheep: the wolves would tear you right down. You could hear them away off in the night. One would howl, then another would answer — howl, howl, howl, then another, way off, howl, howl, howl, till they got up such a roar that it would almost tear you down. The animals we feared most were bears, wolves, catamounts, and rattlesnakes. Deer were thick. Shot one from the house door once.

After I married we moved across the valley westward where we had to tough it. I had toughed it at my father's and now I had to tough it here. Only a half acre was cleared. There we lived for five years without a stove or fireplace. We absolutely had no chimney. We burned wood right against the logs of the cabin and when they got afire we put it out.

That was the Adirondack country at the end of the eighteenth century.

Harpy Land Jobbers

For some people between 1783 and 1800 the northern wilderness meant forests to clear, fields to plant, cabins to roof, and wolves to kill. In those same years, however, another Northern Wilderness existed for a group of men in Manhattan, most of whom never put foot in it. It existed only on the heavy paper of maps spread out under the gentle glow of whale oil lamps in some of the finest mansions in Manhattan. Here the wilderness meant fortunes that might be made in land speculation.

Among the well-known men in the city who studied and marked those maps were William Constable, Dublin-born merchant-prince, aide to Lafayette during the Revolution, banker and importer, a man blessed with influential friends both in America and Europe; Daniel McCormick, Dublin-born bank director and very proper gentleman, one of the last New Yorkers to wear short breeches, white stockings and slippers with silver buckles; and Alexander Macomb, son of an Irish emigrant, grown rich in the fur trade on the frontier at Detroit, owner of a home on Broadway below Christ Church sumptuous enough to serve as the presidential residence of George Washington. There were many others, including Aaron Burr and Gouverneur Morris, to whom land speculation was always attractive. All were unusual and active men; speculating in Adirondack land was only one incident in their crowded lives.

Through their efforts, directly and indirectly, there was introduced into the story of northern New York as strange a collection of characters as ever appeared in any regional history, including a princess from India, an assortment of French nobility, a Dutchman with a scheme for ending slavery in the West Indies, and even Joseph Bonaparte, elder brother of Napoleon.

Among the maps they may have studied in McCormick's

comfortable home, the last private residence on Wall Street, may have been one of 1785 that had written across part of the Northern Wilderness:

> Through this tract of land runs a Chain of Mountains which shew their tops always white with snow. This one unfavorable circumstance has hitherto rescued it from the claws of the Harpy Land Jobbers yet no doubt will furnish a comfortable retreat for many Industrious families.

These "Harpy Land Jobbers" of Manhattan hoped indeed that the region would furnish a retreat for families who would have to buy the land, at a price, from those with the foresight to have bought it earlier. Maps may have shown no detail of any sort, but the location of mountains, rivers, and even swamps was not important. At the moment it was necessary to know only that the land was unclaimed, that it lay where settlers might be attracted to it, and that friends in the state legislature might be useful in securing it.

After the Revolution every state had unclaimed lands and competed for settlers. After 1787 the federal government also hoped to dispose of its lands. Most statesmen in these years, including Alexander Hamilton and Benjamin Franklin, dabbled in land speculation. In at least one large deal speculators were involved with numerous members of Congress. One contemporary called it a scandal "in which many of the principal characters of America are involved." That deal was eventually examined by one of the first congressional investigating committees, but only one man, conveniently dead, received any blame.

Thus the Adirondack land deals, in eighteenth-century terms, had nothing unusual about them except their size. For many reasons it seemed desirable to get the New York State lands into private hands at any cost, no matter how low the price or how conveniently assisted by the legislature. The northern

frontier was not yet settled, and the British, only recently enemies, were in Canada. Many people suspected that they had
their eyes on northern New York. The Revolution left the
state with a debt of $1,167,575, a huge sum, which the governor,
George Clinton, proposed to settle in various ways, including
the sale of the state lands. The first buyer to turn up was the
Crossfield of 1772. The state confirmed his earlier purchase at
twelve cents an acre. The land was divided among many asso-
ciates. A century later the state bought back much of that land
for as much as five dollars an acre.

The largest purchaser of land in the Crossfield grant was
Alexander Macomb. He may never have visited the Adirondack
country but while passing back and forth along the Saint Lawrence as a fur trader he had learned something of the lands of
northern New York. Knowing that much more about them
than other New Yorkers, he probably interested Constable and
McCormick.

In 1791, after the state land commissioners had been authorized to sell "the waste and unappropriated lands of the State,"
Macomb made them an offer. What he wanted was almost all
of the Adirondack country in the north, northwest, and part of
the southwest, as well as all the lands in the northwest that surround the Adirondack region — a total of 3,816,960 acres. He
offered to pay eight pence an acre, sixteen cents, although other
offers for land nearby at eighteen cents had been turned down
as too low. Other details of his offer, no interest on installments
and easy payments, were all in his favor. The offer was confirmed by Governor Clinton in January, 1792, and a first payment of thirty-five thousand dollars made. No sooner were the
details published than cries of "Graft!" and "Corruption!" rose
in Albany and among the beaver-hatted and outsmarted gentry
of Manhattan. Clinton's enemies at once howled that Macomb
was only a front for some Britishers who meant to annex northern New York to Canada; that Clinton was in on the deal and

stood to make large profits; and that Aaron Burr, the attorney general, had arranged the entire underhanded business. (Burr was in on later land deals but was out of Albany while the Macomb transaction was being arranged.) Motions for impeaching Governor Clinton were presented. In time the assembly cleared everyone concerned.

Macomb's name went on the purchase, but it was only one of many interests. Three months after its completion, following the failure of a scheme to sell shares in a new bank, Macomb was bankrupt and in debtors' prison to keep him safe from the anger of many citizens who felt he had swindled them. He made little out of his Adirondack land venture. Shortly after his failure, perhaps by prearrangement, he transferred part of his share in the "Macomb Purchase" to Constable at a slight profit and the balance to McCormick. He then disappeared from Adirondack history.

Perhaps Macomb was only a front man for Constable, McCormick, and others. The best hint of foresighted shadiness showed up two years later when the same legislature passed a bill to fix the price of the remaining two million unbought acres of public land elsewhere in the state at six shillings, thereby giving the Adirondack owners a fine hedge and a handsome paper profit on what they had bought for eight pence. The Totten and Crossfield and the Macomb purchases put most of the Adirondack country into private hands, although over the years the state had to take much of it back for unpaid taxes.

After 1792 the lands of the "Macomb Purchase" were divided, subdivided, and subdivided again. While most of the land buyers eventually lost heavily, one exception was the leading subdivider, William Constable. Unlike others who purchased large tracts of northern New York land, he came and settled on the land a short distance to the west of the Adirondack region. He sold land, rebought it, sold it again. His profits are beyond any computing today. In 1796 he and two partners could report a profit of $74,778.57 on some sales.

Many Irish Americans were among those who dabbled in Adirondack lands. As a result many Irish place names turned up on the early nineteenth-century maps of the Adirondack country, including Saint Patrick, Killarney, Barrymore, Tipperary, and Hollywood, to be replaced by more prosaic names at a later date. Some of the land buyers were just as picturesque. No one in Adirondack history has a more colorful background than one Michael Hogan, to whom McCormick sold twenty thousand acres at a dollar per acre.

He was a ship captain of thirty-eight who had grown rich in the East Indian trade and came to New York for the first time in 1805. With him he brought his bride, the sensation of the day among the rather proper gentry of Manhattan, for she was a princess from India and brought with her a dowry of two million dollars. Hogan was accepted into society at once and soon gained the reputation of giving the best dinners ever served in New York. He set up one of the handsomest department stores the city had ever seen. His land was just north of the Blue Line and up to the Saint Lawrence. One township in Franklin County was named Bombay in honor of his wife's birthplace. A Saint Lawrence village, Hogansburg, is today the center of the Saint Regis Indian reservation. He never visited his lands, but his son lived on them. Eventually Hogan lost most of his fortune and wound up as United States consul to Chile.

The interest in New York lands as a prime commodity for speculation was not confined to wealthy Irishmen of New York. Europeans were interested. Some Amsterdam bankers were particularly eager to buy American land and formed the Holland Land Company for that purpose. Their representatives considered land in Pennsylvania and in central New York and even negotiated with Constable for some of the Adirondack lands.

One representative, Gerrit Boon (a name remembered in Boonville, a village on the edge of the Adirondack country), wrote home about the money that might be made in cheap New York lands and more particularly the fortune to be had from maple sugar that came free from the trees of the northern forest. The Amsterdam bankers knew much about cane sugar, produced in the West Indies by slave labor. The combination of profits and idealism was attractive; maple sugar could mean income and might at the same time drive cane sugar from the market forever and thus end the curse of slavery.

The Dutch bankers authorized Boon to go on with his scheme. He bought almost one hundred thousand acres near the present city of Utica, just below the Blue Line. It was well covered with maple. He picked a small test patch on a hillside and cleared off everything but the maples. By the summer of 1793 he was ready for his experiment at ending slavery except for the troughs to carry the sap down to the stoves. By winter he had what he wanted, in thin troughs of wood.

He waited for the sugaring days in early spring. They came. The sap ran. The sun and the frost at night soon warped the troughs and the sap leaked out. New troughs worked no better. The maple leaves grew to the size of a mouse's ear and sugar season was over for that year. Boon casually reported his failure back to Amsterdam along with his plans for a second try the next spring. For the bankers, once was enough. The land was put up for sale at a loss. The few hundred pounds of sugar that Boon did make cost the company just fifteen thousand dollars, the most expensive maple sugar ever produced in New York history.

Constable was willing to sell any part of the land to small settlers, but they were not easy to find. He wanted men of wealth who could buy acres by the thousand. Thanks to his European connections he knew where to look for them. Maps of land in faraway America, spread on the mahogany tables in London countinghouses or in the luxurious salon of a French château, had an irresistible appeal for many Europeans. They asked only to be assured that the land was actually where the map showed it. Constable's fine reputation guaranteed that.

Less than four months after Macomb had signed over his interests, Constable was in London. He must have been an extraordinary salesman. He sold the high sheriff of London twenty-six thousand acres of wilderness at a shilling an acre. He sold four thousand acres to a wealthy William Inman. Although Inman's son Henry, born in Utica, became one of the important men in nineteenth-century American art, there is no irrefutable evidence, as has been claimed, that he ever painted Adirondack landscapes.

Constable's most dramatic feat of salesmanship took place in a gracious living room in Paris, where he sat talking with an old friend, Pierre Chassanis, a French nobleman. It was an August afternoon in 1792. Conversation was understandably difficult; at that moment revolutionary mobs were raging in the streets outside the house, the king's palace was being surrounded and the king himself was being taken off to prison. In these circumstances, Constable's remarks about his far-off land fascinated Chassanis. It took little to persuade him to buy six hundred and thirty thousand acres for about one dollar and fifty cents an acre, land that had cost Constable less than twenty cents an acre a few months earlier. That handsome paper profit, however, stayed largely on paper, for eventually the purchase was reduced to two hundred and ten thousand acres at fifty cents, part inside, part outside the Blue Line.

With the cries of the Paris mob on all sides as a sales talk, Chassanis was sure he could quickly resell the wilderness land to various titled French families. He set up "La Compagnie de New York," a shareholding organization for founding a New France in northern New York and for colonization, far from the guillotine. Shares were offered, with the land now upped to three dollars per acre. Agents for "La Compagnie" were sent out at once to prepare for the settlers' coming. Maps were drawn by men unhampered by any accurate knowledge; one showed a road running to the edge of a precipice and its continuation right below it. An elaborate prospectus was published which described a portion of heaven rather than of earth. Yet the shares did not sell well.

Some people did buy and planned to move to the promised Eden. About twenty families came in June, 1794. They were obviously people better used to the customs of the French court. They settled along the Black River, just west of the Adirondacks, and named their settlement Castorland, after the Latin name for beaver and the presumed abundance of those animals. Most of the settlers were unfitted for the hard work that the wilderness demanded. They soon found that the agents of the company were incompetent, careless, and much too busy defending themselves three thousand miles away to be concerned with settlers' problems. By 1800, all that Castorland could show for the thousands of dollars invested was one sawmill, eighteen log houses, and eighty-two acres cleared, and another settlement of eleven log houses and one hundred and thirty cleared acres.

Those settlers who were unable to return home resigned themselves to living out their lives here in the backwoods that would never be a New France. Some even liked it. One set down a unique Rousseau-like picture of wilderness life at the turn of the century:

> Our rivers abound in fish and our brooks in trout. Of all the colonies of beaver which inhabited this country and raised so many dams only a few scattering families remain. We have destroyed those communities, images of happiness, in whose midst reigned the most perfect order. Our chief place, Castorville, is a cluster of primitive dwellings. It contains several

families of mechanics of which new colonies have so frequent need. . . . One of the proprietors has a daughter as interesting by her figure as by her industry.

Castorland may never have attracted many settlers but it saw some odd ones. A former forester of Louis XVI, Louis François de Saint Michel, settled in the southwestern foothills of the Adirondacks on Deer River, near Copenhagen, bringing with him his daughter Sophie. It was always a shock for hunters and trappers to come through the wilderness and happen on this man with his European manners, his courtly hospitality, and his daughter, "interesting by her figure." She married another Frenchman and settled into frontier life as if she had been born to it.

While this salting of French settlers in the North Country took place largely west of the Blue Line, the story belongs in Adirondack history. It brought into the Adirondack country an extraordinary man, James Donatianus LeRay de Chaumont. His father had sided with the Colonies-in-revolt and had been an admirer and close friend of Benjamin Franklin. In his father's home, James LeRay, as he was known, had met many a distinguished American. He spoke English perfectly. He had faith in America. And he was an honest man who tried hard to salvage something for the miscast settlers of "La Compagnie."

He was Chassanis's brother-in-law and one of the original subscribers to the colonization scheme.When it failed he bought up many of the shares and came to America to act as agent for other shareholders. In time he bought additional land in the Adirondacks as far east as the present village of Saranac Lake and built himself a home in the Saint Lawrence country. Back and forth to France he went, trying to attract other settlers, trying to help those that he had settled. On one journey he interested Joseph Bonaparte, sold him 160,260 acres of land, and helped him get established in America. His eagerness to aid other people put him through one bankruptcy. At the end of his life he returned for good to France and died in 1840. His son Vincent took over the management of the land and continued to sell it for three to six dollars an acre until 1860. The Compagnie de New York story even has an occasional echo today. Now and then Frenchmen find shares tucked away in the family vault. From time to time some threaten to sue to recover what they claim are their titles to northern New York land. No other remains of Castorland exist today.

Speculation in Adirondack lands continued for the first thirty years of the nineteenth century, but land values slowly fell as better land opened in the West. The early speculating fever did necessitate land surveys, and the area was therefore to some extent explored. After 1795 a few accurate details of the wilderness were added to the map of New York State. In time land that speculators could not sell reverted to the state for unpaid taxes. Until 1883 the state was usually willing to sell its land to any buyer, often at ridiculous prices. In mid-century two hundred and fifty thousand acres were sold to a proposed railroad company at six cents an acre. Some of that land was eventually bought back by the state at a hundred times that price.

When the forest preserve was set up in 1885 the state found that it owned only 720,744 of the 5,000,000 acres in the Adirondack country.

Wilderness Opening

The families who had settled on the fringes of the Adirondack region probably knew little of the activities of the large land speculators and cared less. It was far more important for a man to know that each year saw another acre or two of his holdings cleared, a better dwelling built, another mile or so of rough road opened. By 1815 some families could boast of thirty years' residence in the Adirondack country, time enough to raise a new generation. If life was tough they had learned how to live it. They could take pride in the comment of the author of the first gazetteer published in New York State in 1813: "The rigors of an inland climate in a latitude of 45 degrees north leave little time for the lassitude of idleness or dissipation: a circumstance friendly to moral vigor and to vigor of mind and body."

On the lower lands on all sides of the Adirondacks the settlers, perhaps fifteen thousand by now, lived in a sprinkling of small villages. Near the Champlain shore they were simple little places, even as they are today — Elizabethtown, Westport, Keeseville and others, the patina of age now on them. Thirty miles back on the west were the primitive settlements of Keene Valley and Jay. Behind them the woods were unbroken and only an isolated settler or two lived in them. On the flatlands west of the region were similar small settlements — Boonville, Canton, Gouverneur, and, to the north, Malone.

The woods were no longer entirely trackless. Almost as soon as the first Vermont settlers had their land cleared they banded together to build some sort of road to the next community and to replace the trails that had been marked only by blazed trees. As roads they were little more than tracks from which the larger trees had been removed; they remained like that for decades. In Donaldson's phrase, "they were passable enough in winter but impassable in spring and impossible in summer." A north-south road between Albany and Montreal was completed before 1810, a route that follows most of today's Highway 9. It was not much of a road; it cost all of sixteen dollars for labor and supplies to build a mile. The first road into the interior was begun before 1810. Still in use and still called "the Northwest Bay Road," it was built across the wildest parts of Franklin and Essex counties, to connect the settlements along the Saint Lawrence with those by Lake Champlain. Another was cut from the southern edge of the country northwest, to provide a route to the thriving village of Ogdensburg. In 1815 another road ran around the Adirondack country on level ground from Plattsburgh, north and west. In no time four-horse coaches and lumber wagons were using it. The drivers changed horses every ten or twelve miles, stopping at the little one-room inns that appeared almost as soon as the last tree in the way of the road was cut down and pushed aside.

By 1810 the county lines of today were drawn. The small villages had their own firm government. These early settlers with New England background set up simple rule by town meeting. The settlements were often so far apart that the ballot box had to be carried around to the voters. The Vermonters also brought with them their democratic principles, expressed in their constitution of 1777, which provided that any adult freeman might vote or hold office regardless of property owned or of religion. The settlers were eager for schools but lacked teachers. The best-educated woman in any village usually taught in her home at a dollar and twenty-five cents a week.

The more enterprising settlers built grist mills by streams and the simplest of sawmills. Almost every pioneer family went into the business of making potash out of wood ashes, a medium of exchange which backwoods stores accepted gladly. All a man had to do was to cut down the timber at his back door, burn it, gather the ashes and leach them with water, boil down the lye, and haul the product to market. Thirty cords of wood made a ton of ashes and one sixth of a ton of potash, worth ten to twenty dollars. The settler saved his ashes until he had a large pile, then hauled them to the nearest store. Collectors took them from there, usually to Canada, where the potash was made into soap, explosives, and other products.

Some settlers became lumbermen and cut logs for shipment to Montreal or Quebec. Others went into the shipping business and took lumber rafts down the lake, with sail and oar on the five-day journey to the Saint Lawrence. "Those were the days," one settler said years later, "when nothing more wonderful or adventurous could happen to any boy than being allowed to go to Quebec on one of those rafts carrying with him the skins of those animals which he and his brother had trapped the winter before." The trade with Canada grew. In just two months in 1811 the value of goods through one border customhouse was almost three hundred thousand dollars.

Not all the traffic on Lake Champlain was north and south. From the earliest days settlers traded across the lake with the Vermont shore, getting store goods in exchange for furs or even fish. One of the earliest ferries began to run in 1790. The amount of Champlain traffic was substantial enough to interest one Vermonter, John Winans, who was with Robert Fulton on a September day in 1807 when the first steamboat in history, the *Clermont,* moved along the Hudson. Winans said good-by to Fulton and hurried north. At Burlington he built the *Vermont,* the second steamboat in the world. For seven years it ran up and down the lake, in the shadow of the Adirondacks, the first of a long line of Champlain ships.

One other industry and activity, whiskey making and drinking, vividly marked life on this American frontier. Produced from rye in any of a score of stills in the region, liquor was cheap at twenty cents a gallon. A bucket stood on the counter of every general store on a "Help yourself" basis. A few enterprising settlers made rum of maple syrup, a beverage now mercifully gone from the Adirondack country. Law courts were nonexistent. What simple trials there may have been were held in the primitive taverns and "the bar of justice" had a literal meaning. The amount of whiskey consumed in frontier social life was tremendous; a fondness for it is not unknown in the Adirondack country now, where the tavern keepers are numerous and prosperous.

Only one event, the War of 1812, broke the peace along the Champlain shore in these days and then not for long. The Adirondack people knew little of its causes, but many felt for a long time that the British in Canada had designs on northern New York. Nothing happened until the summer of 1813. On July 31 a squad of Paul Reveres rode through the towns on the Champlain shore shouting, "A party of Britishers have invaded the state and are making for Plattsburgh." As one man told it, "The men sprang for their guns and powder horns, while the women packed cold Johnny-cake and salt pork into their knapsacks, and filled their canteens with rum." In the meantime the British were sacking the village, but by the time the backwoods militia arrived the British had re-embarked. The militia sat in the hills around Plattsburgh eating cold johnnycake for five days, then went home.

In the spring of 1814 the news was more serious. Fourteen thousand British, with regulars who had served under Wellington, were marching on Plattsburgh. The American general, Macomb, son of the originator of the Macomb Purchase, had to wait them on the banks of the Saranac below the village with only forty-seven hundred men, seven hundred of them local militia. A British fleet came down the lake and a smaller American fleet sailed north. The American ships beat the British in a vicious fight. The British army on the banks of the Saranac retreated at once, leaving more than two thousand wounded men behind. The Americans lost fewer than two hundred.

The last cannon shot had echoed in the Adirondack hills. For years after, the people of the North Country sang jeeringly:

Now the battle's growing hot, boys, I don't know how 'twill
    turn,
While Macdonough's boats, on swivels hung, continually do
    burn:
We see such constant flashing that the smoke beclouds the
    day,
And our larger boats have struck and the small ones run away.
We've got too far from Canada, run for life, boys, run.

Other shots continually resounded in the Adirondack country from the rifles of hunters and trappers. The supply of game still seemed inexhaustible. Bounties were set in the Adirondack counties on wolves, panthers, and other animals, including one of two cents in Lewis County for chipmunks. In time the panther and the wolf were rarely heard around the settlements and were pushed into the interior. From the bounty on wolves came an incident which led to a law still on the books of New York State which declares that if a wolf's head is turned in for bounty it must have ears on it.

While wolves howled outside the cabins on the shores of Lake Champlain in 1800 they were killed off fast. Bounty payments dropped sharply in all the Adirondack counties except in Franklin where, from the records of bounties paid, it seemed that all the wolves had decided to concentrate and hold out to the last wolf. There the combined state and county bounty was sixty dollars per wolf, a huge sum of money at the time. From 1820 to 1822 Franklin County hunters applied for more than fifty-five thousand dollars. Since this huge expense had to be shared by the local taxpayers and the legislature in Albany the protests were loud in both places.

The legislators sympathized with the people of Franklin County, who seemed to dwell amid wolf packs, but they asked why it was that no inhabitant ever reported any damage done by wolves and why were so few ever seen. Quite able to smell a wolf, thanks to years in local politics, the legislators did a bit of investigating. What they found out stirred up a scandal that came close to many a worthy country politician and to some of our sturdiest forefathers.

The legislature moved to stop it. It decided to appropriate just one thousand dollars for wolf bounty each year; if one wolf was caught, that was the bounty. If a thousand were caught the bounty was one dollar each. Nothing in zoological history ever wiped out wolves as fast as that law. The legislature added a further proviso. When a wolf's head was presented for bounty, the official had to cut off the ears and burn them at once, even before payment; no bounty was to be paid on any earless wolf. Therein was the secret of the huge wolf population of Franklin County. Wolves in the backwoods could be caught now and then and wolf heads could be bought in Canada and imported. As soon as a hunter had one, he collected his friends. They hurried to the county official's office and promptly put the wolf's head on his desk. As he wrote out the papers, someone moved the head to the window sill of the one-story building. In five minutes another chap was at the desk with a wolf's head, and so on. That night, in the taverns of Chateaugay and Malone many men had sixty dollars each to spend. No one ever directly accused the county officials of connivance — well, not much connivance. They just had bad eyesight and all wolves looked alike to them.

By 1820 a number of isolated settlers were scattered throughout the interior of the woods. Some solitary settlers cleared one place, only to sell it, move on, and clear another. Others were trappers who ran lines as long as forty miles through the central Adirondacks. Some were recluses with shadowed motives, like a mysterious Moses Follensby who lived by a lake west of Saranac Lake, a lake now called by his name. He was the first of the "professional" hermits, of whom the Adirondacks has always had a number; one early guidebook had a heading in its index: "Hermits (also see People)." For years after his death people were sure he had been the heir to some large English fortune. One Jacob Moody, progenitor of a long line of Adirondack guides, came to what is now the village of Saranac Lake about the same time and had no neighbors for ten miles in any direction. Isolated families settled south of Marcy by 1818.

A few individuals were unafraid of the wilderness in the southwest, where a Providence, Rhode Island, merchant, John

Brown, had tried to attract settlers and failed. To this John
Brown tract, now empty, his heirs managed to attract a few settlers by offering a free farm of one hundred acres to the first ten
families to come. A few came and soon left. Others followed,
squatting on the clearings of their predecessors, but they too
went their way in a few years. Now and then the backwoods-
men appeared in the village stores, to trade their furs for six
months' supplies and trudge back home.

The people of the villages paid little attention to the solitary
settlers. Nor did they notice the start of another phenomenon.
Its first recorded instance took place in 1818 when "a group
of Yale men along with a brother-in-law of the president of
Columbia College" came into the southwest Adirondacks not
for wealth, woods, or land, but for a vacation and some fishing.
They rode in from the village of Boonville as far as a team
could go and walked the rest of the way to Beaver Falls. The
solitary resident of the region, one Thomas Puffer, acted as
guide. What fish were caught is not recorded, but one member
of the party lay close enough to the fire to burn his boots and
had to tramp out of the woods in bark sandals.

In spite of that the same party was back again the next year.
As the fish stories spread around, other outsiders must have
followed. In 1830 a lonely hermit in the southwest, David
Smith, snorted, "This place is too much frequented by hunting
and fishing parties." He promptly hiked thirty miles north to
the lake that now bears his name, where he was sure no hunting
or fishing parties would ever come.

The people of the little Lake Champlain settlements ignored
another development taking place just south of the Adirondacks.
At Saratoga Springs, already famous for its mineral waters, a
full-sized and popular tourist center was developing, of frail
board buildings on the edges of the pine forest. Even in 1790
crude taverns had "a dozen respectable people" as guests. In
1808 the village had seven new taverns. A first settler, Gideon

Putnam, was convinced that the springs would draw visitors and built his Union Hall, three stories high, one of the largest hotels in America at that time. Like Paul Smith, Adirondack hotelkeeper sixty years later, Putnam sold lots around his hotel so that guests might build and return summer after summer. After 1815 the three rival coach lines to Saratoga from Albany, each running two coaches daily, were crowded. Many a Southern planter's family was aboard, particularly mothers with eligible daughters, for as Saratoga became increasingly popular the word spread that it was always open season for prospective sons-in-law and that the hunting was good. By 1825 this village could hold a thousand guests. Its reputation for being a mixture of society, politics, gaiety, and sin was firmly set.

By the 1820's spas and summer vacations were becoming fashionable for the wealthy. Resorts still alive and famous — Long Branch, Cape May, and Narragansett — and resorts now dead but the height of fashion a century ago became popular. One that was extraordinarily fashionable was Trenton Falls, just above Utica, where West Canada Creek comes out of the Adirondacks. It was a must for any traveler, particularly distinguished Europeans, en route to Niagara. An early guidebook called it "the most enjoyably beautiful spot among the resorts of romantic scenery in our country." Visitors stood by the rushing water and marveled at the "wild cataract." Today the entire site of the falls and the wild cataract is now filled with a powerhouse, dynamos, and high-voltage carriers. Guests at Trenton Falls one hundred and twenty-five years ago were urged to make short expeditions into the Adirondack wilderness so near at hand — "a flask of brandy swung over the shoulder," the guidebook said, "will enhance the pleasure of the journey."

But Saratoga remained the most popular resort. No visitor to America, from Lafayette down, could say he had seen the country until he had visited it. Washington Irving and James Fenimore Cooper knew it, as did every statesman of the day.

The few English writers who came hunting material for books on America made it a compulsory stop and usually called it vulgar but alive. As at Trenton Falls, a few miles above Saratoga were the unbroken Adirondack woods. It was inevitable that the gentlemen lounging on the piazzas of the Saratoga hotels, bored with billiards, tired of poker games in hot hotel rooms, sick of sipping water three times daily, and even weary of flirtation with Southern belles, might listen eagerly to the tales of that wilderness so nearby, to stories of fine fishing and hunting, and of the novelty of roughing it. They went to see for themselves.

Hotels for them quickly opened on the southern fringe of the woods, the first at Lake George, and one a little later at Luzerne. Here the first of the line of colorful Adirondack innkeepers, George Rockwell, planned his hotel on the edge of the little Hudson. His hotel, of logs and boards, with many a touch later to be described as "Adirondack," opened in 1832. Saratoga loungers came. In time Rockwell expanded his hotel to one hundred and fifty rooms. Perhaps some of the Saratoga adventurers even brought ladies of a sort with them, for a few years later Rockwell was advertising his hotel as "a large three-story building divided up into pleasant high-walled rooms in *suits,* richly furnished and designed for parties who might prefer them to the more public places in the main building."

An 1831 guidebook, *The Northern Traveller,* could say, "There are various routes embraced within the range of the Northern Traveller, — down Ticonderoga to Lake Champlain. The inn to which strangers resort at Lake George is particularly fitted to gratify the eye of taste."

The tourist trade into the Adirondacks had begun. It began with the development of Saratoga, that gaudy front step to the opening wilderness — complete with "bands of colored men dispensing sweet music" and guests arriving "with eight trunks complete with elegant silks and bonnets."

Riches Everywhere

If any word of the growing glamour, prosperity, and gilded vices of Saratoga reached the settlements on the eastern fringe of the Adirondacks a hundred miles away, the people paid little attention. Certainly the strong Vermont strain had no desire to emulate the wretched place. Saratoga and its publicans might get rich, but riches seemed to be all around in the Adirondack land, ready for the taking.

Timber was so abundant, and timber in the early days usually meant the giant white pine, that it was inconceivable to the early settlers that it could ever be exhausted. Timber meant cash, either as boards, as potash, or as charcoal to fire the first iron forges, and more trees were waiting to be cut, just a few hundred yards back in the woods. These first settlers had only homemade axes for tools and tediously rived out by hand with ax and wedge the boards and shingles needed for their own houses. Others hewed long logs square, then elevated them to a trestle over a pit. With a saw blade that cut only on the way down, one man above, one man below with a handkerchief over his face to keep out the dust, rough planks could be sawed out. Then came the water-driven mill, with one blade fastened to the millwheel. Mills had been used earlier in New England with as many as twelve blades worked by the millwheel — "A few such mills will quickly destroy the woods at a reasonable distance from them," one observer reported even in 1701. These gang mills did not come into the Adirondacks until well into the nineteenth century; in steam-driven mills, they had as many as thirty-two blades.

The first simple mills worked the pines that stood nearby. A team of oxen snaked the logs to the mill, one at a time, but it was not long before all trees that were available close by had been cut. The mill either had to close down or move farther into the woods and find some way to get the boards out. The need for lumber transportation led to some of the early road building. Many early inns along the roads began to serve the lumber teamsters; at some it was common to see forty loaded teams tied up at once.

The little mills found they had run out of timber that could be cut and moved economically by road. At the same time one of the earliest lumber firms, the Fox Brothers of Warren County, who had rafted logs down the Hudson to mills at Glens Falls, discovered that it was possible to float single logs in a drive and get them safely to the mill. The white pine giants, some two hundred feet high and seven feet through at the base, were cut into thirteen-foot lengths in winter, pulled by oxen over iced roads to places along the river, then pushed into the turbulent waters in spring and thus sent to the mills. The Foxes first tried it on the Schroon River branch of the upper Hudson in 1813. It worked. In a few years many other groups were doing it; the Adirondack lumber industry had really begun.

Trees that stood deeper in the woods, too remote for the small sawmill, could now be timbered. The smallest streams, stretches of dried rock barely a yard wide in summer, served to move logs in spring. Temporary dams were built on them, the log cut piled below, and when the spring thaw and freshets came, the dam was knocked out. In the rush of cold mountain water, down went the winter cut to some larger stream and on to the mills. The logs were marked with the brands of separate owners, with brands used as in a Western roundup, from the crow's foot, double O, and hawkeye to wine cup and many others. Log driving became a steady and dangerous profession. Through the lakes, without a steady current, they had to be floated, warped, or "kedged" by cables, anchors, and windlasses. No hardwood went in these drives; it was too heavy for river driving. It was to stay in the woods until better roads and railroads made it possible to draw it out.

After 1840 the lumbermen moved inland. French Canadians came into the Adirondack country and proved to be the best of the lumber workers. The lumbermen cut on their own land or land bought from the state at prices as low as fifteen cents an acre. When they had taken the big trees they let the land revert again to the state for taxes. Their cutting did not level the woods; usually they scorned anything under twelve inches in diameter or anything that would not furnish at least two thirteen-foot logs. They did leave tops and trimmings in their trail as ready fuel for forest fire, but fires were rare until the days of hunters, cigarettes, and railroads.

By 1830 the timber that could be easily moved to Ticonderoga was gone and that first great Adirondack lumber town saw its industry vanish. Glens Falls, on the Hudson just below the Blue Line, became the important lumber center. The great spring drive on the Hudson to that town was the lumbermen's event of the year. In time every Adirondack river became a highway for logs. Many companies went into the business and many failed. A river drive could get jammed and "hung up," miss the spring flood, and be unmovable until the following year, with all its cost of cutting tied up in it.

The lumbermen reached the center of the Adirondacks about 1850. At the same time New York was producing more lumber than any state in the Union. A half-million trees and more went into one year's cut, for more than a billion board feet. The industry had its giants, men who controlled all the mills along a river and who watched over the timbering of thousands of acres. A few of them did get rich but more failed. Most of the settlers and their descendants found no riches in lumbering — only careers as teamsters, log drivers, or cutters, and that only part of the year, at wages that rose slowly to twenty-eight dollars a month with board. In spring and summer, like the oxen who pulled the logs, they could return to their farms and work their own fields.

One other product of the woods, the bark of the hemlock tree, used for tanning hides, offered a chance for wealth. Since the wood was thought to be of little value once the bark had been stripped off, the shaft of the tree was left to rot. In the tanning business things worked both ways: In some places the bark was shipped out to tanneries elsewhere; in others, the hides were brought in. This industry continued well through the nineteenth century until other tanning substances displaced hemlock bark and saved some of the trees in the woods.

As men explored the region and searched out the tallest trees they sometimes looked down to the ground. What they frequently saw at their feet excited them more than the trees above them. In many places they saw iron ore in various forms — in black sand on some of the lake shores, in hard rock close to the surface, in harder rock buried deep.

Who the first man was who discovered Adirondack iron is unknown. The rich deposits in the hills behind Port Henry overlooking Lake Champlain were known both to Gilliland and Skene, the early settlers. The British at Ticonderoga may have worked those deposits. The Americans certainly did, for Arnold wrote in his diary in June, 1775, "Sent a boat with Skene's negroes to dig ore." After the Revolution this richest of all magnetite deposits, second only in quality to the best of Swedish ore, was overlooked or forgotten for a time while the first settlers worked the iron ore nearer at hand.

The early furnaces were everywhere along the lower reaches of many Adirondack rivers, wherever a waterfall offered power. The first settlement at what is now Lake Placid was a little forge. All a settler needed to be an ironmaster was a simple firebox to hold ore and charcoal, more charcoal for fuel, and water power to turn a wheel to break down the resultant slag and metal — thus using the Vulcan forge method, one as old as the Phoenicians.

The search for ore bodies took men from their farms; one settler found a deposit near Keeseville and sold the land for eight hundred dollars. Eventually it produced more than seven hundred thousand dollars of ore. News of ore in the Adirondacks attracted New York capitalists, who hired men to search the region. As more forges fired up, more trees roundabout went down. It required six hundred bushels of charcoal to make the one ton of metal from every four tons of ore. Small rolling mills and ironworks opened in some of the villages, but most small forges soon closed down, their operators bankrupt. Knowing little of complex metallurgy, they found impurities in their ore which made it hard to work and difficult to assay. Ironmakers complained that the quality of the finished iron varied widely. Ore deposits ran out or nearby timber for charcoal was exhausted. For the little settler with no resources except hope and muscles, the dream of wealth was soon over, although some men, bewitched, kept trying for years to make their forges and furnaces pay.

The dream also ended almost as soon for the wealthy. One of the early land speculators was James Duane of Manhattan, son-in-law of Constable. In 1824 he brought his whole family to his wife's land thirty miles north of Saranac Lake, and planned a great estate. He built a road in from Malone, cleared a farm, built a sawmill, then discovered, as his daughter said many years later:

> Our land unfortunately abounded in iron ore. Ore bed after ore bed was discovered, worked, and given up. At last, in 1828, they did get fine beds open: Father built a forge and made bar iron which sold excellently at the Clinton rolling mills: the good times looked to be coming. Just then came the freshet which destroyed so many lives and so much property in Vermont and Northern New York and carried off the forge. He built another forge; it burned; another: it was carried off by another freshet. Uncle Robert put up a large blast furnace at

Deer River: their works looked like a village. It was a wonderful treat to go over and see the casting at the furnace. In the long run neither they nor poor papa made by their manufactories.

The hope of great wealth from the iron led to one of the more dramatic and oft-told tales of early Adirondack days, the story of the Sanford bed on the upper Hudson, below Indian Pass. It begins when Archibald McIntyre, a resident of New York and Albany, and some friends, who had been interested in a small furnace near Lake Placid, decided on further exploration. The chief explorer was David Henderson, a friend of McIntyre's and later his son-in-law. As he was about to take off on one trip through the woods in October, 1826, "a strapping young Indian of a Canadian tribe," Henderson reported, "made his appearance, the first seen in the settlement for three years. The Indian opened his blanket and took out a small piece of Iron ore about the size of a nut. 'You want see 'em ore? Me know 'em bed, all same.' "

The Henderson party followed the Indian through what is now Indian Pass and came to the Hudson as it comes off Marcy. Here they found pieces of pure ore, some of the size of a pumpkin, lying in the channel, and below that a ledge five feet high and fifty feet broad that seemed to be pure ore. After a few days of more discovery and more amazement, Henderson and party raced to Albany to buy the land.

En route Henderson bought a lottery ticket and learned later that he had won a five-hundred-dollar prize. "I am afraid," he wrote, "I am getting too lucky in this way to be lucky in other matters." He was right. Twenty years later, in 1845, he died in a wretched shooting accident by the shore of the very lake he had passed on the way to the great ore bed.

Here in the depth of the wilderness, forty miles from a settlement of any size, with no roads, no population to draw on for help, the McIntyre interests worked a small industrial miracle. By 1839 they had a colony named MacIntyre, later Adirondac, and even later Tahawus, complete with bank, school, two hundred workmen, and a road to Crown Point.

The ore was found to make excellent iron, tough and malleable. It could be produced profitably, but one ironmaster who used it complained that it worked slow because of impurities — a token of things to come. Henderson kept trying. A first blast furnace was built above the mine, which meant refined iron could be produced for shipment. A state geologist estimated that the mine held seventy million tons of ore, a figure found too low in later years. By 1844 the furnace was running, "although vexatious and expensive." Inexperienced labor and an inadequate water supply were chronic problems. In September, 1845, Henderson set out with a group, including his small son, to search for more water. By mistake he pulled the trigger of his own pistol, which John Cheney, his guide, had left cocked, and killed himself. A monument still stands lonely in the mountain wilderness by the lake where that incident occurred. It was named thereafter Calamity Pond.

Calamity it was. Henderson's death did not end the MacIntyre operation, but it sped the work toward it. Ore that was sent to other furnaces continued to behave badly. The company was reorganized, failed, reorganized again. Then a combination of floods that washed out part of the workings, the panic of 1857, and the death of McIntyre in 1858 brought the entire operation to an end. Things were dropped just where they were, to the last casting left in the sand. Except for one family, Tahawus became a deserted village, visited only by occasional tourists.

In later years the property passed over to a large private club, for a hunting preserve. Yet the story does not end there. The mines eventually went into profitable operation. That story belongs to the twentieth century. The key to the happier ending was the "impurity" in the ore which had so plagued the first operators. It was titanium, a heat-resistant metal, vital in today's industry and even more important in the day of jet engines.

Other relatively large iron-mining operations in the mid-nineteenth century had varying fortunes. One large deposit at Lyon Mountain was discovered by a surveyor when the iron set his compass awry. Out in the west, near Lake Bonaparte, a Swiss company was excited about the ore available there and built furnaces and forges at a little place to which they gave the name of Alpina. Their operations failed, but not before they attracted the attention of Colonel Benton, an extraordinary gentleman who appears in detail in a later chapter.

More than two hundred iron mines and forges were worked during the nineteenth century. Only one has been more or less successful from its start to the present day — the rich deposits at Mineville, behind Port Henry on Lake Champlain. Here is one of the largest and richest magnetic ore bodies in the world. From these mines came the iron that sheathed the *Monitor* in the Civil War. The first substantial mining in them began in 1804. Some could be worked in open pits. Others had to be tunneled out; by 1852 some tunnels were three hundred and fifteen feet deep. For years ore was brought to the surface, loaded on heavy horse-drawn wagons, and taken to the lakeside, to be sent to furnaces all along the eastern seaboard. More than a quarter-million tons of ore came out annually in good years. The discovery of the Lake Superior beds decreased Mineville's importance but by 1905 thirteen million tons had been taken out. The mines operate today but little raw ore is shipped. Instead it is "sintered," heated and mixed with coke, and the resulting concentrate is sent to the steel mills.

In the 1830's the people in the villages on the fringes of the Adirondacks could not foresee the eventual disappointment ahead in both the lumber and iron industries. Nor could they see any particular significance in the appearance of the occasional tourist who now stared at the mountain scenery. In the small towns the hopes were all for industry. Small factories had opened, making window frames, simple iron objects, furniture, and tools. One man who opened a horseshoe-nail factory in Keeseville, with his own patents, was congratulated on having a source of wealth that would guarantee his heirs and his heirs' heirs untold income for centuries yet to come. A few unpleasant problems appeared in these years. Cholera came over the border from Canada in 1832. Immigrants en route to New York along Highway 9, now so heavily traveled by tourists, fell dead by the wayside, but the disease did not strike the little villages. In the same years the steady stream of new settlers slackened. The Erie Canal, completed in 1825, provided an easy route to the west. Land agents in Albany were no longer able to turn settlers north.

With the tremendous supplies of lumber and iron it was apparent to these villages that the Adirondack region could achieve tremendous prosperity — if! The "if" was transportation. As the first steam-drawn train in America wobbled the seventeen-mile journey between Albany and Schenectady in 1831, the demand for railroads and canals through the Adirondack region mounted. With it went the cry that has never really died out: "Bring industry to the Adirondacks — that is our chief hope for prosperity!"

To be sure, traffic on Lake Champlain thrived. More than a thousand ships were registered at one time as sailing between Montreal and Ticonderoga and lesser lake shore points. In 1823 a canal was completed to connect the lake with the Hudson and the trade of the region turned south instead of toward Canada, but all lake and canal transportation was locked by winter ice. The state legislature became interested in a proposal to build a canal from Lake Champlain across the northeast Adirondacks to the Saint Lawrence and appropriated money to make a survey. The legislature soon lost its interest when the survey showed that such a canal would cost almost two million dollars.

Saratoga was quickly connected to Albany by rail in 1833. In 1845 New York State had six hundred and sixty-one miles of railroad but not one mile touched the Adirondacks. In 1850 a line was built on the flatland north of the region, between Lake Champlain and Ogdensburg. No line was built into the Adirondacks until 1871, when a short road was laid between Saratoga and North Creek, along the upper Hudson. The first line into the central Adirondacks was built in 1885. But from 1830 on, few years passed without some new scheme, survey, or new company making fancy plans and selling fancier stock. All the plans were based on the same premise: Here was a region rich in iron and timber that needed only modern transportation to get it out. Bureau drawers in Adirondack homes eventually held packets of stock in this plan or that and all worthless. Many a route and plan was laid out but none fancier than the proposal of a Vermont engineer for a road across the northeast Adirondacks, between Boston and Ogdensburg on the Saint Lawrence, to bring all the produce of the west eventually into Boston when the canals and riverways to New York were frozen. Taking the description "Siberia of America" literally, he proposed building a roof and sides over the tracks for most of the way and using hinged smokestacks on the locomotives. He could never raise the three million dollars for that scheme.

None of the prospectuses for the various roads mentioned what the railroads might do to the woods, for there was no concerted conservation movement before the 1870's. The lumber was there for the taking, if only it could be moved profitably; by taking it, a man was contributing to progress and supplying needed raw material for a growing country. Only one of the early prospectuses foresaw the possibility of the tourist trade: "The Adirondack Lakes would force themselves upon the attention of the public and during the hot sultry months of summer be filled with thousands in search of recreation."

The early agitation for railroads, the booming lumber trade, the growing iron industry, all interested Albany. On the porches of the Saratoga hotels, crowded with "cabinet ministers and ministers of the gospel, office holders and office seekers, humbuggers and humbugged, fortune hunters and hunters of woodcock," state politicians also gathered and heard tales of the vast wild land to the north. In 1836 the legislature decided to find out about the resources of the Great Wilderness as well as of other parts of the state and ordered a geological survey. For the Adirondack region the governor, William L. Marcy, appointed Ebenezer Emmons of Williams College, the most eminent geologist of his day. He began his work in 1837.

The opening wide of the wilderness to tourist, sportsman and summer visitor was just ahead.

Wilderness Open

Thirty years in the history of a region is barely time enough for one generation to mature, for another to pass on. Only a short thirty years separate two contrasting descriptions of the Adirondack country. The first was that of Emmons in 1843:

> It is a region of country as little known and as inadequately explored (except by comparatively few individuals) as the secluded valleys of the Rocky Mountains or the burning plains of Central Africa.

Just thirty years later a writer in the *New York Times* lamented that the Adirondack country had

> . . . fallen from that estate of fish and solitude for which it was originally celebrated. Railroads, stages, telegraphs, and hotels have followed in the train of the throng who rushed for the

wilderness. The desert has blossomed with parasols and the waste places are filled with picnic parties, reveling in lemonade and sardines. The piano has banished the deer from the entire region.

That was somewhat exaggerated; there still are deer and hunters who find them, and some parts of the Adirondacks even today have yet to see a sardine. In spirit it was accurate; within thirty years the Northern Wilderness became a tremendous resort area.

How that change came about is difficult to explain fully even now, when it can be seen in retrospect. The tenor of the times, the slow-rising interest in life outdoors, the continuous production of more leisure, more money, and a growing leisure class were all part of it. One thing is sure: The printed word had much to do with it.

The reports of Emmons's survey attracted popular writers. After 1839 a steady trickle of stories about travel and adventure in the Adirondacks appeared and were widely read. The trickle grew to a steady stream. One by one the dangers and difficulties were minimized. People came to see for themselves — people of means for the most part, for a summer vacation was still beyond the great mass of Americans working six days a week, ten and twelve hours a day.

The discovery of the Adirondacks by literary visitors had begun before Emmons, although it was not widespread. In the spring of 1836 a little woman, complete with veil, floppy hat, notebook, and pencil came from Saratoga to Lake George "in double gig and light cart for luggage." She happened to be stone deaf and lacked any sense of smell or taste. That did not keep her from being one of the most indefatigable travelers and travel writers of her day. She was the famous British authoress Harriet Martineau. She had seen Saratoga and cared little for it. Now she was headed north, on the same route thousands of Adirondack tourists take today. She wanted to see things for herself and, as she said, "Everyone who has heard of American scenery has heard of Lake George."

Back in London in 1838 Miss Martineau published a detailed account of her travels: "When we came to Caldwell [on Lake George] men were busy cleaning in preparation for summer company. The Lake House painters and cleaners were busy." She took the boat up Lake George, and as she looked at the mountains on the west she summed up the region: "What a wealth of beauty is there here for future residents yet unborn."

Emmons's own accurate reports on his work were eagerly read. How he came to call the high peaks the Adirondacks has been told. With him on some parts of his journey went a group of friends, including Charles J. Ingham, and also a meteorologist, W. C. Redfield. To Redfield belongs the honor of the first magazine article ever done on the region, a report of a trip with Emmons and an account of how the party climbed "the High Peak of Essex" which Emmons named "Mount Marcy":

> We immediately found ourselves entangled in the zone of dwarfish pines and spruces. These gradually decreased in height until we reached the open surface of the mountain, covered only with mosses and small alpine plants, and at 10 A.M. (Aug. 6) the summit of the High Peak of Essex was beneath our feet. Around us lay scattered in irregular profusion, mountain masses of various magnitudes and elevations, like a vast sea of broken and pointed billows.

The news of the first climbing of Marcy reached Manhattan. On one man its effect was electric. A popular magazine of the day was the *New York Mirror,* a weekly journal "devoted to literature and the Fine Arts, embellished with fine engravings and Musick arranged with accompaniments for the Pianoforte." Its editor was a little man, fiery in his enthusiasms, named Charles Fenno Hoffman. In spite of the loss of one leg in childhood, he had traveled considerably and knew something of the Indian tribes of western New York.

Less than six weeks after Marcy had first been climbed an excited Hoffman was in the Adirondacks. To his paper went his breathless dispatches: "I am detained here at Whitehall for three hours on my way to visit the source of the Hudson . . ." His columns were sandwiched between music for "Beats there a heart on earth sincere" and "The light of other days," and beside poetry signed "James G. Whittier" and "W. C. Bryant." To the little editor, climbing Marcy had some deep meaning. He searched out John Cheney, who had helped to guide the Emmons party. Cheney knew his mountains. He listened to Hoffman tell his wish and he shook his head; he could not help a one-legged man up the steep sides of the peak. Hoffman insisted on trying, but the going got too tough. On the gray side of the mountain, Hoffman broke down and wept. For him, forever, the top of Marcy was to be unattainable.

Just what attention his continued series of articles in the *Mirror* attracted, particularly among the idle gentlemen yawning on the verandahs at Saratoga, is unknown. They did attract the attention of a London publisher. The first popular book of travel and adventure in the Adirondacks ever written appeared first in England in 1839. It was reprinted later in America. Its two volumes, only a small part of them on the Adirondacks, were titled *Wild Scenes in the Forest*.

Read today, the only thing wild about the book is in its title. What Hoffman wrote was a simple account of a trip into the mountains. It lacked the purple prose that was to mark many a later book on the region. He told of his trip a few miles into the interior to MacIntyre, of meeting with John Cheney, of a little hunting, and repeated a few of John's stories, the first reporting of the many guides' stories that were to come.

For the first time the city dweller could read of life in the Northern wilderness. Hoffman told of bears, of wild gorges, of the great rock slides of Indian Pass, of panthers met in guides' stories if not in the flesh. He told of meeting one settler who complained that the Adirondacks were already being spoiled. That theme rises and falls through Adirondack history. This was its first statement. Hoffman never revisited the Adirondacks. As has been told, he was responsible for suggesting "Tahawus" as the most fitting name for Marcy. His book brought no new settlers and may have attracted only a few hardy visitors. It set a pattern for later books that would bring visitors by the thousand.

Hoffman did not go far into the interior, but that was no longer all unknown. John Todd, a Boston clergyman, followed Emmons's trail as far as Long Lake in the central Adirondacks in 1841 and found eight or nine families lumbering and farming. He returned in 1842, found three more families, and added proudly that all the people of Long Lake were members of a temperance society. That distinction did not endure.

In the mid-forties two smart young journalists were on the staff of the *New York Tribune*. One was Henry J. Raymond, associate editor, a man for whom journalism was life. In 1846 he left that paper, with dreams of having a paper of his own. Six years later he founded the *New York Times* and was its first editor. One of his closest friends was Joel T. Headley, an ex-minister turned reporter. Headley took Raymond's place on the *Tribune* but his health broke and he quit, to become one of the most widely read authors of the mid-nineteenth century. Two of his books, *Napoleon and His Marshals* and *Washington and His Generals,* were in many parlor bookcases. A master of the bombastic style, Edgar Allan Poe called him "the Autocrat of All Quacks."

Yet Headley is an important figure in the further opening of the Adirondacks. He was one of the first to report a fact that was to draw thousands to the region in later years: Many people sick with a variety of diseases seemed to improve in the woods. He went to cure what he described as "an attack on the brain." Following two journeys he published *The Adirondacks,* or *Life in the Woods,* written as letters to Raymond, who had hoped to make the same trip. It was a popular book and reappeared in many editions between 1849 and 1875. What Headley wrote was not only the best description of the Adirondack country at mid-century but the first popular report of the seemingly infinite stock of fish and game to be had for the taking. Many a man, as he put the book down, must have wanted to grab his tackle and rush off to the Northern Wilderness at once. For, as Headley wrote:

> Arriving at a clearing I had hardly swallowed some dinner before I donned my India rubber leggings and plunged into a splendid stream nearby after trout. The very first cast I made, I took one and kept taking them till the end of two hours I had fifty fine fellows.

Headley wrote of every quarter except the unsettled northwest. He was not always accurate in his details but he always had a good story. He fished on Raquette Lake and Long Lake, Piseco Lake and Lake Pleasant "where fishing has become a business." Wherever he went, the fishing was perfect. On Moose Lake,

> A judge and his lady are accustomed in summer to come from the western settlements and camp for two or three weeks at a time on its shores and fish. The lady, accomplished and elegant, enjoys the recreation amazingly and once caught herself a trout weighing nineteen pounds!

Or,

> My friend had great sport here one day. He did not fish over an hour and yet in that short time, took a hundred and twenty pounds of trout and left them biting as sharp and fast as when he began.

Many other collections of tales of hunting and fishing in the Adirondacks followed in the next twenty years. All were larded with camp-fire philosophy and the prettiest sentimental approach to the necessity of having to shoot a deer or of having to club it to death with a boat oar. The books sold well and were widely read. Most extraordinary of all writers to come was the Honorable Amelia M. Murray, maid of honor to Queen Victoria, who visited the region briefly in the autumn of 1856, along with the governor of New York, Horatio Seymour, and his niece. She went in from Elizabethtown, armed with tea, biscuits, lemons, portable soup, and arrowroot. Out of the wilderness at last, at Utica, she reported, "Three days were necessary to recruit and repose myself."

By 1850 a few new hotels appeared, often in remote places. Some backwoods families found a new livelihood in offering shelter to sportsmen and tourists. That shelter was always plain. The wilderness might be opening but it was still largely trackless. A new occupation appeared, that of Adirondack guide. Many a lone hunter found he could get paid for doing the very thing he liked best to do.

How many sportsmen the writings of Headley and others may have attracted is beyond knowing now, but they did come. Shortly thereafter men began to complain that in easily accessible lakes the fish were gone. A fisherman at Lake George said, "A few years ago the lake abounded in lake trout which were frequently caught weighing twenty pounds. Their average weight at the present time is not more than a pound and a half and they are scarce at that."

Those city people too busy to read of or visit the Adirondack country now found lithographs of it in front of their eyes in living rooms, clubs, bars, barbershops — wherever Currier and Ives prints were hung. In the early fifties that firm began to issue reproductions of various Adirondack scenes, done by "perhaps our greatest sporting artist," Arthur Fitzwilliam Tait. An Englishman of thirty-one, he arrived in New York in 1850, determined to paint life out-of-doors. His talents were recognized at once by other American artists and by the firm of Currier and

Ives. For the next fifteen years they eagerly bought his paintings. He headed for the North Woods and eventually had his own camp on Long Lake. Travelers through the Adirondacks told of coming suddenly on a tall, handsome, tweedy stranger out hunting, armed not with rifle but with palette and canvas. Today collectors search eagerly for copies of "Sunrise on Lake Saranac" or "Brook Trout Fishing," offering hundreds of dollars for prints originally sold for a dollar. Their wide sale did not please Tait; he complained that it interfered with the sale of his originals to collectors.

As vivid publicity about the Adirondack region spread, it attracted the attention of a new group of railroad promoters. Their plan was to build from Saratoga westward through the central Adirondacks to Sackett's Harbor, on Lake Ontario beyond Watertown. In their first prospectus they even offered two alternate routes. The company had a state charter. It managed to buy two hundred and fifty thousand acres of state land at six cents an acre and hoped to mortgage that land to British capitalists and thus get the money to start the road. In spite of these assorted blessings the company ran out of money about 1853 and glowing adjectives describing the iron and timber resources did not attract new funds.

With the foresight of twentieth-century lobbyists the directors then organized a publicity junket, hoping that influential and wealthy prospects might see for themselves and come home and tell others. Unlike the junkets of today this one had no luxuries, no smiling hostesses, no free liquor — only a one hundred and fifty mile walk in the woods. Raymond of the *Times* accepted the invitation to go along. The result of that trip was a series of four articles which appeared in his paper in the summer of 1855, entitled "A Week in the Wilderness." They are fresh and vivid Adirondack source material.

They describe a journey, largely on foot, between Saratoga and Lowville, through the heart of the Adirondack country. As Raymond explained:

The Directors set on foot an Exploring Expedition and invited fifteen or twenty gentlemen of wealth, character, and position to visit the region and study its character and capabilities for themselves. I had the good fortune to receive an invitation also . . .

Raymond covered much the same territory as Hoffman and Headley. Starting at Luzerne, which was

. . . known to the more adventurous of Saratoga loungers, not less for its picturesque beauty than its excellent hotel and the superb dinners of venison and trout which await those who are fortunate enough to fall into the hands of Rockwell . . .

the party continued north, then west, visiting Long Lake, the Tahawus works, and out at Lowville. Raymond did offer a clear picture of life at one of the early backwoods hostelries, at a place west of Schroon River where a Vermont farmer had arranged his house to care for tourists. He wrote:

Bed time brought new anxieties. The house had only two rooms beside the kitchen, which was hardly large enough to hold the stove, on the ground floor, and the same number above. These were all of the smallest size and over twenty people, besides the family, were to lodge there somehow or other. I only know that the Chief Engineer [of the railroad and of the expedition] told me my room was No. 16 on the second floor front and he did me the additional favor of pointing out the corner of the garret which answered to that description. Before dropping asleep I had a glimpse of a floor carpeted with sleepers.

Raymond was impressed by the tremendous supply of timber and iron and urged the building of the railroad. Although he never returned to the Adirondacks, that journey had its effect on him a few years later. It had no effect on the railroad promoters and their hopes. By 1863 the company had twice reorganized and was bankrupt. It passed into the control of Dr. Thomas C. Durant, one of the builders of the Union Pacific, and an important Adirondack figure after 1870. Durant built the first part of the line, the only part ever constructed, from Saratoga to North Creek, in 1871, the first railroad to come deep into the Adirondack country. When it was built its trains were not overweighted either with lumber or iron. What they carried in great number was tourists. From 1850 more and more people were finding the North Woods.

One old hotel register, of the Raquette Lake House, opened in 1856, tells something about the visitors who came in its first fifteen years. By 1871 the hotel had entertained twenty-five hundred guests. A party appeared in 1864 about whom some one noted in the register, "All drunk." Yet in July one guest wrote, "Going home to Chicago where there is whiskey," and another added, "Been temperance man for 8 days from necessity." In August of the same summer one gentleman commented, "Been sleepless all the time. My home is Heaven, my rest is not here." And one guest named Foster arrived with two girls, whose coming was noted in the register:

> How Happy would Foster be with either,
> Were t'other fair Charmer away.

In Civil War years the Adirondack country sent to the armies the usual high quota of expert marksmen that the area has contributed to all wars. Some of the Adirondack men, however, went to war from Vermont, where volunteers were paid seventy-five dollars, a better rate than in New York, a proof that the Adirondack people inherited something from their Vermont forebears. The real effects of the Civil War on the Adirondacks were indirect but important. War incomes meant that many people of moderate means could now follow the custom of a summer vacation. In Saratoga, always the Adirondack gateway, the long-caricatured Southern planter, wife, and honeyed daughter disappeared forever. In their place were Northerners grown rich on the war. The small stream of tourists into the Adirondack region continued to rise, even if the Grand Tour only meant a day in Glens Falls, where the bars were filled with roistering lumberjacks, and a boat ride up Lake George and Lake Champlain, picnic baskets by Lake Luzerne, or a daring trip by coach into Saranac Lake, where one Colonel Baker's hotel already had many a famous name on its register. Here the visitors might even have the same experience that befell one New Yorker who left an expensive fishing outfit on the porch overnight and was surprised to find it safe in the morning. The colonel was not surprised. "By Godfrey, sir," he said, "your things are as safe here as in the Bank of England. There's not a Republican within ten miles of here." *

By 1865 the wilderness was indeed open, but there were men who did not like it that way. By 1865, some who could boast of twenty summers spent in parts of the Adirondack wilds marked the changes. One man lamented, with fancy similes full awash, "We shall have large American hotels everywhere rising like splendid icebergs, suddenly brought down upon us as by the current of travel and migration and sweeping down from the old Arctic of wealth to summer seas of common sympathy and use." For others the important change was not in the way people were coming into the woods but the change in the woods themselves. The lumbermen were in the central Adirondacks in the early 1850's. They were still interested in the bigger trees, but the acreage they cut showed on many a hillside. There were stretches of the Adirondacks that had been lovely in 1850 but showed only water-soaked tree stumps by 1860; here lakes and rivers had been dammed, sometimes by lumbermen for their drives, sometimes by steamboat operators.

To most men the Adirondacks were still a storehouse filled with riches that should be gotten out; any other attitude was

* From *A History of the Adirondacks*, by Alfred L. Donaldson. Copyright, 1921, Century Company. Reprinted by permission of the publishers, Appleton-Century-Crofts, Inc.

inimical to the progress of America. When a conservation movement did rise in America, after the 1870's, its rise was speeded by spreading concern about saving the Adirondacks. Yet the seeds of that movement were planted by visitors to the Adirondacks even before the Civil War. Those who spoke out were few and their voices solitary. What they had was a new idea — that something of the Adirondack woods should be saved for future generations. The idea was so new and so against the spirit of the times that it found little support.

S. H. Hammond, a journalist who followed Headley, stated it in 1857 in his book *Wild Northern Scenes*. His statement was a remarkable vision of what a group in 1894, sickened by the continuing rape of the woods, did write into the state constitution. Writing particularly of the country around the Raquette River, he said:

> Civilization is pushing its way even toward this wild and for all agricultural purposes sterile region, and before many years even the Rackette will be within its ever-extended circle. When that time shall have arrived where shall we go to find the woods, the wild things, the old forests? Had I my way I would mark out a circle of a hundred miles in diameter and throw around it the protecting aegis of the constitution. I would make it a forest forever. It should be a misdemeanor to chop down a tree and a felony to clear an acre within its boundaries. The old woods should stand here always as God made them, growing on until the earthworm ate away their roots and the strong winds hurled them to the ground, and new woods should be permitted to supply the place of the old so long as the earth remained.

George Dawson, editor of the *Albany Evening Journal*, was saying much the same thing in the fifties. Verplanck Colvin, a boy then growing up in Albany, may well have read Dawson's articles from time to time and wondered what the man was talking about. In time Colvin found out for himself; in time his voice was to call more loudly and more effectively than any other, "Save the Adirondacks!"

Stories of mounting damage to the Adirondack region must have come down to Manhattan during the Civil War. On a hot August afternoon in 1864 Henry J. Raymond, editor of the *Times*, sat down to write an editorial for the morrow. In the heat of that Manhattan summer he may have remembered a walk in the Adirondack woods almost a decade before. He wrote lovingly of them now and he added:

> And here we venture a suggestion to those of our citizens who desire to advance civilization by combining taste with luxury in their expenditures. Let them form combinations and seizing upon the choicest of the Adirondack Mountains, before they are despoiled of their forests, make of them grand parks owned in common, and thinly dotted with hunting seats, where, at little cost, they can enjoy equal solitude and privacy of sporting, riding, and driving, whenever they are able, to seek the country in pursuit of health or pleasure.

That editorial, urging conservation in private if not public hands, was the first metropolitan newspaper mention of the need for some sort of "Save the woods" program in the Adirondacks. Raymond never followed up his suggestion, for he died a few years later and the paper was sold. In later years, however, and down to today, no voice has been sturdier or less afraid to speak out for the preservation of the Adirondacks than the *New York Times* and later the *New York Herald Tribune*.

Isolated as these voices were before 1870, they were a measure of the change in the Adirondack country during the preceding thirty years. In 1840 Emmons could write happily in his first report that "The axe has been laid at the root of the tree and ere long where naught now greets the eye but dense and impassable forest will be seen the golden grain, the sleek cattle browsing on the rich pastures." Now a few men said, "Save the woods." Yet the changes in those years were small and slow compared with changes that lay just ahead. One of the most far-reaching came about because a young Connecticut clergyman visited the Adirondacks on a fishing trip in the summer of 1864.

His name was the Reverend William Henry Harrison Murray.

The Parson Was a Liar

In 1868 the fashionable and conservative Park Street Congregational Church of Boston was seeking a new pastor. The news reached Boston that down in Connecticut, Reverend William Murray, an extremely handsome man of twenty-eight, was as promising a young clergyman as could be found. A group of parishioners went to hear him and were so moved by a really great gift of oratory that they forgot to ask about his hobbies. He was offered the post in Boston and accepted it. His first appearance crowded the church. Not only was he a fine speaker and a virile young married man with a lovely wife. He had some pretensions to writing. After his trip to the Adirondacks he had written about his experiences for a Connecticut newspaper. Everything seemed settled for a sparkling career in the ministry until his Adirondack sketches appeared in book form in April, 1869.

This small book, *Adventures in the Wilderness,* or *Camp Life in the Adirondacks,* was in many ways like the earlier volumes of Hoffman and Headley. A city man goes into the woods, has various hunting and fishing experiences, meets with a unique guide, and advises other city people to do the same and gain new health and strength. Either the timing of the book's appearance matched a growing desire to get out-of-doors or Murray caught some note others had missed; the effect of the book was phenomenal. By June, 1869, the book had created a stampede to the woods. People came in such droves and with such weird ideas of the comforts and excitement to be found that the phrase "Murray's fools," remained part of Adirondack speech for decades.

In later years historians have read and reread that book, trying to understand why it should have had such an effect. For one thing, it was the first Adirondack guidebook, with specific instructions on routes, a few hotels (which he did not overdescribe), activities, costumes, and adventures. Other books had told of adventure; Murray told how "you too might have them." He made the Adirondacks sound not only attractive but attainable. The area might still be wilderness but it was wilderness a man or woman could easily enter, find simple but comfortable hotels and perhaps, as he had done, land two huge trout on one cast, catch deer by following them in a boat and jumping out and hanging on to the stub of a tail until the animal gave in, and shoot a high waterfall in a guide boat and live to write about it.

His tales may have been slightly elongated but not much more than those in earlier books. He appointed himself an authority on the Adirondacks, on fishing, hunting, and everything else connected with the outdoors and may really have believed that he was. Add to this the fact that the book obviously had to be true in every line because one of Boston's most distinguished clergymen had written it, and that may explain in part its extraordinary effect. To explain it fully one must have been alive in 1869, weary of the city, beset by a threatening business panic, and moved by Murray's words:

> You choose the locality which best suits your eye and build a lodge under unscarred trees, and upon a carpet of moss, untrampled by man or beast. There you live in silence, unbroken by any sound save such as you yourself may make, away from all the business and cares of civilized life.

That would set any man at an 1869 desk dreaming and perhaps even hasten him to the railway station. En route he might stop and pick up his wife, for, as Murray pointed out, "There is nothing in the trip which the most delicate and fragile [lady] must fear." He also offered some advice "in respect to what is more appropriate and serviceable for a lady to wear in the wilderness." His list included:

> A net of fine Swiss mull, gathered into the form of a sack or bag, with an elastic to slip over the head. Fix the elastic inside the collar-band and you can laugh defiance at the mosquitoes and gnats.
>
> A pair of buckskin gloves, with armlets of chamois-skin or thick drilling, sewed on at the wrist of the glove and buttoned near the elbow so lightly as to prevent the entrance of flies.
>
> For the head, a soft felt hat, such as gentlemen wear, rather broad in the brim. This is light and cool for the head and a good protection from sun and rain. . . .
>
> A short walking dress, with Turkish drawers fastened with a band tightly at the ankle.

Thus attired, Murray's lady of 1869 was ready for the woods. The sight of her, with net over her face, man's hat on her head, long gloves in place, and her short walking dress with Turkish drawers fastened tightly at the ankle probably sent all wild life scurrying and may explain why panther, moose, and catamount disappeared forever from the woods.

That took care of the ladies, but what about hunting and fishing? "Well," wrote Murray, "every person has his own standard. . . . With a guide who knows his business I would undertake to feed a party of twenty the season through and seldom should they sit down to a dinner lacking trout and venison." Murray generously gave much of the credit for his own adventures to "Honest John" Plumley, a superman in the woods. It was not only sportsman and wife or vacationist looking for something new whom Murray lured to the Adirondacks, but the invalid; this most unhappy sequel is reported in another chapter. As for cost, Murray made that even more delightful. He estimated that guide, railway and coach fare, and a month in the woods with guide would cost about one hundred and twenty-five dollars. That may have been true before the book appeared; it was not true thereafter.

The crowds poured into the woods and forgot what Murray had emphasized about simplicity. They found that many hotels were primitive dwellings. They searched out John Plumley and found him nothing more or less than a good Adirondack guide. They hunted for "Buttermilk Falls" which Murray had shot in a guide boat, so he said, and found no place by that name. Nor was there a "Nameless Creek" where trout bit not one by one but, like the creatures entering the Ark, in pairs. What was worse, Murray had not gone deep into the woods where the lumbermen were working, but stayed on watercourses, and had seen little of the lumberman's work. Thus, even in a year when millions upon millions of feet of lumber were coming out, he could write, "In the Adirondack wilderness the lumberman has never been. No axe has sounded along its mountain side or echoed across the peaceful water." Finally, there were no hotels every ten miles down the road as people thought Murray implied, though he never did.

The stampede into the woods in June was a stampede out in August. Every stagecoach was filled with bitter people. They cried, "Liar! Murray wrote a re-lieable book. In it he lies over and over!" He was attacked in magazines and papers. Murray could say in his own defense that he had done very little exaggerating — no more than a fisherman returning home at night from any pond. People pointed to his remarks on lumbering as showing how little of an authority he really was, and there Murray was vulnerable. Not for years, even while Murray took pride in the name of "Adirondack" Murray, did the cry of "Liar!" die out.

The effect of the book on the Adirondack country was great. Its effect on Murray was greater. The last thing he ever expected when he wrote it was to produce a best seller, to earn a fortune, to become a controversial figure, and to garner columns of publicity in every magazine of the day. Murray wrote another dozen books, mostly on the outdoors, none of which ever duplicated his first success. The book also had another effect on Murray, a rather spectacular one. Understandably, it disconcerted the staid members of the most fashionable church in Boston to have their eloquent shepherd called a liar on every side. They were moved by the eloquence of his speech but nonetheless squirmed in their pews. Worse was to come. The Boston newspapers had dug into the Reverend Murray's hobbies and found that his favorite sport was breeding racing horses and betting on them on week days. He was also busy organizing various companies to publish papers, to build a new racing sulky — all most improper for the pastor of a sedate Boston church. His sermons were still golden-worded, for Murray was a great orator, with more than the amount of innate ham that sometimes goes with great oratory, but — ! The church was relieved when he resigned.

He left the church to found one of his own. In 1880, after rumors of bankruptcy and shady finance, he quit that. He was reported in Texas, Canada, Europe, Africa; but whatever he was doing could not have been as bad as the gossip reported back in Boston. He divorced his wife (who left to study surgery abroad and was the first American woman to receive her diploma in Vienna). He turned up again in Boston, then appeared in Montreal, where he ran a restaurant. Dressed in a white robe, serving food, he attracted many ex-parishioners from Boston to see their former pastor. He then turned lecturer and lived until 1904, long after the Adirondacks he knew had ceased to exist, if ever they did exist at all.

Whether the Adirondacks would have been "discovered" at

this time without Murray's book is beyond saying. More than any one man in Adirondack history, Murray gets the credit for the widest popularization of the region. Before 1869 it would have been difficult to name fifty hotels in the entire Adirondack area; some were hotels in name only, rickety buildings with roofs against the weather. By 1875 there were more than two hundred, some with several hundred rooms and the latest improvements.

The invasion had immediate results in creating a new interest in the Adirondacks in Albany. In 1872 the legislature, after many a prodding, ordered a complete topographical survey made of the region so that it could be accurately mapped for the first time. The young and enthusiastic Verplanck Colvin was appointed as surveyor. In the hubbub of that session of the legislature one member did show that the concern expressed by a few men over the future of the woods was having an effect. A measure was introduced to create a state park commission and "to inquire into the expediency" of converting the timbered regions of the Adirondack country into a state park. A commission was set up. It "inquired" for many a year before any majority in the legislature cared to listen.

A more disastrous result was the continued depletion of fish and game, and increasingly loud protests. The cry "Where are the fish?" was nothing new; it had been raised beside some Adirondack lakes as early as 1850, but it goes further back in history than that. An English poet, with the barely printable name of Thomas Bastard, summed up the fisherman's problem in 1598:

> Fishing if I, a fisher, may protest,
> Of pleasures is the sweet'st, of sports the best.
> Of exercise the most excellent,
> Of recreation the most innocent:
> But now the sport is marde and watt ye why:
> Fishes decrease and fishers multiply.

Following Murray the fishers did multiply, but that was only part of it. Trout hogs, with fantastic catches of any size of fish, ignored the simple early game laws, but there was no one about to enforce them except lackadaisical local constables. The demand of the hotels for trout to put on their tables led them to hire fishermen to supply the demand. These fishermen in turn looked for easier ways to get trout. The result was loud explosions of dynamite on quiet nights in back ponds, a lake surface covered with gasping and dying fish, and more trout for breakfast in the hotel dining room.

The result was the obvious. "To find fish and game" a visitor said in 1880, "you must go to the solitary and secluded lakes and streams." No less an authority than the Reverend William Murray complained in 1877: "I have not put my fly rod together four times in four years. The Adirondack waters will have to be stocked by artificial means before a fly rod is needed on them and it will take six years to do it." Coming from "Adirondack" Murray, of all people, that was a little too much. A critic snapped back: "I fully agree with Murray but much of it is due to overdrawn descriptions in Murray's own writings."

Although an old law forbade the hunting of deer before August 1 and after January 1, it went unobserved in the early 1870's. The methods of hunting put all the odds on the hunter and few on the deer: "hounding," the use of dogs to chase deer into a lake where the hunter could go after them in a boat and club them to death; and the use of lights at night for "jacking." Few hunters made any distinction between buck, doe, or fawn. Hotels served venison in and out of season; out of season, the name changed to "Adirondack steak" or "mountain lamb." The appetite for venison seems to have been unlimited; many hotels listed it on the menu for breakfast.

Forest and Stream summed up the whole wretched development:

The trout hog, the deer butcher, the dynamite cartridge fiend, the steel trap deer stalker, and the like are increasing instead of decreasing. Between the fish hog, the night hunter, the pseudo-sportsman and the like, this grand old region is becoming yearly less and less like its old self and in a few more years will witness the entire destruction from a sportsman's and nature lover's point of view.

Even "Adirondack" Murray came in for criticism, for the magazine said, "This man who talks about sportsmanship boasts of having killed five deer in July."
Compared to other men in the woods, Murray was a piker.

The years that followed Murray's book, thanks to it in part and to the growing interest in out-of-doors life, were the Gilded Years of the Adirondacks — 1875 to 1910, when the region was at the height of its popularity and fashion. The fame of the luxury of the Adirondack hotels, of the lavishness of Adirondack private camps and hunting lodges, of the saltiness of Adirondack guides spread wide. By 1900, a quarter-million guests were coming to the Adirondack resorts in one short summer, and that before the day of the automobile. The wilderness had opened and had found itself an industry. It was an industry not based on lumber or on iron, as many people had long hoped; its natural resources were lakes, mountains, and the woods. They were eternal, or so it seemed. The prosperity of the area appeared forever assured.

Nothing could ever alter the mountains or lakes. The woods had no such guarantee of permanence. A threat to their future was in the making. It began in 1866 when a small mill was opened on the upper Hudson to make paper from ground poplar. Within a year paper makers discovered that chemicals could be used in place of grinders to make wood pulp with less effort, and that spruce was by far the best wood for paper making. The chemical process also meant that small trees, down to those three inches in diameter, could be used. The Gilded Years opened to the sound of ten thousand hammers building new hotels and adding wings to old ones. But on the wind was the increasingly noisy sound of axes in the woods and the happy shouts of a new breed of lumbermen. In the Adirondack woods they found spruce in abundance, giant virgin spruce and seedling trees side by side, a fortune ready for the cutting.

It had taken thirty years to open the woods of the Adirondack country. To some worried men in the 1870's it seemed that it would need only a few more years to wipe out those woods entirely.

IV

Adirondack
Originals

One Vast Boardinghouse

An old-timer who had been coming to the Adirondacks for many summers looked around shortly after 1870. He summed up what he saw: "The day is coming when it's all going to be one vast boardinghouse. You can still go to dinner in a flannel shirt but as the snobby New Yorker and snobbier wife turn up the old set fades away."

It never was really quite as bad as that. The visitor to the Adirondacks after 1870 had his choice of varied places in every part of the region except in the northwest quarter, and on every lake of any size. The day of the forty-five dollars per day hotel, with white dinner jacket and plaid shorts *de rigueur*, was still eighty years off, but among the two hundred hotels building or expanding and charging five to thirty dollars per week for room and board with extras, a visitor could find novelty and even luxury.

The advertisements of the 1870's show what he might expect to encounter. He could choose the Leland House at Schroon Lake, capacity three hundred, whose proprietor advertised: "The society here is of the best class, scarcely any of the rowdy elements finding its way in, for the bright skies, the waving fields, the far reaching forests, and the great grand freedom of the mountains possess little that is congenial to the tastes of such." Further north, he could find the Beede House at Keene Valley announcing: "Two new bath rooms have been added, one for ladies and one for gentlemen." Or he might select the Rainbow House north of Saranac Lake, capacity sixty, which advertised: "Here all conventional restraint may be thrown off and all feel thoroughly at home. Connected with the house is a taxidermist's office."

If the visitor wanted a vacation without taxidermy he could rough it at John Moore's at Tahawus, capacity forty: "Terms: $8.00 per week. Mrs. Moore will accompany ladies on their mountain excursions when desired." He might find a bargain at the Cranberry Lake Hotel, deep in the woods, capacity sixty, its rates one dollar per day, five dollars per week. He could measure the boast of the landlord of the Fenton House, on Beaver Lake, capacity one hundred and seventy-five: "More deer and trout than in any other part of the Adirondacks." Or he might try the first tourist "cabins" in the world at Indian Lake, where Chauncey Hathorn, hermit for years, had suddenly tired of hermiting and set up tents and a central dining hall and charged a dollar a day for tent and three meals.

The history of one small hotel, the Forge House, a popular hotel near the First Lake of the Fulton Chain, sums up much about many Adirondack hotels. Opened in 1871, it was managed first by a young couple who had trekked into the wilderness a few years earlier carrying their baby son in a pack basket. The hotel began as a building of rough-sawed spruce boards, with thirteen rooms and attic space for guides. Its dining room had two tables, one for guests, one for guides. Year by year thereafter it grew larger and fancier. Like many of the hotels, it frequently changed hands, although no other hotel changed quite as often; before the Forge House burned in 1924 it had had twenty-one different proprietors.

Even in its first years its register showed visitors from all America. The Forge House was in the wildest area of the region, but before it was open a year three hundred and forty-eight guests had come and gone, including thirty-two women. The hotel remained open during the winter and twenty-four guests showed up during those months. One of them was an Indian chief who signed the register as Na-San-Ni-Ka-Wa-Na-Wa-Na-A-Na-Ko-Wa-Ne, but added meekly that people called him Bill. On the register in these early days are the boasts of the sportsmen: "Have been here since the 27th of July. Caught 350 speckled trout, 5 salmon. Shot 17 woodcock, 22 partridges, 2 deer."

All Adirondack hotels, no matter where located, had some things in common. All advertised trout and venison dinners until the wonder is that one fish or one deer was left in the woods for later generations. Almost all the hotels were financed and managed locally, and used local help. The distinction between the simple and the fancy inns was sharp. "In the fancy hotels the washroom's got toilet soap," one guide said. "Good yellow bar soap's good enough for the ones that don't put on style." The days of the large corporation that numbers an Adirondack hotel or two in its chain and moves the help to Florida in winter and back to the Adirondacks in summer were still far off. Every hotel had its own company of guides for hire. All Adirondack hotels were built of wood and easy prey to fire. Only a few were winterized and stayed open the year around. Most were built with all the decorations and adornments that a nineteenth-century builder could load on them and, to a twentieth-century eye, differed only in degrees of hideousness.

One unique problem all hotels had to contend with during the Gilded Years was the problem of invalids, particularly people with tuberculosis. Murray's book helped to bring them, but many came because they heard of other people who had recovered their health. "There is scarcely a hotel in the wilderness which cannot write a sorrowful record," *Forest and Stream* reported in 1892, "scarcely one which a few years ago did not

have the appearance of a sanatorium more than a summer resort." By 1890, once Dr. Trudeau had proved the infectiousness
of the disease, most hotels were advertising "no invalids."

Hotel colonies or resort centers grew in only a few places,
on the shores of Lake George, Lake Placid, and Schroon Lake.
Most hotels were isolated, each on its lake. The key to a backwoods hotel's success, therefore, was transportation; for most
that meant four- and six-horse stagecoaches. After the railroads
came in, stages continued to run for some years, but many a
remote hotel failed when the railroad passed it by.

While the coaches did run, with everyone getting out at tough
hills and everyone's heart in his mouth as a coach tried to brake
down a steep hill, they were very much part of an Adirondack
summer. Some did a forty- or fifty-mile trip into the woods in
a day at three dollars and fifty cents per passenger. Various
hotels of which not a trace now stands were crowded half-way
houses on the stage routes. Competition was keen between stage
lines and hotels with their own stage lines. It was not unheard
of for a stage to pick up a passenger for one hotel and drop
him "by mistake" at another, miles from the one where he had
made reservations.

Many hotels without coach lines or railroads managed to
keep filled by means of little lake steamers that brought the
guests to them from some coach-stop point. In time steamers
plied almost every lake of any size, making remote points accessible and angering fishermen, who choked in the black wood
smoke from the funnels and tossed about in the wakes. They
were variously loved and hated, and are all gone now.

The two largest hotel centers, Lake George and Lake Placid,
where rows of hotels stood side by side, developed at different
times. Lake Placid grew slowly. It had only one hotel in 1876,
a date when Lake George could boast of twenty. As the Gilded
Years began, Lake George set out to be most gilded of all the
Adirondack places. After all, it had to compete with Saratoga in

luxury or at least offer luxury that the ladies and gentlemen of Saratoga would not sneer at.

Even the Saratoga hotels and every hotel in the Adirondacks anywhere in the 1870's took a poor second place to the Fort William Henry Hotel at Lake George. A hotel by that name had been built back in the fifties, but it was decrepit and failing. In 1868, the Roessles from Albany and Washington, one of the few "outside" families to come to the Adirondack hotel business, arrived to show what a resort hotel could really be. They knew places like Paul Smith's deep in the woods, and other backwoods hotels had their own charms, which Lake George could not meet. They set out to compete by sheer luxury, in terms of 1868, and rebuilt the old Fort William Henry. What they produced was a building four to six stories high, with a mansard roof three hundred and thirty-four feet long just above the shore of the lake. It had broad piazzas twenty-seven feet high and rows of thirty-foot Corinthian columns. Either it was designed by no architect, by a mad architect, or it just accumulated, for it was a mixture of every school of architecture, with greatest emphasis on the gingerbread. At its center was a dome flanked by two towers, while at the east end of the building was another tower almost as high.

One visitor wrote:

> Under the dome is the general office which is also a point of general interest, made bright with the plumage of fair ladies: fresh and clean, with just a touch of color blending with its white and gold and elegant in its rich simplicity.

The description continued:

> It has offices for the stage companies, telegraph office, cigar, and bookstand, drawing rooms, bijou room, and a large billiard hall. On Thursday of each week during the season a "grand hop" is held in the parlor and every evening between the hours of nine and ten the great doors of the dining room

are thrown open and, with the sound of many slippers, a stream of ministering waiters issues forth, bringing cake and delight and ice cream to all who will partake thereof. The place needs 200 employees to operate it and listed among those employees, to make the season complete for the guests, are a stage manager, a prompter, and a fine art critic.

With tableaux and charades it is easy today to figure out what the first two did, but it is hard to understand the functions of the art critic.

The Fort William Henry offered all this to nine hundred guests for the highest rates in the Adirondacks — thirty dollars a week up. Unlike any other Adirondack hotel the Fort William Henry could boast of its own gas for lighting, manufactured on the spot. It became one of the great hotels of America at the period, an attraction for foreign visitors and a magnet for the many who wearied of Saratoga. The railroad that came to it from the south in 1882 only increased the hotel's prosperity and prestige.

Its luxury did not stay unchallenged. For a time it was rivaled by Prospect House, just below the village of Blue Mountain Lake and thirty miles from any railroad, one of the most extraordinary hotels ever built anywhere. In 1879 an active young man, Frederick C. Durant, was working in his father's sugar refinery in New York City. His uncle, Dr. Thomas C. Durant, railroad builder, who appears in some detail in the next chapter, had returned to the Adirondacks, a region he had known since boyhood. He hoped to make part of it a rich man's playground. The young nephew wanted to help. In 1879 he bought land and planned a hotel, deep in the woods in the area which his uncle and his cousin William West Durant were planning to develop. He started at scratch on the shores of Blue Mountain Lake; he first had to build a sawmill to prepare the lumber for his building.

What he built was a large wooden box of a building, T-shaped, with little ornamentation outside, two hundred and twenty-five feet wide, facing the lake, with a twenty-foot piazza on most sides. Its six stories were built from lumber sawed on the spot and put together by neighborhood craftsmen. It had three hundred rooms, many baths, fireplaces, and an elevator worked by steam. More astonishing for this remote hotel, every bedroom had an electric light powered by two dynamos with steam from a wood fire. Prospect House was the first hotel in the world thus equipped, beating Hotel Everitt in Park Row, Manhattan, by a year. Into the wilds Durant brought such unsylvan things as a wine steward, "Veuve Cliquot," consommé of green turtle, Negro waiters, a primitive sort of steam heat for autumn guests, running water in every room, bowling alleys, and a two-story outhouse reached from the second-floor piazzas, so that people on the upper floors would not have to descend to ground level. Rates for this luxury hotel, which held five or six hundred guests at times, were not as high as at the Fort William Henry; twenty-five dollars per week in the summer months, fifteen dollars in off season.

The idea of continuous activities sparked by a social director, now so common at today's summer resorts, is not new. Prospect House furnished amusement for guests — afternoon and evening concerts, "Mrs. Jarley's Wax Works," masquerades, bowling contests, and water fetes. One New York society editor wrote in 1883:

The grand masquerade ball at the Prospect House was one of the greatest events of the Season. The large and magnificent parlor was brilliantly illuminated with a thousand electric lights and filled to repletion with the elite from every clime. Such an amount of dazzling beauty, such beautiful figures robed in costly attire, such a brilliant flow of wit and humor seldom grace the halls of prince or potentate.

Prospect House was filled during the eighties. The Tiffanys, Astors, Stuyvesants, Biddles, and other fashionable names were on its register, along with distinguished names from London and St. Petersburg. In the nineties the hotel began to run into trouble. The railroad from Utica north, built in 1893, did not come near it. The depression of 1893 hurt it. Even when full it had never made money; Frederick Durant was a fine builder and a splendid host to his own small circle of friends, but he did not mingle with the guests as did other more colorful inn-keepers and lacked the sort of personality that brought guests back year after year to the same place. In 1898 he lost the hotel to his brother Howard on a mortgage foreclosure. The brother was no luckier; even changing the name of the place to Hotel Utowana did not help. In 1900 typhoid broke out in the area; in 1903 two cases occurred in the hotel. The fear of typhoid's lingering in a place where it had once been was real in those days. That ended Prospect House as a resort. It stood empty for years. As if to scorn Adirondack tradition, no fire ever touched it. Finally, in 1915 it was torn down. Today only traces of rubble show where what was called "an uncanny wonder of the wilderness" once stood.

Unlike Prospect House, some Adirondack hotels enjoyed fabulous prosperity for fifty years and more; they were usually hotels whose proprietors were natural, genial, vivid characters.

The tradition of the salty innkeeper goes back to George Rockwell of Luzerne, one of the first men in the business. Even in 1840 guests delighted to hear him talk about pioneer days, as he stood stolid and solid on the verandah of his hotel by the Hudson. "I was born right across the river here," he would say. "There were twelve of us and ten of us grew up and it never cost three dollars a year for a doctor." According to an old guide-book he could hold a crowd of guests entranced with an oration on the only proper way to raise children: "Give children lots of exercise and lots of salt pork too if they want it and they'll never die with the consumption, and while I'm speak-

ing of it, pork is the only thing necessary to take into the woods
— pork and potatoes — the pork's the best kind of seasoning
in the world for fresh fish. I remember going into the woods
with a man once, as nice a man as ever lived, but one of those
dainty fellows who would get sick if he smelt fried pork. He
took in extras of all kinds, dried beef, relishes, pies, and no end
of cake: well, it happened to rain a little as it will sometimes:
his things got wet, cake all soaked up, and someone sat down
on his pies and the poor fellow thought he would have to starve,
and I just split a trout open on the back, broiled it on a stick,
at the same time letting the gravy drip from a piece of pork that
I held just over it: and he tried the fish, then a piece of pork,
and when we went out he could eat just as much salt pork as I
could."

The list of colorful hosts was long. There were the Chases,
Mr. and Mrs., who founded and ran the Loon Lake House from
1879 to 1937. Ferdie Chase slowly lost interest in hotel management and wound up sitting out his years against the barn in the
sun, whittling and swapping stories with the guides. It was Mrs.
Chase who became the legendary figure — a short little woman
who wore a red wig and was seldom seen without a green
sweater. For years guests returned for fine food and to replenish
their stock of stories about Mrs. Chase. One often repeated told
of the day a wealthy man arrived with a party of guests and was
annoyed to find the dining room filled. He stated loudly and
nastily that he was not accustomed to waiting. Mrs. Chase assured him that the staff would do its best quickly. When his
party were shown to their table it was the best in the room, set
with fresh flowers and served perfectly. When the dinner was
over he went to Mrs. Chase. "I have never eaten such a dinner,"
he said. "I shall be back here often. How much do I owe you?"

"You owe me nothing," Mrs. Chase said.

"But — but I can't accept that. Why, I couldn't possibly return here again if I don't pay you now."

"That's just what I thought, mister," Mrs. Chase said. "Good-by, sir."

These and all other innkeepers were overtowered, in legend and physique, by a tall, big-boned giant of a Vermonter. His name was Apollos Smith but everyone called him "Paul." Tales about him fade today as men who knew him personally pass on. Living in the Adirondacks from 1850 until 1912, Paul Smith saw with his own shrewd eyes the opening of the wilderness and the development that followed. In many ways he helped with it and grew rich by it.

He began the most fabulous of Adirondack careers by working on Erie Canal boats and coming north to hunt whenever he could. His favorite place was in the unbroken wilderness at Loon Lake, in the northeast quarter. He became a guide at a little house there that took in a few big-city hunters. The combination of expert woodsman, superb hunter, and fabulous storyteller that was Paul Smith impressed them. They persuaded him to build his own inn. In 1852 he opened Hunter's Home, for men only, a few miles from Loon Lake. It had a living room, a kitchen, a dormitory overhead, and a bar — a barrel of whiskey in the living room with dipper attached, four cents a drink.

From the first his guests included important doctors, lawyers, and businessmen. Many times they asked him to build another and better hotel, where their wives might come and see something of wilderness life and meet Paul Smith. They offered to finance him. In 1858 Smith went a few miles southwest to Lower Saint Regis Lake, ten miles northwest of Saranac Lake. To its end his hotel bore no other name than "Paul Smith's." It began as a frame building, not particularly attractive even among the architectural monstrosities of the time, with seventeen rooms. Although no railroad was nearer than forty miles, this backwoods hotel grew each year, to one hundred rooms, then five hundred, and sprawled along the shores of a lovely lake. As it expanded its reputation grew. Part of its success belonged to Paul Smith's wife, whom he had courted by hiking thirty miles through the winter woods to her home. She rarely mixed with the guests but did all the cooking and managed the help. In 1872 Paul Smith's charged fifty cents a meal, two dollars and fifty cents a day for room and board. Only Lake George rates were higher. Over the years rates went up to thirty-five dollars a week, with many an extra; Paul Smith would have felt it sinful to undercharge.

As Paul Smith's grew it continued to attract a fashionable clientele. In the nineties the New York City papers carried regular social-note columns from Newport, Narragansett — and Paul Smith's. A society editor could report in 1891:

> While the charity ball at Paul Smith's on Tuesday was not as large as the annual charity dance in New York yet it lacked little in brilliance. The company of distinguished ladies and gentlemen gathered on the shore of St. Regis would have done honor to any ballroom in the world. The silks, satins, laces, diamonds, and fine clothes generally made the woodmen's eyes stick out with wonderment at the fortunes thus displayed. Some of the ladies went so far as to send to the city safe deposits for their jewels. Paul Smith beamed on his guests as a genial host should, and pointed to them as proof that they represented $160,000,000 of cold hard cash.

Life at Paul Smith's was different from the days when only an occasional lonely hunter or trapper walked the trackless woods. Charles Hallock, first editor of *Forest and Stream,* described it at the height of its season:

> Great is the stir on the long summer evenings — ribbons fluttering on the piazzas, silks rustling in the dress promenade; ladies in short mountain suits, fresh from an afternoon picnic; embryo sportsmen in velveteen and corduroys of approved cut, descanting learnedly of backwoods experience; excursion parties returning, laden with trophies of trout and pond lilies; stages arriving top heavy with trunks, rifle cases, and hampers;

guides intermingling, proffering services, or arranging trips
for the morrow; pistols shooting at random; invalids, bundled
in blankets, propped up in chairs; old gents distracted, vainly
perusing their papers; fond lovers strolling; dowagers schem-
ing; mosquitoes devouring; the supper-bell ringing. Anon
some millionaire Nimrod or piscator of marked renown drags
in from a weary day with a basket of unusual weight, or per-
chance a fawn cut down before its time. He receives his hon-
ors with that becoming dignity which reticence impresses, and
magnificently tips a twenty-dollar note to his trusty guide.
After supper there is a generous flow of champagne to a selected few upon the western piazza, and the exploits of the
day are recounted and compared. The parlors grow noisy with
music and dancing; silence and smoke prevail in the card-
room.

With a sense of humor that often had an edge, Paul Smith
became as much of an attraction as anything in the Adirondacks.
In addition he had an infallible ability to make close friends
with some of the most important men of his period, to make
them admit that here in the woods he was their superior. People liked him and people disliked him and always intensely.
One of the latter said, "He was one-third court jester, one-third
shrewd beyond measure, and one-third robber baron who robbed
the rich to care for the rich — himself."

On the other hand, Dr. Trudeau, the tuberculosis pioneer,
who arrived at Paul Smith's sick and ready to die, found him a
tender and kindly man, even willing to keep his place open in
winter at considerable inconvenience, on Trudeau's request,
just to oblige a friend. Smith did not care what people thought
of him. No one could deny that he was an original — a combination of shrewd Vermonter, frontiersman, and Yankee businessman, a giant who was cynically amused to find that because a
man stayed himself, people of different backgrounds were eager
to pay good money to enjoy his company. They paid. When
Paul Smith heard that one of his coaches to the railroad had

been held up and robbed on the way out he laughed. "Fool of a highwayman, holding up passengers after they've left here. What did he expect to find on them?" Many guests noticed his shrewdness. He was once told by a clerk, "I forgot to put a charge for a pair of rubber boots on the bill of some guest and I've forgotten which one." Smith said, "Put a charge of a pair of boots on every guest's bill. Most of 'em won't notice it."

He had nothing servile about him, none of the fawning and hypocritical "the customer is always right." The way Paul Smith saw it, the host was not only liable to be right most of the time but considerably smarter. If you liked the way Paul Smith ran his house, you were welcome to stay, that is, if he liked you. More than once in his career he looked over a new arrival, disliked what he saw, and said, "Don't bother to unpack, mister. Coach out leaves in the morning." Many people did like the way he ran things and came back year after year, including some of the leading families of Manhattan — the Harrimans, Reids, and Vanderbilts.

The success of the hotel, even in the sixties, convinced Paul Smith long before most people that the real industry of the region would be the summer people. He was the first to encourage them to buy land — from him — and set up a tent camp of their own, and later on, permanent structures; they remained part of the Paul Smith summer colony and came to him to buy supplies. In the early seventies Smith began buying land, particularly if it had lake frontage. He bought one parcel of thirteen thousand acres around the Saint Regis lakes for twenty thousand dollars. A few years later, he sold just five of those acres for precisely twenty thousand dollars. This settlement, mostly on Upper Saint Regis Lake, was the first of many groups of private camps in the Adirondacks. A Saint Regis camp was a hallmark of aristocracy that many a family envied and relatively few secured. Smith knew the value of catering to snobbish social distinctions and admitted only those people he believed qualified by wealth and position. In a few years he was able to say, "There's not a foot of land on the lake for sale at the moment and there's not a man on it but what's a millionaire and some of them ten times over." It all meant more income for him. In one season in the nineties he took in more than seventy-five thousand dollars.

Perhaps the sharpest criticism chronically leveled at Smith was his attitude toward the game laws. Since they interfered with his guests' pleasure, he felt for years that they were bad for business. Game was there for the killing and he once taunted a guest who refused to club a swimming deer over the head, "When you eat venison, and I notice you eat plenty, do you ever think that maybe what you're eating was clubbed to death? Does it taste any different?"

Paul Smith died in 1912, about the time the first automobile was coming into the Adirondacks. In his last days he rode in one, not realizing that it would be the instrument to change the course of Adirondack life. Before his death he had one last brush with the conservation groups who were trying to protect the woods. In 1908 his power company — for he had acquired water-power sites and even a railway spur — decided to build a dam at Franklin Falls; several hundred acres of state lands were flooded and the trees killed thereon. The Association for the Protection of the Adirondacks publicized this violation of forest law. Paul Smith and his group ignored the charge and even the injunction brought against them and built the dam. The suit dragged through court after court until 1912, when a decision was rendered in favor of the Paul Smith Company. That company still supplies power to the Saranac Lake area of the Adirondacks.

The end of the Paul Smith story is brief. After his death the hotel continued under the direction of two sons. As the season of 1930 closed the hotel burned to the ground and was never rebuilt. The sons died. The entire estate, including ownership of the power company and thousands of acres of land, went to found Paul Smith's College, the only institution of higher education in the Adirondacks. It specializes in two subjects Paul Smith could have taught to any faculty — forestry and hotel management.

Another man stands out in the history of Adirondack hotels, a man different from every other figure in it. He was Melvil Dewey, no woodsman, guide, or backwoods character, but a graduate of Amherst, who, before the age of twenty-one, had worked out a scheme for book arrangement that would simplify the work in many of the world's libraries. Although other men had built big hotels at Lake Placid before Dewey came in the early nineties, Lake Placid owed more of its growth and its reputation for fashionableness to Dewey than to anyone else. He built no hotel; what he built was the Lake Placid Club, with a selected membership, never open to the general public.

Melville Louis Kossuth Dewey, soon shortened to Melvil to save time, was as serious-minded a boy as ever stood on the platform of a small country school at Adams Center, Massachusetts, and delivered an oration on the intolerable evil of wasting time. At seventeen he was teaching that to a country-school class. At eighteen he was converted to the metric system and argued for it the rest of his life. He was also saying, "If time then be so precious at the close of life, why is it not just as valuable now?" He wasted none.

As an undergraduate at Amherst, working part time in the library, he thought out a simple system for classifying books — the Dewey Decimal Classification System. Hitherto, libraries had arranged books alphabetically, paying no attention to subjects. The waste of time in finding books was appalling. By dividing the fields of knowledge into ten parts, by subdividing and further subdividing, Dewey produced his system. Continued work in the field made him the father of modern library science.

He became an advocate of simplified English spelling. Although he did not start the movement to do away with the time wasted in learning the spelling intricacies of English, he led it all his life. He used his system at every opportunity, even though the guests at the Lake Placid Club were sometimes baffled by the words on the menus. One newspaper announced that it agreed with Dewey in dropping "ue" from "catalogue" and suggested doing the same thing with "glue."

Because Dewey had hay fever and his wife was bothered with rose cold, they came to the Adirondacks for relief. Paul Smith advised them to settle at Lake Placid. They secured five acres on the east side of Mirror Lake, and in 1891 the Lake Placid Hotel Company was formed. Invited members could buy stock in this company, which managed the Lake Placid Club. From 80 members in its first years it grew to 1,263 in 1919, with a collection of sprawling buildings, complete with dairy, poultry farms, golf courses, lecture hall, seventy-two acres where families could spend the summer and seventy-eight hundred acres of forest and farm land.

Dewey and the club brought winter sports into the Adirondacks in 1904, when six guests shoveled snow off Mirror Lake to get an appetite. Eventually he saw ski runs, toboggans, and crowded trains at Christmas and New Year's bringing guests to the club for a long series of traditional festivities.

Dewey had been librarian at Columbia University, secretary of the State Board of Regents, and then librarian of the State of New York. A man of firm ideas, with an unshakable conviction in the correctness of them, he was in one crisis after another. He was important not only in setting up modern library practices, but in the formation of the state's education policies. His idea behind the Lake Placid Club, as one writer described it, was to form a "backwoods university," "a place where congenial people might meet," where "the country's best will exchange ideas before the open hearth."

To guarantee that the guests would be "the country's best" by his own standards, Dewey set stern rules of discrimination. As T. Morris Longstreth stated in his book *The Adirondacks,* club guests were graded as: "Class C — common client, welcome, neither specially advantageous or disadvantageous"; "Class B — some talent, some distinguishing traits that make him desirable"; "Class A — those admirably suited to further the ideals of the Club"; "Class D — doubtful or deficient characters"; "Class E — unsuitables who, if already in, must be eliminated, if still out, must be excluded for the protection of the rest." *

Whom Dewey cared to have in his club was his own business, but one grossly worded paragraph in club literature from its earliest days shocked many people: "No one will be received as member or guest against whom there is physical, moral, social, or race objection, or who would be unwelcome to even a small minority. This excludes absolutely all consumptives, or rather invalids, whose presence might injure health or modify others' freedom or enjoyment. This invariable rule is rigidly enforced: it is found impracticable to make exceptions to Jews or others excluded, even when of unusual personal qualifications."

As the chief power behind the club, Dewey had a right to publicize that if he chose, but a number of the leading Jewish leaders in New York City thought it disgraceful that a man on the public payroll as state librarian and influential in matters of public education should be responsible for such blatant anti-Semitism. They asked that he be dismissed from his public post. In September, 1905, after a reprimand from the Board of Regents and because of other factors, Dewey resigned. The Board of Regents did add, "It has been established to the satisfaction of the committee that the regulation excluding Jews is not due to any personal prejudice on the part of Mr. Dewey."

* Copyright, 1917, Century Company. Reprinted by permission of the publishers, Appleton-Century-Crofts, Inc.

If that were so, as Dewey insisted, that made his club's policy all the more reprehensible. After 1905 Dewey devoted most of his time to the club. Despite the official assurance from the Board of Regents of his freedom from personal prejudice, never did his club change its racial restrictions on members or their guests.

Dewey died in 1931, when the club was floundering after the 1929 depression. In his last years he continued to think up elaborate schemes, one after the other, including a "Lake Placid" in Florida, to bewilder his backers and the club's financial advisors. The army took over the club as a reconditioning center during World War II and made many needed repairs. Today, after various reorganizations, it continues, and is still an important part of Adirondack life. Conventions, overriding social taboo and social classification, are now welcome during fall, winter, and spring. Liquor is now served, a complete turnabout from the days when Dewey would not hire a bellhop if he smoked or drank, or let in one guest who did not rate up to the club's standards.

Since the club was a private organization it cannot be judged as hotels are judged. It has been a tremendous part of Lake Placid life and responsible for the fashionable veneer which that village acquired, some of which still lingers. To many Adirondack people the club has always seemed a place apart. Few ever went through its doors except as help. Others would never go into it, even on invitation. Its bigoted snobbishness would not merit comment if the club had not pretended to Adirondack leadership and to the finest of American traditions. By maintaining its anti-Semitism, the club augmented and reinforced the discrimination that marked and marred so many Adirondack resorts.

Anti-Semitism in the Adirondacks was something brought into the region and was very real for many years. The Flume Cottage at Keene Valley advertised in 1894, "Hebrews will knock vainly for admission." A few years later the Brightside on Raquette Lake was advertising, "People suffering from pulmonary troubles not taken. Hebrews need not apply. The proprietor is a sportsman and very freely imparts information of interest." Today, many hotels that were anti-Semitic have changed completely; a number are largely Jewish resorts. Anti-Semitism, once a nasty reality in some Adirondack villages, has decreased and Jews are among the civic leaders. Lake Placid now has a number of hotels that cater particularly to Jewish guests; in recent years the village has attracted many European refugees, who have found the scenery reminiscent of central European resorts and who feel at home there.

A New York State law now forbids discriminating advertising; most Adirondack hotels abide by it in spirit and letter. Now and then some hotel slips around the law and hints well its point of view. One Lake Placid hotel advertises, "Guests will enjoy our Christian religious library." People who do not enjoy that sort of slick evasion of an ugly fact shun not only the library but the hotel.

The Adirondack summer hotels did well during the first part of the twentieth century. In time a combination of changes hurt them and finally closed most of them.

In 1912 an advertisement of the Grand View at Lake Placid hinted at one change that was imminent. It proclaimed: "Bath houses, golf grounds, steam heat, modern bath rooms, pool, baseball, no mosquitoes, no hay fever. Symphony orchestra and special inducements to young men in bachelor's hall." Then, after the assurance, "Pulmonary cases not taken," it added a sentence that was the handwriting on the wall: "Special accommodations reserved for automobile parties."

In thiry years the tourist cabin and the motel would also offer that, and far more conveniently.

A Camp Is a Camp

"When you talk about Adirondack camps," an old guide said, "you always have to say what kind of camp. 'Camp' means more things up here than a porcupine's got quills. Mine's a one-room shack back in the woods to use in hunting season. That's a camp. Some of the people in the village build a platform down on state land in summer and put up a tent. That's a camp. And some people can't live in the woods without they have a forty-room house with more servants on the place than trees and boatmen, and dance teachers and waiters and waiters to wait on waiters and that's a camp."

That sums up the definition of the word in the Adirondack country. "Camp" means any place in the woods where people live. But "camp," as it was used in the more colorful periods of Adirondack history, meant usually the summer homes of the rich, the luxurious layouts where "roughing it" was a phrase without much meaning. Down in the city the owner might boast about his "Adirondack hunting lodge." That sounded far more fashionable. Up in the woods he always called it a camp.

In the 1890's Paul Smith could look around the shores of Upper Saint Regis Lake and say, "I tell you, there's no other spot on earth where millionaires go to playing at keeping house in log cabins and tents." That may have been the "peak" in the development of the private camp, but the really lavish camps were elsewhere. The two hundred and fifty thousand dollar layout, which set a new style in American architecture, began in another part of the Adirondack woods. As the possession of an elaborate Adirondack hunting lodge became fashionable, the wealthy families of America — Morgans, Vanderbilts, Whitneys, Lehmans, Lowes, Harrimans, Rockefellers, and Lewisohns — as a rule built their camps in remote and isolated places surrounded by hundreds of acres of land for privacy. Here the owners might stay a few months, weeks, or only a few days in the year. The remainder of the time they were the residences of caretaker and staff — in some cases as many as fifty people. Elsewhere men of less impressive wealth formed clubs to buy up large sections and set them aside as private preserves. Each member had equal privileges, and in some cases his own lakeside camp.

The first man to build an Adirondack camp as a shelter in the woods is unknown, but it is easy to guess what he built. It was a shanty of logs, roofed with the bark of one or more trees, the simplest sort of frontier structure in regions where wood was plentiful.

One Platt Rogers came as "summer camper" to Westport shortly after the Revolution, and William Lawrence, a New York merchant, spent summers on his land in the extreme western part of the area in 1820. Not until after the Civil War, however, did people in any number begin to say, as they looked out from the windows of the early hotels, "This is a good place to spend the summer; let's buy land and have a place of our own." A few campers erected simple log cabins in the sixties. One, on the Third Lake of the Fulton Chain had crossbeams over the living room to make sleeping quarters for any woman who dared venture into the wilderness. A wealthy bachelor of New York City, Rufus Wattles, built a camp on an island in Lake George, but it seems to have been a tossup whether his greater interest was in catching lake trout or lady tourists. Some Manhattan bachelors who had a camp at Lake Meacham, north of Paul Smith's, brought in their lady friends and scandalized the neighborhood.

Those few who did buy land at this time were content to set up tents and live in rustic manner. It was that way in the early days on the land around Paul Smith's. Even this simple camping could be complicated. Mildred P. Stokes Hooker, daughter of a New York financier, came as a child in these early years to a camp on one of the islands in Upper Saint Regis Lake. Her story of the departure of the family for their summer in the north must have been repeated in more or less the same detail by other families going to Blue Mountain Lake and elsewhere in the Adirondack country:

> Patrick left in the afternoon with horses, Muggins and sport (a pug and setter), and a truck load of freight. Papa chartered what they call a special parlor horse car direct from 42nd St. to Ausable for $100 and we take in it our horses, carriage, all camping outfits, extra trunks, stores, etc.

The family and other luggage followed the next day:

> Anson Phelps Stokes, wife, seven children, one niece, about ten servants, Miss Rondell, one coachman, three horses, two dogs, one carriage, five large boxes of tents, three cases of wine, two packages of stove pipe, two stoves, one bale china, one iron pot, four washstands, one barrel of hardwood, four bundles of poles, seventeen cots and seventeen mattresses, four canvas packages, one buckboard, five barrels, one half barrel, two tubs of butter, one bag coffee, one chest tea, one crate china, twelve rugs, four milkcans, two drawing boards, twenty-five trunks, thirteen small boxes, one boat, one hamper.

As Paul Smith began to sell camp sites in the early seventies, the first of the families who were to make Millionaires' Row at Bolton, on Lake George, began to plan their terraced lawns, cast-iron deer, and marble steps. No one could call those "camps." The day of the lavish camp was almost at hand, although it was some years before a man would buy a barren hilltop because he liked the view, erect an expensive "hunting lodge" and then, because he also liked the woods, pay a landscape architect to move a solid acre of woods around the house, complete to the last rock and old stump.

In 1884 William West Durant, a young man of twenty-four, educated in British schools and European universities, was in

Egypt doing archaeological research. He was in the happy position of being able to do anything he fancied, for his father was Dr. Thomas C. Durant, tremendously wealthy railroad builder. The doctor had studied medicine, but after a few years of practice gave it up and went into business. Railroads interested him most; by 1861 he was dreaming of a railroad to the Pacific. He became the leading figure in the building of the Union Pacific and shared all the glory, scandal, profit, and headache that its completion brought. Even when concerned with getting tracks across the Rockies Dr. Durant had an interest in the Adirondacks; he had lived some of his early years in Albany and had known the region. When the Saratoga-Sackett's Harbor scheme failed in the early sixties, Dr. Durant reorganized the company and eventually completed forty miles of road from Saratoga to North Creek in 1871, a road still in use today, with added trackage to extend to Tahawus and the titanium mine. After that he had other railroad schemes, including one that involved some questionable stock manipulation, but his real interest was in the Adirondacks, around Blue Mountain Lake. This area he proposed to develop as a playground for men like himself, the men of great wealth of the period. Most were his friends. In this dream he felt he needed help and sent a letter to his son in Egypt.

The son answered. He would come and he would help. In 1876 he arrived at Raquette Lake, and to his father's delight not only took up all the grandiose plans his father had conceived but expanded them. For the next twenty-five years William West Durant was the outstanding man of the Raquette Lake region, with dreams and projects never seen before or since in the Adirondack country.

Father and son set to work. Together they organized a fast coach line to Blue Mountain Lake from North Creek, the railroad end, and thirty miles off. William's cousin Frederick came to build Prospect House. William West Durant had his own plans for hotels and club, but first he wanted a suitable residence for himself and his family. He drew up the plans and supervised the construction of what he called Camp Pine Knot, on a point on Raquette Lake. That one camp set the whole following style of Adirondack architecture as Donaldson described it:

> It became the showplace of the woods. Men took a circuitous route in order to gain a glimpse of it and to have been a guest within its timbered walls and among its woodland fancies was to wear the hall-mark of the period. Before it was built there was nothing like it: since then, despite infinite variations there has been nothing essentially different from it.*

What Durant designed was basically simple. He took the best features of the early Adirondack log cabin and combined them with the decorative features of the long, low Swiss chalet, to make a style of building that blended most perfectly with its woodland and lakeshore setting. The idea of Swiss influence, so common in decoration, in gables, balconies, and other details copied later in the lavish Adirondack camps, may have been something Durant remembered from his years in Europe. It may also have come, consciously or unconsciously, from an Adirondack building that preceded Pine Knot in its use of Swiss ornamentation along with gables, verandahs, and similar features. This was the Wayside Hotel at Luzerne, which Durant knew.

Durant's first structure was two stories high and had balconies and porches. It was built of logs, with taste and dignity. When he needed more room he secured it not by building onto the house, but by building a separate house, thereby setting one of the most prominent features of Adirondack camp architecture. In time he added more buildings, and then, since inclement weather is common, he connected them all by separate runways, a standard feature of many old camps. An elaborate boathouse,

* From *A History of the Adirondacks*, by Alfred L. Donaldson. Copyright, 1921, Century Company. Reprinted by permission of the publishers, Appleton-Century-Crofts, Inc.

often built elsewhere with a music room and dance floor above, went with the Durant camp.

Durant built two other lavish camps — Uncas, on Mohegan Lake, and Sagamore, on Shedd Lake. Durant even winterized one camp and brought parties of guests from New York through forty miles of winter wilderness for a sort of vacation they had never known before. He had many plans for the area he loved, including fancy camps, fancy hotels, and fancy transportation. To get tourists and visitors to Blue Mountain Lake, which the Utica-Montreal line did not touch, he built the most unique railroad ever constructed in America — three fourths of a mile, standard gauge, between the portage at the end of the Marion River to the first of the Eckford Lakes. His cars were old horse-cars from Brooklyn drawn by an elevated railroad engine. He hoped that a passenger could board a sleeping car at Grand Central and by a combination of train, barge, and the Marion River railroad, arrive at Blue Mountain Lake. Not wanting to risk its cars on an Adirondack lake, the Pullman Company did not co-operate.

While busy with his plans Durant had family trouble. He faced a suit by a sister for his administration of his father's estate. He was sued for divorce. His backer in many of his plans had been Collis Huntington, wealthy Californian, whose money had come from the Central Pacific and Southern Pacific railroads. Durant sold Pine Knot to him. He sold Uncas to J. P. Morgan, who rarely visited it. By 1900 Durant was in deep and counted on his good friend Huntington to help him out. Huntington arrived in the Adirondacks in the summer of 1900. A few days later he died of a heart attack at his camp.

That ended Durant's great dream, for Huntington's executors would not honor the promises made to Durant. Durant went bankrupt in 1904. In 1916 he was clerking in a North Creek hotel, gallant and without bitterness, often serving the men he had once employed. He lived until 1934. His three camps survive. Camp Pine Knot is a summer camp for the New York State Teachers College at Cortland. Uncas and Sagamore Lodge are privately owned.

At the height of Durant's career he estimated his Adirondack wealth at one million one hundred and twenty thousand dollars, but everything went at a huge loss. One of the large land buyers was Dr. Seward Webb, son-in-law of William H. Vanderbilt and builder of the railroad from Utica north. Webb became a great landowner on his own, amassing more than 112,000 acres. He set up a preserve and a camp, Nehasane, deep in the woods. It survives today and is owned by Webb's son. It can only be reached by the railroad, at the Nehasane station. That is a unique station. The New York Central, by ancient agreement with the Webb family, will not sell a ticket to that station unless the prospective purchaser can prove he has been invited by the Webbs.

The fame of Camp Pine Knot spread far. In the next years scores of places basically like it but with assorted modifications went up in many parts of the woods. Logs were used at first with the bark on, but later were peeled and varnished; the bark was subject to attack from borers and disintegrated in spite of all sorts of anti-bug coatings. One handsome camp, the Pruyn camp at Newcomb, south of the main range, used more than fifteen hundred large trees to build its five buildings. In time the logs were replaced with sawed timber and rough-sawed boards, painted brown and trimmed with green, but birch slabs, with bark attached, made paneling for rooms and ceilings.

Most camps had a number of buildings, connected by runways and usually covered. Some camps even had a separate building for each "room" of the house — one for dining room and kitchen, one for living room, one for library and study, and a number of bedrooms, so that part of the camp could be closed off when not fully occupied. To these buildings were added others for the help, as well as boathouses and ice houses, so that a large Adirondack camp often resembled quite a lakeside settlement. In some cases a number of related families secured land and built a separate house for each family, with one common dining room and kitchen. Most camps were not winterized. Great native stone fireplaces provided the heat. Unfortunately, no way was ever found to make the camps fireproof and fires destroyed many over the years.

Since these were "hunting lodges," although the only hunting done around many of them was for places to sleep extra guests, the interiors were decorated in backwoods manner, with snowshoes, guns, and mounted fish. "Things made out of things" appeared everywhere — chandeliers made of deer horns, lamps made of old guns, and many a deer's hoof was made part of a coat rack. The prized decorations were mounted animal heads. Panthers, tigers, and assorted African specimens were neighbors on the wall with the local deer, beavers, birds and fish, and even a whole flight of flying ducks might be suspended from the ceiling by wires.

The first camps may have been built more or less by inspiration; in time professional architects were called in. Even Addison Mizner of the Coral Gables, Florida, boom development tried his hand at one. Several New York firms built some of the later camps, but they followed what the local carpenters had emphasized before, that the houses had to be built to the contour of the land, that sleeping porches were desirable, that it was a poor idea to plaster walls and a worse one to use wallpaper. The most successful of the later camps were built by W. L. Coulter and later by William G. Distin and William H. Scopes, all of Saranac Lake. It was Will Distin who had a fabulous order from one New York client. He approved Distin's sketches for a camp, then said, "I'm leaving for Europe. I want it built and finished the day I return." As the camp neared completion the owner cabled, "Will arrive Thursday. Please buy dishes and fittings, and have roast lamb for dinner." The owner arrived. China, silver, flowers and roast lamb were on the table.

While most camps were built in Adirondack style, sometimes with lavish additions, one camp was built on Upper Saint Regis Lake in the classical Chinese manner, complete with pagodas and carved Ming dogs on pedestals. A number of spectacular camps, and sometimes odd ones, appeared in scattered parts of the Adirondack country. On the east side of Schroon Lake a German, Wilhelm Pickhardt, set out to re-create an old German baronial estate. With buildings in the proper Germanic style, his estate lacked wild boars, a species of animal life common on such estates. He planned to import them but found that they needed acorns for food. So he first planted oaks, then brought on the wild boars. The oaks may have lived, but the boars escaped when the first winter storms broke the fences.

The shores of many lakes, including Lake Placid and Lake George, were eventually lined with fine camps on small land holdings. They may not have been Adirondack hunting lodges in every sense of that snooty phrase, but many were far more luxurious and enduring.

The most pretentious camp — and that is stretching the word camp as far as it will go — was built southeast of Tupper Lake in 1893 by Edward Litchfield, a retired Brooklyn lawyer. Here he bought about nine thousand acres, including three lakes and two ponds, and surrounded the entire area with wire fence eight feet high. He built a model French château of stone and concrete, with walls three to six feet thick. It had tall towers, a great hall filled with animal heads, and an art gallery. It looked as out of place in the deep Adirondack woods as an Adirondack lean-to would appear in a Versailles garden. In addition, Mr. Litchfield brought in moose, elks, beavers, and many varieties of birds, and set guards to patrolling the fence line. Fallen trees in winter storms and the ability of poachers to get through any fence either let the animals escape or led to their killing. Litchfield Hall still stands and is used by some of the family today. Few Adirondack people have ever seen it; it is six miles back in the woods, reached only by its own road.

Since most camps were far back from main roads, the year-round Adirondack people never knew much about them from personal experience. They visited few and were guests at fewer. What information they did get, and it makes a fascinating chapter of Adirondackana, came from people who worked at these camps or from tradesmen. The development of the big camp started a new Adirondack profession — that of caretaker, a man who usually lived on the camp throughout the year, even deep in the woods in winter, and in summer was overseer of a large group of workers. Every camp of any size had its roll of private guides, waiting the pleasure of host and guests. The caretakers were a faithful group, with a loyalty to the camp owner rarely broken. Most could boast of thirty and forty years in the same job. Many residents of the Adirondack area today were raised as children on camps where their fathers were caretakers. Marriages between wealthy camp owner and caretaker's daughter were not unknown.

Of some of the camp owners there were many tales. One caretaker complained that he had to hire ten guides, and guides were hard to find. "You see, the Missus has a rough camp back in the woods and she has twenty guests at a time," he said. "She decides each week to rough it for lunch at the 'rough camp.' So in the morning a maid goes round to each guest asking whether he'd like squab or filet mignon and what kind of cold soup and dessert. Then all the lunches are put in pack baskets. I need a guide for each two guests to cart the stuff so they can rough it."

One camp mistress on the Saint Regis Lakes used to come in a private car which was towed on the Paul Smith line from the junction by an old trolley car that Smith used for locomotive. When the lady heard that statistics showed that the last car on the train is the one that figures in many railroad wrecks she bought a baggage car. That was attached behind her private car for the four miles to Paul Smith's, to make a two-car train through the wilderness. In the case of another camp, husband and wife were divorced but each insisted on sharing the camp. An additional house was built. For years wife and husband number two and husband and wife number two, along with numerous children of the assorted marriages, spent pleasant if involved summers.

As the number of private camps increased, more groups of wealthy men, even groups from the Middle West, formed clubs and bought up land for their own use as a preserve. These clubs raised their own trout to stock lakes and streams, set their own conservative game laws, forbade deer hounding, hired caretakers and guides, and let the timber cutting under strict control. Invariably they put up "No Trespassing" signs.

The largest club formed, the Adirondack League Club, still survives. Organized in 1890 by a New York City group, it bought 104,000 acres in the far southwest corner of the region, at four dollars and seventy-five cents an acre. On it were 93,000 acres of "primeval forest" of which not a tree had been cut, and more than twenty-five lakes, many of them favorite fishing spots in earlier days. The club was limited to five hundred members. Over the years judicious timber cutting was begun; the owners of the shares have received a fine income and their shares have increased in value.

By the nineties more than thirty such clubs owned thousands of acres, to which should be added the thousands of acres in the hands of the big camp owners. By 1892 the State Forest Commission reported: "Fully one-fourth of the Great Forest is held in private preserves by clubs, associations, or individuals." The Adirondack natives found more fences and more "No Trespassing" signs on land where they had been accustomed for decades to hunt and fish freely. Ill feeling became inevitable. To be sure, the camps and preserves did create jobs, but only for relatively few people. That did little to placate most of the guides, who were used to conducting their patrons wherever game was plentiful and now found an armed gamekeeper blocking a favorite trail.

Resentment even spread outside the Adirondacks. Some citizens in the nineties petitioned the legislature to buy up all preserves. The petition was tabled. In any case the state had no such money available.

The defenders of the large preserves argued that they added to the county's taxable values and offered protection against forest fires. That was true. Their constant patrol and safety measures did prevent forest fires. The year 1899 was a bad fire year in the woods, but not one fire touched any private preserve. The owners of camps and preserves, many of them influential men in New York State, threw all their support to the proposal in 1894 to keep the woods "forever wild." For that reason alone, if for no other, the proposal was fought bitterly by many Adirondack citizens who charged that it was just a rich man's scheme to lock up the woods.

It was many years before the feeling between preserve owners and Adirondack people died out; a generation of men who had walked the whole woods freely had to pass on before it could go completely. It did not vanish without bloodshed, this in the least populated part of the Adirondacks, the northwest section. There William Rockefeller bought land that completely surrounded the little village of Brandon, even the main road to it. He posted the land; the people of Brandon could go nowhere without trespassing. Rockefeller offered to buy out all the landowners in the little town. Most accepted the offer, but not without bitterness. One old French Canadian, Oliver Lamora, held out. He trespassed again and again, was hauled into court, and when he was found guilty the metropolitan press built up a big story about the lone woodsman fighting great wealth. Then Lamora claimed he had a right to fish the ponds on the Rockefeller land because they had been stocked by the state, but it was held that where private land completely surrounds a lake, the lake is also private, or at least the owners have the right of exclusion.

While the Lamora case dragged on another landowner not far away was Orlando Dexter, who bought seven thousand acres in Santa Clara and fenced and posted it. When his Adirondack neighbors annoyed him by poaching and trespassing he retaliated in every possible way. The situation did not last long. As he was driving to the post office one afternoon in September, 1903, someone fired a shot. Whoever fired it was a marksman. Dexter fell to the road dead. His murderer has never been caught or named.

The Dexter affair came in the middle of the Rockefeller-Lamora case. Rockefeller took no chances on another shrewd shot from behind a tree. For a time he lived as weird a life in his large and luxurious camp as has ever been lived in the Adirondacks — on an estate that bristled with private detectives, patrols of armed guards, and watchers from platforms in the trees. In time Lamora died and Rockefeller had peace on his land, but the memory lived for many years.

The preserves and clubs survived the years better than did the private camps, but that story belongs to the twentieth century. The word camp is still a common word, but since 1920 it has had a new meaning. It may now mean one of four hundred sites around a lake shore under state supervision, with families from all over New York State summering in peace for two weeks on *their* land.

Courteous Scoundrelly Guides

"The Adirondack guide is born, not made," one admirer wrote in 1879. "He falls so to speak out of his log cradle into a pair of top boots, discards the bottle for a pipe, possesses himself of a boat and a jackknife and becomes forthwith a full-fledged experienced guide."

Other backwoods parts of America attracted sportsmen, appealed to families of wealth as sites for summer homes, and became vacation areas. None ever produced that paragon of woods lore or that shrewd rascal — depending on who did the reporting — known as the Adirondack guide. The Adirondack guide was portrayed variously as a limitless fount of stories and yarns, a tracker with the skill of a bloodhound, a better shot than Annie Oakley, a chef who could take baking powder, flour, and salt and outcook Delmonico's, and an all-knowing rustic philosopher in unchanging costume, his trousers hung from loose suspenders, a felt hat with trout flies in the hatband on his head, and a watch chain dangling into a side pocket. His proudest boast was that he could take a city man into the woods, shoot his deer for him, drag it out, cut it up, and knock down anyone who said the patron hadn't shot it.

Not everyone shared the high opinion of the guides. In the 1890's when the profession had attracted the same percentage of scoundrels as any other calling, one visitor reported:

> A more impudent, lazy, extortionate, and generally offensive class (with, of course, exceptions) than these gentry would be hard to find. The angler or hunter subjected to their tender mercies has cause for congratulation if he escapes from the wilderness with a whole skin after surrendering to the sturdy beggars his choicest tackle or accoutrements, furnishing unlimited drink, tobacco, and cigars, submitting to the outrageous overcharges, caprices, and insults and listening to the lying boasts of these windy humbugs who guide their prey in the manner and direction which best suits their own convenience.

Among the guides who have trodden the Adirondack woods in the last century some may have been like that. Many were not. Many were selfless and loyal beyond any measure. It needed infinite loyalty for a guide to take some wealthy city sportsman into the woods, nurse him through three weeks of delirium tremens and convince everyone, including himself, that it was just a bad case of pneumonia.

The first solitary settlers and trappers in the woods needed no special training to be guides; either they knew woodcraft or they perished. Into their solitude came explorers and hunters, willing to pay these men for what they did every day of their lives. Some of the early guides seem to tower over their successors as high peaks over hummocks. They were unique and extraordinary but their fame was due in part to various writers who found in them a new type of American and put them vividly on paper.

The first guide to appear in detail in any Adirondack chronicle was John Cheney. Born in New Hampshire, Cheney had come from Ticonderoga into the wilderness south of the main range about 1830, bringing with him, gun, dog, and pack basket. Hoffman, who was first to write of him in 1838, described him as "A slight looking man of about seven and thirty, a man that lived winter and summer in the woods — honest John Cheney, as staunch a hunter and as true and gentle a practiser of woodcraft as ever roamed the broad forest." Many another description followed that. Had Cheney been able to read he would probably have been the first to blush at what some outsiders wrote. Even at the age of seventy-three he was still "running the woods," a gentle, wise man who instantly won the respect of outsiders, a man as at home in the woods as others are in their own living rooms. Many Adirondack guides in the years that followed were made in the same mold.

A number of Indians were among the early guides. Most famous was Mitchell Sabattis, a member of the Abenaki tribe. With an aged father and a beautiful sister who slips mysteriously through pages of early Adirondack history, Sabattis lived and guided in the Long Lake region. His career covered a whole century, from 1800 to 1906. Other early guides were no less able, if not as famous. One was Chris Crandall of Lake Meacham, the only one-legged guide in history. Although he had lost a leg hunting, he was able to do everything a guide should do except to walk down a stream pulling a boat after him.

An early guide of another sort lived in Keene Valley. He was Orson Phelps, far better known as "Old Mountain" Phelps. No great hunter or trapper, he was that rare person in early Adirondack history — a mountain climber. He lived for one end, to popularize the Adirondacks and to make New Yorkers realize that they had in their own backyard a place where, as Phelps, who spoke his own variation of English, said, a man can feel a sense of "Heaven-up-h'isted-ness." He was born in Vermont in 1817 and later wandered on to Keene Valley. In this loveliest of valleys, at the foot of Marcy, he settled down forever. Anyone who ever saw him remembered his long body and short legs, woolen shirt and butternut-colored trousers, and his limp light brown felt hat with yellowish hair that grew out of it like some nameless fern. His long beard was red. Phelps's opinion of soap was to the point. "Soap is a thing," he said, "that I hain't no kinder use for." As for water for bathing purposes, he declared, "I don't believe in this etarnal sozzlin'!"

Occasional visitors carried away stories of Old Mountain. His fame grew. He even began to make a living guiding people up the mountains. Guide them he did, for people flocked to Keene Valley to see the "primitive man." Those who came marveled at what he could do with the English language. When asked where the morrow's hike might lead, Old Mountain liked to say, "Waal, I callerlate, if they rig up the calleration they callerate on, we'll go to the Boreas." For him a hike over a beaten track was "a reg'lar walk," while off the beaten track was "a random scoot." Marcy was his favorite mountain; he climbed it hundreds of times, from all directions. It was he who picturesquely and accurately named Haystack and the Gothics. In old age he kept himself alive to his eighty-eighth year selling guidebooks and pictures of himself. He died in 1905.

In the Gilded Years of the Adirondacks every hotel of any importance had guides waiting around the boathouse, much like taxi drivers at a railroad station. These "hotel guides" were the lowest rank in their profession. They were paid by the hour; they might put in a few days hunting but were more likely to spend an afternoon rowing an old lady around a lake. One rank up were the "house guides," attached to one private estate and paid by the month and ready to serve their employer at any time. The aristocrats of the profession were the "private guides." They had their own clientele, up from the city for a week or month, who reserved time in advance and paid well.

Most guides worked hard in spring, summer and autumn and were glad to lay up for the winter. With good reason one hamlet near Paul Smith's, where many guides wintered, was called "Easy Street" (and still is), although the guides have long passed on. No matter what rank in the profession, hat, suspenders, pipe, and watch chain always marked the guide.

By 1890 the guides were being paid a base of three dollars per day. They earned it. A good guide provided the boat and pulled at the oars for twenty or thirty miles a day. At portages between lakes the guide did the carrying, using a yoke that fitted over his shoulders; up came the boat, bottom up, and what looked like a beetle with long narrow shell moved through the woods on two legs. (One travel book said, "A gentleman will assist in this arduous labor.") A guide had to know the spring holes for trout and the depths for lake trout. In deer hunting he put his client on a likely runway, then circled around and tried to drive deer toward him: the guide used dogs as help until their use was forbidden by law.

He had to know where to find the best camping spots, how to pitch a tent or build a temporary shelter of bark, to make balsam beds, set the fire, and keep smudges going day and night. He knew how to cook trout, venison, and flapjacks and how to supply them. He knew how to skin, not pluck, a partridge. In addition he had to carry the pack basket of supplies, sometimes a load of sixty pounds. He earned his three dollars.

Each Adirondack guide worked in only one part of the country and took pride in being known as a "Lower Saranac," a "Loon Lake," a "Blue Mountain," or a "Lake Pleasant" guide. He never guided a party outside his own district. He would guide a group to another district, then return alone, unless, by chance, he could pick up some party headed his way. The visitor had to pay the guide for the time he took to get back alone, a custom which led to much abuse, for the guide tried to find some party to go back with him by whom he would likewise be paid.

Probably the most difficult job the guides had was to take their client's equipment over the portages between lakes. It took a strong man to move a boat as well as several hundred pounds of gear several miles. Out of the need for that job came the guide boat, an Adirondack contribution to outdoor life. It was, and still is, "a canoe built like a rowboat," as one outsider described it. The credit for building the first one usually goes to Mitchell Sabattis. The builders who followed took off extra weight until they could make a boat sixteen feet long that weighed about seventy-five pounds without equipment. Many guide boats, in an emergency, have carried four and even six men across a mountain lake in an autumn storm, pulled along by one pair of broad oars. The boats had to be stormworthy; few guides ever learned to swim. "Don't worry none in this boat," one guide used to say. "You're as safe in it as you are in the Lord's pocket."

The guide boat's best joints were cut from naturally shaped spruce roots. The three tenths of an inch planking was of local pine or cedar. The planks were laid flush, not overlapping.

Following the sawing, beveling, and fitting, they were fastened to the ribs with brass screws and the joints were nailed with copper tacks. The heads of these five thousand tacks and three thousand screws, left bare, were the decorations of the boat, which then got several coats of clear varnish. The guides used to say, "It takes a man with know-how a whole month of long days to make one boat." Two men at Saranac Lake, Theodore Hanmer, now ninety, and his son Willard still build them.

Boat, pack basket, and rifle were not all of the guide's stock in trade. Most of them were storytellers. They added much to Adirondack folklore. If the great number of stories which they knew and which, in retrospect, they seemed to tell around the clock, were not all based on personal experience, they were at least the guide's in the manner of telling. "Well sir, I remember one day I was hunting in the swale over to Ampersand," a guide would say, "and I'd fired my last bullet. All I had for a weapon was a bottle of iodine when along come a ten-point buck. I hit him with that in the tail. The iodine itched and the deer started scratching and by the time I cotched up to him he'd rubbed hisself all away. All that was left was a pair of antlers. I got 'em home over the fireplace." Or it might be a tale of the guide who shot himself in the neck but didn't stop his hunting. "Hell," he said, "I've hit plenty of deer in the neck and they went right on running. Didn't seem to hurt 'em none."

As a storyteller no one surpassed Mike Cronin, guide and teamster. He was unique, however, in that he had only one story. It was the tale of how he drove Theodore Roosevelt out of the woods below Marcy in September, 1901, after Roosevelt, then vice-president, had received the news that President McKinley was dying from an assassin's bullet. Mike drove the last lap of that midnight journey to North Creek over the worst of roads.

A few years ago someone wrote that Mike knew all the while from a telephone call he had overheard that McKinley was dead and that Roosevelt was really president even as he raced along the mountain roads, but Mike said nothing to Roosevelt, "because," he explained in fine guide fashion, "he never asked me. All he said was 'Hurry!' " In any case, Mike went through night, mist, and shadow, by peril and precipice, and delivered the president safely to the waiting train.

In the years that followed Mike told the story ten thousand times. Each time freshly remembered details were added until it was quite a story. "It wasn't the bumps or ruts that was bad," Mike used to say. "It was the steam, red-hot steam right in front of me and them as doesn't believe that just wasn't there. Yes sir, red-hot steam coming out of the flanks of them horses. As I remember it, there was one minute that was real bad, going round one curve. We went too wide and the carriage and one horse were out in the air, over the edge, ready to fall. Why didn't they? Mister, I just whupped the other horse up, that's why, and he pulled his mate and the wagon right around, gentle-like."

Mike never seemed to remember to tell one astounding fact in the whole episode, that each of those black horses had two hundred hooves. If Mike liked a listener well and if the listener didn't look too skeptical, Mike presented him with one of the genuine horseshoes that his black team wore on that ride. There used to be about four hundred homes in the Adirondack country that proudly treasured a genuine shoe from Mike's black team.

By 1890 the profession of guide had deteriorated. The rich men from the cities were blamed — "they pay big wages, secure a big slaughter, all to have the satisfaction of a big brag." At least one guide boasted of a tip of one thousand dollars for two weeks' work. At the same time the guide's prosperity often depended on his ability to get a deer for his client. Those who were not particular how they got them or in what season gave

the entire body of guides the reputation of being game slaugh-
terers and outlaws.

To check some of the evils the more legitimate guides formed
the Guides' Association, a backwoods trade-union, in 1891. Its
members agreed to uniform rates and to observance of the game
laws. Its membership lists named six hundred and twenty-six
men as qualified. Most of the names showed New England origin; few were French-Canadian. Among them were the old
names of the Adirondacks — Moody, Stickney, Martin, Russell,
Manning, Betters, Plumley, whose children and grandchildren
today are proud of being known as "old guides' families."

Those old guides began to go in the early part of the twentieth century; none took their place. When the demand for the
services of those who lived on decreased, some became permanent caretakers for camps. Some became game wardens. After
1908 all guides had to register with the Conservation Department. More than a thousand guides continue to register even
today; they are mostly men regularly employed, but always willing to quit the job during hunting season. They follow a
memory rather than a profession.

The first of the "old" guides was John Cheney. The last?
Les Hathaway died in December, 1952.

Les was a dapper little man with trim moustache and laugh-
ing eyes. He looked a distinguished sixty-five but always insisted he was much older. The spring before he died he was
saying, "I'll never see eight-nine again" which meant he was
born in 1863. People laughed and said, "That's just Les, exaggerating as usual." Les never minded what people said. He was
old, that was sure, and he liked to say, "There may be people
around who've lived as long as I have but there ain't many who
remember as much."

During most of his years Les Hathaway had been a private
guide. He didn't care much for house-guiding. "I was one once,"

he said, "for a man on Upper Saint Regis. I lasted just two weeks. Most of the time I didn't do nothing except paint the boathouse. Then one afternoon the boss came out in what I guess you call formal clothes. I remember he was also wearing gloves and in July at that. 'Les,' he said, 'I want you to row me. I must make a call.' So I rowed him across the lake, him sitting in the stern as formal as a funeral. We go to a camp where some newcomers had just arrived. My boss went to the door but the camp owner wasn't home, only a maid. You know what he does then? He leaves a visiting card! How do you like that — a visiting card in the Adirondacks! I quit the job next day. That wasn't what I called guiding. It wasn't even camping. I'm not even sure I'd call it living."

The people whom Les served for fifty years and more were usually wealthy men up from the city, men in important places, used to giving orders and having them obeyed. In the woods it was different. Here the guide was the boss. Back in the city these men may never have had anyone talk back to them. Here they took it from Les and liked it. Les used to tell of one man who carried a flask of liquor on a fishing trip and sipped it himself, explaining to Les, "I never let a guide drink." Les agreed, "That's right. One drunk in the boat is enough."

One man used to come up to the woods every autumn and go out with Les for a month. While many a multimillion-dollar decision was awaiting his return, he was hunting contentedly with Les, happy at being with someone who was completely honest, frank, and unimpressed by him, doing the dishes after supper and doing them over again if Les didn't like the way he had done them. When he died and the newspapers printed a long list of his achievements, Les read it and snapped, "Didn't say nothin' about him being one of the best dishwashers in the North Country. And I taught him, too, all he knew." Les could have added that his clients usually got their deer. Les was modest about his great skill in hunting. "All it means," he used to say, "is that a man knows more than a dumb beast. What's special in that?"

What was different about Les Hathaway was that he kept his strength and his sharpness to the last day of his life. He outlived all his clients. After that he offered gladly to take anyone into the woods in season, whether they paid him or not. The rest of the time he worked at any jobs he could find. He had his faults, but they were easily forgiven and forgotten. He'd never refuse a drink with a friend and he had many friends. During the summer it was hard to keep him on the job of mowing golf-course greens because he knew too many streams to fish. He was the first to admit his faults. "Any strong pine has moss growing on it," he used to say. "Don't hurt the pine none."

In all his long life Les was rarely out of the Adirondacks. "I was born in 'em and I'll die in 'em," he said, "and you couldn't ask for a better place to be born or to die. Some employer of mine once wanted me to come out to California with him and I almost went. Then I saw some pictures of the country. I wouldn't have nothin' to do with the sort of mountains they got, mister. The trees don't go all the way to the top." Like most of the guides, Les stuck to just one section of the woods, the area around Saranac Lake. "There's maybe only a couple hundred square miles I know but mister, I know 'em. Every rock and every stump on 'em. The trouble with people today is they're so busy coverin' ground they ain't got time to notice what's on the ground they're coverin'."

Les had his stock of stories, and good ones. Just how much truth was in them never seemed important. A friend once overheard him telling a man about a deer he had shot the week before. "Yes, sir," Les said, "an eight-point buck and all of two hundred pounds." A little later the friend overheard him telling another man about the same deer. "Got him last week," Les said. "Six prongs and all of a hundred and sixty pounds."

The friend asked Les, "What did you change your story for, Les?"

"Well, mister," Les said, his eyes twinkling, "I sorta size up the man first and see just how much he'll believe."

By the end of his life Les was a good friend of the forest rangers and the game wardens. They often looked in on his shack when he was out in the woods alone, just to make sure he was all right. Like many old guides, Les had been a man who took deer when he wanted them, regardless of any law. "We grew up before there was any conservation laws," Les used to say. "When a man was hungry he went and shot a deer. And I've been hungry some." Les used to pride himself on outwitting the wardens. He liked to say, "They never had me once."

He often told one story about the way some young warden kept after him, as Les knew, and finally caught him ten miles back in the woods, sitting beside a pack basket filled with fresh meat. "This time I got you with the evidence," the warden said. "Off we go to the judge."

"Yep," Les agreed, "but you got to carry the evidence. The law can hang a man but it don't say he has to tote his own gallows."

The warden picked up the pack basket, which weighed about fifty pounds, and lugged it out of the woods. Les followed behind like a carefree beagle. They got to the judge. The warden was about to present his case when Les said, "Judge, is there any law about letting a man buy a calf, skin it out, and take the meat into the woods, just to have it handy in case he gets hungry?" At that, Les opened the basket and took out the meat. "You can see for yourself, Judge," Les said. "That's veal, not venison. Sorry it was so heavy, Warden."

That was how Les told it. There probably wasn't a word of truth in it, because people always claimed you never could believe a word Les said.

He had another story about wardens. Les came on a salt lick

where a couple of men were killing deer and trucking them down to fancy city restaurants. Les couldn't squeal on them because that was against his code. Instead, he told a warden he knew where the biggest beavers in the Adirondacks lived and all black at that. The warden went along to see and the trail happened by chance to lead through that backwoods slaughter yard with its salt bait. The warden forgot the beavers and a little later caught the deer killers. Les said the whole thing was a coincidence. "Anyway," he added, "those guys deserved the jail they got. That kind of outlawin' ain't legal."

Most of his stories were about hunting. Not long before he died he had gone out into the woods alone. The way he told it he got up some time about dawn, climbed in his little boat, and paddled up the river. He hiked six miles to his hut in the back-woods. In no time he spotted a fine eight-point buck, four hundred yards off, so he said, much too far for any kind of shot. He fired anyway. The deer went plunging down the hill.

Les, so he said, didn't follow as other hunters might have done. He went up the hill and just over to the other side. In a half hour along came an eight-point buck. Les shot and killed him. "It takes a smart man to out-think a deer," Les said. "That deer figured most hunters would chase downhill after that first shot so he went a short ways, hid, then came back up the hill and I shot him. How do I know it was the same buck? Mister, he had the point of one antler chipped right off when I clipped him with that first shot. I remember seeing it fly. How could I see at that distance? Mister, I saw well enough to hit the point of the antler at four hundred yards, didn't I?"

Anyway, Les brought many a deer out of the woods in his last years, and by himself. People said that only proved Les was always exaggerating his age. No man past eighty or beyond, as Les claimed to be, could do that, not even a sliver of Adirondack hardpan like Les.

On the last afternoon of the 1952 hunting season Les came

down the river, a deer in his boat. He died the next morning. The local paper ran his obituary. One sentence read: "He was born at Franklin Falls on July 10, 1862." When people read that they said, "What do you know! Les was really ninety. Maybe some of his other stories did have some truth in them after all."

That was an old Adirondack guide, and just about the last of them.

The Top of Pisgah

On a gentle hillside that overlooks one of the loveliest of Adirondack views, the valley of the Saranac River, is a statue by Borglum. It is a life-size bronze of Dr. Edward Livingston Trudeau. He sits in a cure chair, a blanket over his legs, and looks out over the hills. The hillside slope is that of Mount Pisgah, a minor Adirondack peak. It is fittingly named. It was "to the top of Pisgah" that Moses was told to go to behold the Promised Land — "and lift thine eyes westward and northward and southward and eastward."

The statue belongs there, on the grounds of Trudeau Sanatorium. More than anyone, it was Dr. Trudeau who made part of the Adirondack country a promised land for thousands and whose lifework helped build Saranac Lake, one of the unique villages of America. Dr. Trudeau was the father of modern tuberculosis therapy. The thousands who have beaten the disease and lived lives of deepened usefulness all owe something to the tall, thin, gentle-faced man who came to the Adirondacks in 1873 to die — and enjoyed forty-three more years of life.

Trudeau, the son of a New York doctor and a French mother, was raised in Paris. When he returned to America at seventeen he was headed for the navy. Tall and attractive, he was the gayest of the smart social set in the city, the well-born young men around town. In later years as these rich young men became richer and important, they were vital and useful contacts for Dr. Trudeau. Flitting happily about as a gay young man of twenty, his only serious interests were hunting and fishing. He and his crowd even went up to Paul Smith's for one trip. He never forgot it.

He might have gone on to be a colorful but frothy naval officer had his elder brother not caught tuberculosis. For most people that was a death sentence. Until the end of the last century little that was accurate was known about the disease. Doctors believed it was caused by the disintegration of the blood; when the body was unable to dispose of such waste products, tuberculosis resulted. Until 1860 there were no sanatoria for the tuberculous. Some of the big city hospitals had wards where the sick might lie quietly until the end. Standard cough mixtures were the only medicines. Any changes in temperature in the sick room were considered dangerous and windows were kept tightly closed.

Trudeau nursed his brother and shared the same tightly closed room with him, only to see him die. That death had its profound effect. Trudeau went into a stockbroker's office, a more serious-minded young man. He met the girl he wanted to marry. She let it be known quickly that she was not interested in marrying a butterfly, even a well-to-do city-bred sort. Against the bets of his friends that he would never finish the course, Trudeau decided at once to study medicine.

He did finish it, only to break down with tuberculosis, as many a young doctor has done since. Feeling he had only a short time to live, he decided to spend that time where he had once been happy, at Paul Smith's, and to use his last strength hunting. He went in the summer of 1873. The story of his early days is now part of Adirondack legend: how a guide carried him from the stagecoach to the house, saying, "You don't weigh more'n a dried lambskin"; how Trudeau sat in bed shooting at targets, just to keep in practice.

Trudeau recovered sufficiently to return to the city. He was back again ill in the Adirondacks in the spring of 1874, this time with wife and children and determined to stay the winter. His own physician, Dr. Alfred Loomis, encouraged him to do it, but other doctors assured Trudeau it would kill him. He survived that winter and the next. His health improved so much that he decided to stay on, having shown for any to see that fresh air and even winter air do not necessarily kill the tuberculous. Now at home in the hills, the doctor decided to find some permanent residence; he found it in the river-edge hamlet of Saranac Lake. He was in fair health once more, able to go hunting, particularly after foxes on a hillside behind the village.

Even though Trudeau proved in himself that life outdoors could help the tuberculous, he was not the first to discover it. Beginning with Dr. Benjamin Rush, surgeon in Washington's army, a small number of doctors had been suggesting it for almost a century. A Louisville doctor, William A. McDowell, wrote in 1843 of the value of four meals a day, outdoor air, and graduated exercise. He even suggested, thirty years before Dr. Trudeau came to the woods, "summer residence in a northern mountain region." At the same time, in proposing moderate and regular exercise, he wrote:

Dancing or fencing is to be preferred. Jumping rope may be advantageously substituted. Although a few hops over the rope may comprise the extent of ladies' ability in their first efforts, yet by perseverance they will find themselves in a few weeks able to prosecute it for three or four consecutive hours without fatigue.

The Adirondacks sanatoria never saw anything like that.

Nor was Trudeau the first man to sense the value of the Adirondack region in helping the tuberculous. The first doctor ever to settle in the Adirondacks, a Dr. Asa Post, came to Elizabethtown from Vermont in 1792 "for the cure of his consumption." In 1852 a local historian said, "In my explorations of the country I have met with repeated instances of individuals who had reached their forest homes, in advanced stages of pulmonary affection, in whom the disease had been arrested and the sufferer restored to comparative health." Similar reports brought a steady trickle of invalids to the Adirondacks in the fifties and sixties. But the great rush started after Murray's book, in 1869. It brought invalids, even advanced cases that could barely stand the stage ride to Paul Smith's, in almost as large numbers as it brought tourists.

Many a hopelessly sick person in a large city, lying in a sunless, airless room, was shown pages in the Murray book. He must have been strengthened at once in hope and even in health when he read the story this reliable clergyman, obviously a man not given to exaggeration, had written. Murray told of one young man in New York whose death was merely a matter of a little time. He went to the Adirondacks to go to some woodland camp. A guide loaded him into a boat on a mountain lake and laid him on a couch of balsam branches. Murray wrote:

> The boat went its way down the lake with its load of living and dying. This was in early June. At the end of the first week he could walk by leaning on the paddle. The second week he needed no support. The third week his cough ceased entirely. The second week of November he "came out", bronzed as an Indian and as hearty. In five months he had gained 85 pounds. This, I am aware, is an extreme case and, as such, may seem exaggerated: but it is not.

After reading that, the sick came to the region and continued to come for the next thirty years. When they heard of Dr. Trudeau they began to throng the rude boardinghouses and the hotels in Saranac Lake. Trudeau was there in winter and came in one day a week from Paul Smith's in summer.

Saranac Lake was not much of a place. A Philadelphia clergyman, Reverend John P. Lundy, was a patient there in 1877.

During his stay he wrote a book, *Saranac Exiles,* which he signed "Not by W. Shakespeare." He had sense enough not to publish it until after his departure. He liked the place little, even though he seems to have recovered his health sufficiently to live until 1888. To him the place was "the miserable hamlet of Saranac Lake." He wrote:

> To the everlasting honor of Saranac Lake it must be said that it has no lawyers or news editors to do the mischievous and harassing headwork of keeping the community in an uproar of needless excitement and agitation.

And, he added:

> One good doctor of medicine Saranac Lake has, the intrepid and heroic invalid, Trudeau, ready and willing to give his best advice to his needy sick friends, and to the very poor who cannot afford to send for some distant physicians, without money and without price.

In 1882 news reached Trudeau that the German bacteriologist Koch had discovered the tubercle bacillus and its relation to the cause of the disease. He shifted dramatically from his concentration on the care of the sick to research into causes of their sickness. He never had any great reserve of strength, but collecting what he could, he went off to New York, as curious and willing as any college freshman, to learn what he might of the new science of bacteriology.

He returned to Saranac Lake. In the most primitive surroundings, Trudeau founded the first tuberculosis laboratory in the world. In a short time he satisfied himself that tuberculosis could not occur, no matter how poor or mean the environment, unless the bacilli were present. The rabbits that he used for this most fundamental tuberculosis experiment ran on a little island near Paul Smith's hotel during a whole summer. Guests shook their heads at the earnest absorption of the tall man who watched them, and did not realize that what he was learning would change the world's attitude toward tuberculosis as an infectious disease.

In addition to research, Trudeau had another live interest. For the most part, the Adirondack cure was only for the well-to-do; in terms of the times, hotel rates were high. What Trudeau wanted was a place where people less fortunate might come and be under intelligent control. In 1858 a Dr. Brehmer in Silesia had written a plan for helping the tuberculous. He believed that climate was not the only all-important factor and that the invalid was never injured by exposure so long as he was accustomed to live out-of-doors. Where he lived was not so important as how he lived, and he must live under careful regulation of his daily life — of air, food, rest, and exercise. Many a tuberculosis specialist was saying the same thing ninety years later. Brehmer's ideas led to the founding of a health center at Davos in Switzerland in 1860.

Trudeau knew of Brehmer's work. He believed, as he wrote, that the Adirondack country had some special virtue for the sick; this he felt was due to large amounts of ozone in the air, produced by the woods, and to the resinous odors from the evergreens. He also knew that sick men went elsewhere and recovered. It was clear that it was not so much the climate or geography as how those factors were used. With help from his wealthy friends at Paul Smith's, Trudeau was able to plan his own sanatorium. It was located on the hill behind Saranac Lake, his favorite fox-hunting ground, bought for him and given to him by the guides with whom he hunted. In 1884, a one-room cottage, painted red, opened with two patients as the start of the Adirondack Cottage Sanatorium. (It kept that name until after Trudeau's death.) Its first patients were two factory girls; one lived to return to the fiftieth anniversary of Trudeau.

This was the first private nonprofit sanatorium in America; costs were fixed so low that part of the patient's bill had to be met from outside contributions. Today Trudeau runs on the same basis; there is always a deficit. Other semiprivate sanatoria eventually opened in or near Saranac Lake, including Stonywold, Gabriels, and, in the 1930's, Will Rogers for the theatrical profession.

One ex-patient told of early days on the side of Mount Pisgah:

> Unless desperately sick no one was put to bed. Patients were allowed to exercise but when fatigued they rested in chairs on the porches. In the absence of enough steamer chairs heavy wooden armchairs were used, tipped back on their hind legs, while the feet of the patient were inserted in a cracker box in cold weather: soapstones were placed in the boxes and the patient sat huddled up and mummy-like, in strange headgear, in fur coats, or wrapped in heavy shawls. Once a month Dr. Trudeau examined each patient and brought fresh courage to him to continue on with the cure.

In those early years the sole charge for everything was five dollars a week; it rose to eight dollars in 1913. (Bedfast patients today pay seventy dollars.) In the first years those who came had to leave the train at Ausable Forks, forty-two miles off, drive or be driven sicker than death over the worst of roads to arrive at the lonely little village in the middle of the hills. Dr. Trudeau welcomed each patient personally, and was able to make each one feel that someone cared. That greatest asset of Saranac Lake functioned from the start. No patient ever needed to tell a doctor that he felt his case was helpless — he could look at the doctor; along with Dr. Trudeau, almost every medical man who has attended the tuberculous in the three quarters of a century that Saranac Lake has functioned as a health center has himself been a patient.

The first years' figures showed something like 25 per cent of the cases arrested. The basic regime set at Trudeau continued with little change for years, but as new ideas in surgery and newer ideas in the use of drugs came along, the Trudeau staff adapted its regime to them. In Dr. Trudeau's time, when he knew no drug he could give a patient except a sedative, he saw many a "hopeless" case leave, arrested. He could take pride in that, although, as the most modest of men, he never mentioned it. That had to balance the grief of his personal life; he watched two of his children die from pulmonary disease. His second son, Dr. Francis B. Trudeau, has helped to maintain his father's traditions to the present time.

From the earliest days, Dr. Trudeau's sanatorium attracted young doctors as patients. When they were well many stayed on, either with Dr. Trudeau or in private practice in the village. They continued the Trudeau traditions: the best of care for the patient, together with the most advanced research into the cause and cure of tuberculosis and, later, into the whole field of pulmonary disease. Saranac Lake has never lost that duality and the reputation of its facilities became world famous. That has continued; a Point Four sanatorium built in Santiago, Chile, in 1948, was named Trudeau Sanatorium.

Among those who arrived sick, recovered, and stayed on were Dr. Lawrason Brown, who began the first occupational therapy in America at Trudeau in 1903, and Dr. E. R. Baldwin, who broadened the research program. Dr. Leroy U. Gardner aided in research and carried on some of the first studies in America on the relation of silica and other dusts to lung diseases, and helped in the creation of some of the earliest labor safety laws. These men sought no monopoly for their knowledge; they shared it gladly. Many of the tuberculosis centers in America that opened between 1900 and 1930 were staffed by men who had studied, and often been cured, at Saranac Lake. The Trudeau School for medical personnel — thirty days of intensive training annually in all that is new and best in the study of pulmonary diseases — was opened in 1916 and still continues. It has trained men in the Public Health Service and many more from overseas. So broad and generous has been its training that many townspeople complained that through the Trudeau School and other teaching arrangements the tuberculosis specialists were "giving away their secrets" and helping to undermine the village's economy.

Out of Trudeau's work came a unique village. Since his sanatorium would not take those who could pay their way in full, the village developed a large private sanatoria industry. When the infectious quality of the disease became known, tourist hotels refused to take invalids. They were not even welcome as residents in some of the villages. The result was the appearance of many boarding cottages in Saranac Lake after 1890, run exclusively for the sick and served by those doctors who had remained as private physicians.

As Saranac Lake's reputation grew the number of cottages increased. By 1920 more than one hundred and fifty of them, with room for four to thirty patients, cared for the two thousand patients who were in the village. The big screened porch, a part of the cure, became a feature of Saranac Lake architecture. Many cottages were run by devoted people, often nurses or even ex-patients, who felt that the career of caring for the sick was a service and acted accordingly. Some, however, saw a fine opportunity to get rich. Costs in the cottages were usually moderate; many cottage owners kept patients after their resources had run out. Others put on new charges at every opportunity. In 1905, Alfred L. Donaldson the historian, himself a patient and well-to-do, wrote:

> Whether at Saranac or at Bloomingdale,
> Whether the milk be sweet or slightly stale,
> The price of eggs keeps rising day by day,
> Oh! if we could but take the cure by mail!

Among the thousands of patients who dwelt for a time in the little Adirondack village were many who were famous. Most distinguished was Robert Louis Stevenson, who came to America in 1887, intending to go to Colorado for his health. When he heard of Dr. Trudeau he came to the Adirondacks. He arrived in early October to be Dr. Trudeau's patient and stayed through a cold winter until April of 1888. Even though he felt better at Saranac Lake he cared little for the place. He found it "A bleak blackguard beggarly climate, of which I can say no good except that it suits me. . . . The grayness of the heavens here is a circumstance eminently revolting to the soul." Most of the time he wrote. He finished twelve essays as well as two thirds of *The Master of Ballantrae*. Occasionally he stole away to a pond nearby to ice-skate. The rest of the time he dreamed about getting away to warmth, sun, and private yachts. The village keeps the Stevenson Cottage as a shrine, with his cigarette burns still on the mantle, caring far more for the memory of the man than ever he did for the village or the Adirondacks.

Perhaps no one as famous ever came to Saranac Lake in the years that followed, but the list of well-known people is long. It includes President Quezon, who died there; many theatrical people, including Eugene O'Neill and Lila Lee; ball players, including Christy Mathewson, Branch Rickey, and Larry Doyle; and members of families famous in politics and business. In recent years many distinguished South Americans have come. A few years ago the chief of staff of one South American country lay ill in a Saranac Lake nursing cottage. The president of that country, as an act of courtesy and friendship, made a flying trip to the Adirondacks to see him. The village gave the statesman a parade. President and chief of staff swore eternal friendship in the sick room and the president went home. A short time later the chief of staff sneaked out of town without telling his doctor, took a plane home, and immediately led a revolt that threw the president out.

The village has a large stock of "patient" stories. One young man arrived and promptly won the reputation of being the best-behaved patient ever to come to town. He not only seemed to sleep all night but slept soundly all day, from early morning until dinner. A doctor, returning from a meeting in Montreal after midnight, stopped in at a bar in Plattsburgh to find the "good" patient raising Cain in the barroom. The young man admitted that he could not stay in bed at night. He waited until dark, then took off every night, to return about 6 A.M. and get in some sound sleeping.

One man, completely well, once took the cure and rested most of the day with a revolver beside him; he was the bodyguard for a New York gangster's sick brother and for more than a year did what the invalid did. Another young man arrived very sick and stated that he would follow all the doctor's orders and rest, but one afternoon each week he had to be up and about his business. On that afternoon he vanished for some hours. Later it was found he was a photographer's model and even while desperately ill was posing for fashion pictures somewhere in the woods, to show what the well-dressed sportsman was wearing.

The most flamboyant story is that of a Latin-American millionaire whose daughter was curing in town and wanted to see her brother's wedding, scheduled for a Caribbean island. Her father promptly chartered two airplanes, placed bride and groom, guests, wedding cake, and champagne aboard, and flew everything to the Adirondacks. Enough champagne was poured at an open house to float an Adirondack guide boat.

In the village's population today are many ex-patients, lawyers, contractors, and businessmen of all sorts, who came to the place as patients, got well, and stayed on. In the village, for the same reason, are people of twenty nationalities, to make this backwoods Adirondack village a cosmopolitan center in miniature. The village has benefited in tangible ways from those who sought health in it. Much of the equipment of a fine local hospital has been given by grateful people. William Morris, New York theatrical agent, once a patient, brought his top stars, including Jolson, Harry Lauder, Eddie Cantor and Sophie Tucker, to play benefits which in successive years raised money for the Jewish Community Center; for the Methodist Church; to settle the mortgage on the Catholic Church; and for a Children's Day Nursery. He and Sime Silverman, founder of *Variety,* a former patient, proposed the Will Rogers Sanatorium for theatrical people.

With such a large patient population Saranac Lake was a natural target for all peddlers of nostrums and gadgets. For years the tuberculosis experts in the village had to show patiently that each new one was of questionable value. Machines for breathing, glass helmets to admit special gases, vaccines, and secret drugs were each boomed in turn until each went bust. One doctor arrived and opened a sanatorium to cure tuberculosis with a serum made from turtles; he left in a hurry three months later.

For many years it was known that if a patient returned to the same environment and work in which he had previously broken down, he might well break down again. To change this, a group of Saranac Lake doctors and ex-patients set out to start some sort of rehabilitation program. In 1935 they opened the Saranac Lake Study and Craft Guild, now the Saranac Lake Rehabilitation Guild. It has been run largely by ex-patients ever since and is now supported by the state, by private contributions, and by small fees from pupils if they can afford them. Training courses have been offered in sixty subjects, so that when he is well a butcher can leave the place trained as a radio operator, or a dancer can return home retrained as a secretary; their cure is that much more complete. One Guild specialty has been the training of ex-tuberculous patients from all over to become X-ray operators for the Public Health Service mobile detection units that search out the disease in American offices and factories. Many of those units in America today are manned by people trained at the Guild in Saranac Lake.

Saranac Lake's health industry was at its peak in 1922, when more than sixteen hundred new patients came to the village in one year. Those already there were staying two, three, and four years and longer. Many patients were veterans of the First World War. At this time a fateful decision for the future was made by some of the doctors, who were the most powerful men in the village. The Veterans Administration proposed building a five-hundred-bed hospital just outside the village. For various reasons, some logical and many fearful, the influential doctors prevailed on the Veterans Administration to build that sanatorium elsewhere. It was built eighteen miles down the road, at Tupper Lake, where Sunmount Hospital, with a payroll of four hundred and ninety, has been an important factor in the economic life of that town. For that decision many of the townspeople never forgave the doctors, no matter how well reasoned their arguments.

The opening of Sunmount and the depression of 1929 closed the first of the cure cottages. From that time to the present the trend has been steadily lower, although there have been ups and downs. Higher costs, more state institutions, modern surgery, and finally, the discovery of drugs which permit more or less satisfactory cure at home have all helped to becloud the future of Saranac Lake as a health resort.

As the health industry declined, some people in Saranac Lake were content. In early days, and perhaps even today, Saranac Lake meant tuberculosis to many people; some tourists scooted through the village as if it were a plague spot. In truth, thousands of vacationers have come and never met a sick person, but this reputation as a health center has split the village. There were always those who wanted to see the village forget the health industry and concentrate on its tourist business and who would gladly see the last tuberculous patient on the train — even though the health services in recent years have made up more than 50 per cent of the village's year-round income. The arrival of a small shoe factory in 1953 has led to hopes that more small industries may come, to provide a year-round payroll in addition to the tourist trade.

At the same time others have tried even harder and continue to try to rebuild the village as a health center. They point out that there will be work for a place like Trudeau to do for many years in repairing damaged lungs, even if a quick and sure cure for tuberculosis were found on the morrow. They believe that the superb private medical and surgical staff — more than forty doctors in a village of seven thousand — who are still loath to leave a place they love can be put to some other vital use. They believe the superb equipment of the Saranac Lake General Hospital and of the laboratories can find some way to serve and continue to serve humanity. They believe that there is room for a cancer treatment center in the area, particularly for work with lung cancer. They believe that with the experience in rehabilitation, as centered in the guild, Saranac Lake can offer to take polio victims and the victims of industrial accidents, retrain them, and make the town a leading rehabilitation center.

In the long run these people believe that while the tourist trade may continue to grow, the village's best hope is in its eighty-year-old reputation as a "Town of Second Chance." That second chance was once given the tuberculous. It can be given as willingly and as expertly to people with other disabilities.

The best symbol of it remains. It is Dr. Trudeau in bronze, in his place just below the top of Pisgah, looking at the hills in which he taught men to find new hope.

·❧ V ❧·

Adirondack Manmarks

Men have come to the Adirondacks country with varied motives — for wealth, a career, a refuge, health, or inspiration. Some have just come for the summer.

This stream of outsiders into the area is a distinctive part of any Adirondack chronicle. Some appeared mysteriously and left nothing but legends or old wives' tales. Others stood like one of the great white pines; when they went they left a place not easily filled. Many who have come stayed only a short time and left little or no impression. Their variety shows the broad appeal of the Adirondack country in all its written history. The list is long.

It includes Viscount Châteaubriand, famous in French literature, who traveled the southern edge of the region in 1791 and thereafter wrote, in the manner of Rousseau, about the goodness of nature and the goodness of man living close to it. It includes Ralph Waldo Emerson, James Russell Lowell, Louis Agassiz and a group of other distinguished intellectuals, who spent part of the summer of 1858 by Follensby Pond west of the Saranacs. Their guides quickly called the place "the Philosophers' Camp." Longfellow had been invited but refused when he heard that the lofty Emerson was going to take a gun. No gun was ever fired and nothing else happened except that Emerson wrote a ten-page poem on the experience — not much of a camping trip and not much of a poem.

Other literary figures knew the region. James Fenimore Cooper visited it early in the nineteenth century and used the Lake George area as background for some novels. Mark Twain had a summer camp on Lower Saranac Lake for many years: one of his favorite guests was Irvin Cobb. Edward Judson, better known as Ned Buntline, the father of the penny dreadful and master of the paper-backed thriller, discoverer and promoter of Buffalo Bill, lived at Eagle Lake, south of the Blue Mountain Lake, off and on for five years after 1859.

In addition to Theodore Roosevelt, two other presidents, Cleveland and Coolidge, summered in the Adirondacks and made that region the location of the summer White House. Artists came, the most famous, Winslow Homer, American watercolorist. Many of his most popular works show Adirondack scenes. Rockwell Kent has lived and worked at Ausable Forks for many years.

Many musicians have lived in the Adirondack country. Lotte Lehmann, Louise Homer, and others spent their summers on the west shore of Lake George. Gershwin and Grace Moore were Adirondack visitors. Artur Rodzinsky still lives at Lake Placid. A large group of theatrical people have always come to the woods; for many years Elizabethtown was like a bit of Broadway in summer with Leon Errol, Otto Kruger, and a large portion of the membership of the Lambs Club. Harry Lauder, as perennial guest of his agent William Morris, was a familiar figure on the streets of Saranac Lake and at the golf club. Al Jolson played a benefit in the same village in 1927 and broke all theatrical records by staying on stage alone for three hours, an astonishing show of repertoire, stamina, and ability to hold an audience.

The assortment of outsiders has been a wide one, from John Jacob Astor, who skirted the Adirondacks in 1785 as he paddled north on Lake Champlain to buy furs, to Chester Gillette of

Cortland, New York, who drowned his mistress Grace Brown in Big Moose Lake in July, 1906, providing the incidents and murder trial which inspired Dreiser's *An American Tragedy*. It includes Charles Herreshoff, whose descendants designed yachts for international competition — a cultured gentleman, raised in the court of Frederick the Great, who tried to make the family fortune at what is now Old Forge and shot himself in 1819 when his mine was flooded. It ends with a troop of Seminole Indians who came to dwell by an Adirondack roadside in the summer of 1953 to wrestle alligators for the edification of passing tourists.

Most of these Adirondack visitors were transients and in time went their way. There were others who stayed on for years or for a lifetime. That list is long, too. The tales told about them are many and colorful.

My Uncle Napoleon

When the American vessel the *Commerce* docked in New York from Bordeaux in August, 1815, one of its passengers was a portly man of forty-eight, a French merchant who called himself M. Bouchard. The mayor of New York was at the dock to greet him, an unusual honor for a simple French merchant. At the best hotel in the city the manager treated the Frenchman with special honor, but, alas, all the rooms were taken. The American statesman Henry Clay had the best suite in the hotel. A word from the manager and Clay not only gave up his suite but invited the visitor to a lavish dinner.

The next day the portly M. Bouchard went strolling on Broadway. An old man, veteran of the Napoleonic wars — Waterloo had been lost just two months earlier — happened to notice the stranger. With the greatest reverence he dropped to his knees in the middle of a Broadway sidewalk, bowed, and said, *"Votre Majesté!"*

The stranger acknowledged the courtesy and said, "I may pass under the title of Count de Survilliers but here in America I may sagely avow the truth. I am Joseph Bonaparte."

That begins the most glittering of the stories of all who ever came to the Adirondack country. Some of it has been retold many times. But much hitherto unknown, particularly of the consequences of Joseph Bonaparte's coming, is told here for the first time.

Joseph was the elder brother of Napoleon. He was a soft man, gentle and fond of the luxuries of life — fine wines, fine paintings, fine women. He had only one request, that he have them, in plenty. For five years as king of Spain, he was disliked by the Spaniards, and was finally driven out by Wellington. In those five years, with the usual Bonaparte talent, he had piled up quite a fortune and a magnificent collection of paintings. He helped to finance his brother's return from Elba. After Waterloo Joseph, who more or less resembled his brother, offered to take his place as prisoner and let Napoleon escape to the United States, but Napoleon rejected that. Next best, Joseph decided, was to get to the United States himself and prepare a place where his brother might someday come, that might even rise to be a New France.

An old friend, James LeRay de Chaumont, buyer of North Country lands, had dropped in at Joseph's villa at Blois a few days after Waterloo. "Well do I remember," Joseph said, as the century-old brandy was being passed, "that you spoke to me formerly of your great possessions in the United States. If you still have them I should very much like to have some in exchange for a part of the silver I have there in those wagons and which may be pillaged any moment. Take four or five hundred thousand francs and give me the equivalent in land." De Chaumont demurred at such a blind purchase, but Bonaparte insisted, saying, "I know you well and I rely more on your word than on my own judgment." Bonaparte gave no clue to why he wanted that land.

A tentative deal was arranged. Bonaparte became the owner of 160,260 acres for about one hundred and twenty thousand dollars but eventually cut that down by three quarters. The lands ran from the flat Saint Lawrence country up the western slopes of the Adirondacks, hilly land, not particularly good, and sparsely settled.

So Joseph came to New York in the hope of setting up New France. He soon left the city and moved to Philadelphia, where he had a close friend with whom he had corresponded for years. This was the eccentric merchant and millionaire Stephen Girard, landowner, shipowner, and wealthiest man in the city. In the next months the news from France made clear that Napoleon, tightly guarded on Saint Helena, could never escape. The idea of a New France was pointless.

In 1818 Joseph made a quick visit to northern New York to see his land. If he had any idea of settling there he quickly abandoned it; life in such a wilderness had no appeal. He did not return for ten years and then only for a few short weeks in three summers. On his first journey he did discover the delights of Saratoga and returned to it every summer thereafter. It was at Saratoga that he received news of the death of Napoleon.

Joseph decided to be a country gentleman. He bought land at Bordentown, New Jersey, up the Delaware from Philadelphia on the main post road to New York. Here he planned to build as exquisite a small estate as possible and live the life of a cultured English gentleman, under his new motto, "Familiar with misfortune, I have learned to help the wretched." Thanks to help from the shipping connections of his friend Girard, Joseph was able to send an emissary to France to recover the wealth he had buried in a garden and to bring back part of his art collection. To occasional callers at Bordentown, and many of the famous men of the period were delighted to be entertained by a Bonaparte, Joseph sometimes showed crowns, swords, and other jewels, in all worth five million francs.

His art collection, the finest in America, included works by da Vinci, Raphael, Rubens, Van Dyck, and Titian. In his later years he sold occasional pictures whenever he needed cash. He took pride in showing his pictures. But if he had a very proper guest, particularly one of his Quaker neighbors in Bordentown, Joseph liked to display the full-size nude statue by Canova of his sister Pauline, casually pointing out to the embarrassed listener both the fine points of his sister's form and the sculptor's skill in copying them.

He had left a wife and two daughters in France. His wife did pack her trunks to come but never got beyond the gangplank. His daughters came for a time but for the most part Joseph seemed to be the sad and lonely man of the world, secure in his little garden. In fact, it wasn't like that at all. A contemporary who knew the Bonapartes well said of them, "It was characteristic of them to have a wife in every country where they spent much time." Joseph did not delay, once he arrived in Philadelphia. He found some local lady, name unrecorded. He tired quickly of her, and "before long he arranged a marriage between her and a local politician of some prominence, who knew the history of his bride and loved her none the less for it. Her dowry was handsome and she saw Joseph Bonaparte no more."

In 1818 he went into Philadelphia from his estate one day and met a girl of eighteen named Annette Savage. The legends say that he found her clerking in a store when he went in to buy a pair of suspenders. No legend tells accurately who she was except that she was "a Quaker girl of good family." However, the last of the Joseph Bonaparte line in America, who died in 1937, wrote to an inquisitive inquirer just before his death:

"Allow me to disabuse your mind. Annette Savage was not a Quaker girl but from Virginia, of the Savages of Virginia Station."

Whoever she may have been, she was a pretty and hot-tempered brunette. Joseph never mentioned her anywhere in his continuing correspondence with Stephen Girard nor in any other papers except in his will, in which ten thousand dollars was left to "the offspring of Joseph Bonaparte by a Miss Savage." He could not keep her in Bordentown. He rented a place up the Delaware, six miles to the north at Trenton, and installed her in it. The house still stands. She bore two daughters, one in 1819, the other in 1820; the older died in an accident when two years old and is buried in a Trenton churchyard. The surviving daughter was Caroline, a lovely brunette with a face in which the Bonaparte lines were written deep; the few pictures of her bear a close resemblance to Joseph's own mother Letizia.

There is no way of knowing the sort of life which the young Annette and her small daughter lived at Trenton, waiting for the occasional visits of Bonaparte. The good people of Trenton were as aloof as the burghers of Bordentown and she was alone most of the time. In 1824, without him, she went to Paris with her small daughter. Joseph might have wanted to go but he was barred from returning home. Little Caroline played in Paris parks and went to Paris sweet shops. Her mother met a Parisian silk merchant, Alexis de la Folie, and married him on April 27, 1826, at the mayor's office and later at the Protestant church. The report of the marriage was published in a Philadelphia newspaper on June 13 but upset no one, including Bonaparte. She came back. Financial relations continued between him and Annette for some years, even as she went on to bear de la Folie five children.

In 1828 Bonaparte revisited the land he owned in the North Country to examine it in more detail. With a gay entourage he went north by way of Albany, visited as usual the booming spa at Saratoga, went out to the west by the Mohawk coach, then into the woods by boat. The land pleased him even though he found little of it level. One lake (now called Lake Bonaparte) on the extreme west of the Adirondack country particularly attracted him. The hunting was fine, the companions gay, and there were even gold dishes for picnics in the woods. Joseph had a log fortress constructed at what is now called Natural Bridge, and built a lodge high on a point on the east of Lake Bonaparte. He gave the name Diana to his township that contained the lake. That name and the name of the lake are all that remain of Bonaparte in the North Country today.

He must have recommended the country to Annette and her obliging husband, for he offered them land on which to settle in the little town of Evans Mills, New York, just north of Watertown. Here she and de la Folie settled. If Bonaparte saw her on his visits north no one reported it. In 1832 he gave her additional land valued at eleven thousand dollars. He did not see her after 1837, when he returned to Europe for good, to die in Florence in 1844. His pictures were auctioned from time to time after his death and brought almost a quarter million dollars. Most of them were sold to Europeans and are now in European galleries.

In the meantime his daughter Caroline was growing up in the Saint Lawrence country, far from any of the advantages which Bonaparte children in Europe had enjoyed. She was a good-looking girl and free from any overwhelming pride in her Bonaparte ancestry. A few miles up the road in the small hamlet of Oxbow, the local physician, a Dr. Benton, had four sons. One, Zebulon Howell Benton, was a tall, slim young man, gifted with words, and with far more ambition than to follow his father as country doctor.

"Hole" Benton, as he was called, lived until 1893. He is still a fresh memory in the minds of some of the older people in the North Country. If ever there was a promoter and born actor it was "Colonel" Benton, the title being self-acquired somewhere in his career. He married Caroline de la Folie, as she now called herself, in 1838, in as lavish a wedding as the backwoods town of Watertown had ever seen, with four horses in tandem drawing the coach, and a footman in uniform. That was the way a niece of Napoleon Bonaparte should have been wed, or at least that is the way a prospective nephew of Napoleon Bonaparte, by marriage, thought she should be.

From now on the Bonaparte story is the Benton story. No more strangely costumed figure ever appeared in the Adirondack woods than Colonel Benton. Being a nephew of Bonaparte, if only by marriage, he wanted no one to forget it. Shortly after the wedding he adopted the costume he wore the rest of his life — cocked hat, even as Napoleon, a ruffled shirt and white stock, even as Napoleon, and a long Prince Albert coat, almost military in cut. In Napoleonic manner he was usually photographed with hand in coat.

By North Country standards, Caroline was a wealthy bride, with land and money from her father. She loved her tall, attractive husband deeply and bore one child after the other, until she had seven. Five lived to maturity. Four had the Bonapartian names of Charlotte Josephine, Zenaide Bonaparte, Zebulon Napoleon, and Lewis Joseph; the youngest, Thomas Hart Benton, was named after the senator from Missouri, probably on the Colonel's whim. Although he was no relation of the senator's, Colonel Benton often boasted of his political contacts. (The American artist Thomas Hart Benton is not related to the Zebulon Benton family.) As Caroline began wedded life in a neat brick house in Oxbow, which still stands, she must have been flattered by her husband's plans. He had two objectives — to grow as wealthy as possible so that a Bonaparte nephew and niece might live in Bonaparte style, and, eventu-

ally, to have his wife recognized and legitimized by the Bonaparte family.

Family scandal broke out before he could start after either
objective. Annette, the mother, and de la Folie were living in
Evans Mills, New York, when de la Folie died. For years
people in the North Country whispered that Annette had murdered him. His death was mysterious: he was well in the afternoon and dead at evening, but Annette would call neither
doctors nor help. Instead she called a gravedigger and had her
husband buried at once. There were many tales of North Country marriages to which this attractive and restless woman seemed
a threat — tales told by aged grandchildren who remembered
how "that de la Folie woman certainly upset Grandpa. Grandma
was awful glad when she up and married someone else." She
did marry a man named Henry Horr about 1840 and went to
New York. She then disappears from any recorded history, but
there is reason to believe that she died in 1864 or 1865. What
Episcopal cemetery is the burial place of this mistress of a king,
this "Savage of Virginia," no one knows. A long search for her
burial place has never located it.

In the meantime her son-in-law Benton, hat, cloak, and pose,
was building his career. His plan for making his fortune was
simple. Iron ore was plentiful in some of the lands his wife
owned. Benton was a fine figure in the fashionable hotels of
Manhattan, where many a stranger, attracted by his costume,
found him quite a conversationalist. The sportier business
circles and the Wall Street brokers came to know him well.
Eventually his conversation ran on the same line to the same
end. With his important contacts, his knowledge of geology and
mining, he could help any enterprising man with some spare
cash to double his money easily in the iron-ore lands of the
Adirondacks. Part of that was true; there was ore, but it was
difficult to get out. But as proof of his integrity and high social
standing he usually mentioned casually, "My wife Mrs. B., you

know, is a niece of Napoleon Bonaparte. Quite so!" If anyone checked they found that part of the story was most certainly true. They were then willing to believe that the Colonel's integrity might be as well founded as his family background.

With his wife's money and land behind him Colonel Benton was in one deal after another. In the long run all failed. In addition, the Colonel was never loath to talk about his investments in South America and Mexico, most of which had no basis except in his imagination. One story tells how he operated. In New York one day he dropped in on a real estate auction where they were selling a theater. The Colonel, with almost no cash but conscious of the effect his costume was producing, kept raising the bid as he felt a Bonaparte would have done, until to his surprise he found the theater knocked down to him. He quickly excused himself "until he could go to bank to secure money for payment" and hurried off, to get to a train north as fast as he could. While leaving the auction he bumped into a man who said, "I do hope they haven't sold that theater yet. I want to buy it." Benton said cheerfully, "They've sold it to me, my good fellow. Of course, if you would really like it — " and sold it at a profit.

All the while Caroline was raising her children and teaching them French, which she knew well. She frequently took off to the nearest fortuneteller — another Bonaparte trait — to see how her future was shaping. If she was ever troubled by the occasional stories of how her husband had sold the same piece of woodland to six or seven speculators in New York, she said nothing publicly.

About 1851 Caroline insisted on moving to Philadelphia, Pennsylvania, for the sort of schooling her children could not get in the shadow of the Adirondacks. For some years they lived on Pine Street in a fashionable part of the town and mingled with the best of Philadelphia society. A golden chance had risen for the Bentons. Napoleon III made himself emperor of France in 1852 and he was a cousin of Caroline's — if he chose to admit it. To his occasional prospect for land sales Benton now told a new story — that he and his wife had just returned from France, where the emperor had entertained them handsomely. That was less of a falsehood than a premature announcement of a dream to come true. To make it come true, money was needed and the proper introductions had to be arranged. Furthermore, Caroline was more interested in her children at the moment than in traveling to France for an uncertain reception from an unknowing cousin. That could wait.

The Colonel was with his family only now and then. He had found a new interest. In the forties a Swiss group had built a town called Alpina and a forge at the far west end of Lake Bonaparte and were trying to make iron. Benton sold stock in a million-dollar company to buy them out. Transportation was a serious problem. With persuasive speech and genteel manner he went to work on some of the politicians of Lewis County, in which Lake Bonaparte was situated. He succeeded in persuading them to put up a county bond issue to build a railroad to his furnace at Alpina. The taxpayers of Lewis County were paying off that bond issue down into the twentieth century. The road, with rails of maple, was started but the money ran out.

Like others before him, Benton now became obsessed with the thought of getting iron out of the abundant ore. His family stayed on in Philadelphia but he settled at Alpina in the backwoods, trying experiment after experiment and even running one furnace charge. More letters went off to Philadelphia asking his wife to arrange to mortgage more land, to sell land, to raise money on which he could draw.

Not until 1867 was Caroline willing to consider a journey to France. By then it was urgent. As Benton's iron-making schemes failed, the family had had to move from one less fashionable address in Philadelphia to another. The last of the upstate land was mortgaged now and the balance in the bank was small. The only hope for the Bentons was that the magnanimous Napoleon III might see fit to bestow an annual pension on his cousin. Benton set about using what political influence he could find in Washington to get the necessary introductions, but it was really Mrs. Benton who arranged them, thanks to the Philadelphia dentist who looked after the Benton teeth. He was a friend of Dr. Thomas Evans, dentist to Napoleon III and an influential man at court, for Napoleon was rarely without tooth trouble. By the autumn of 1869 everything was arranged. An upstate banker supplied three thousand dollars for the journey. Caroline sailed for France with two of her children. The trip turned out to be a miserable piece of bad timing.

On her return she published a small book, *France and Its People,* a glorification of the Bonapartes. Except for an occasional short paragraph it was as impersonal as a guidebook. In Paris the memories of a childhood visit more than forty years before when she was five were still fresh. "Before starting out for the day," she wrote, "I was desirous of finding some familiar spot and, from memories of childhood, soon stood within the arcade that was all gay and dazzling with rare and elegant merchandise. There was the toyshop that had been my delight: a few steps onward the confectionery where I had parted with many bright coins." Later she met the emperor. Although she did not tell it, the traditional story is that he greeted her with the remark, "By your face I can see you are a Bonaparte." Tradition also insists that he granted her a pension of fifteen hundred dollars a year — scarcely worth the journey — and made her daughter part of the court and put one son in military school. There is no proof that any of these things happened. The source and proud disseminator of these stories was the Colonel back home.

She did attend one royal party and she reported a conversation with the emperor. "I considered Mr. Lincoln one of the kindest hearted, one of the most noble men that ever lived," he told her. "I was surprised," Caroline commented, "though upon reflection I knew that the honorable nature of men is ever respected and admired, even by those with whom they differ in sentiments, creed, and politics."

She reported without a trace of emotion what must have been a highly emotional moment, a visit to Les Invalides. "In the chapel to the right," she wrote, "as you enter, stands the sarcophagus of Joseph, King of Spain, the eldest brother of Napoleon I. It is of black marble, white veined, and bearing no inscription except 'Joseph Bonaparte.' "

But Caroline's days as part of royalty were few. In July, less than five months after her arrival in France, Napoleon III declared war on Prussia. By September he was a prisoner at Sedan, with more on his mind than the problems of a relative from the village of Oxbow in the distant State of New York. Back home the Colonel was giving out many stories about the way his wife had gone to the front, where she was the only one of his family permitted to console Napoleon in his captivity. Actually, once the war broke out, Caroline never saw her cousin again. She stayed in Europe until the following February, gathering second-hand stories of the emperor's fate. The Prussians released him. He went to England, where, Caroline could report, "through the kindness of friends I have been favored with details. At Dover he was received by an enthusiastic gathering of all classes."

Then she was home again, walking the muddy streets of northern New York towns. The last hope of the Bentons had failed. Their financial affairs were in a mess, with mortgages piled on mortgages. A judgment of fifty-three thousand dollars was filed against one of Benton's ventures. Land and money were gone. The upstate banker who had always liked Caroline and helped her was himself bankrupt, partly because even he had become involved in some of the Colonel's land and stock schemes. That finished the Benton marriage. Caroline settled in Watertown and gave French lessons, and may have been helped by one of her sons, Zebulon Napoleon, who was showing the same talents which his father had for selling the same stock twice. The aging Colonel still wore his costume and lived by himself in the deep woods at Alpina. From time to time he came into Watertown to add details for any who would listen, even small boys, of the regal glory that had been his when he and his wife ran the Napoleonic court.

In 1885 the local paper in Richfield Springs, then a popular watering place below Utica, ran a small ad: "Mrs. C. Benton has located permanently in Richfield Springs and will teach French orally and theoretically. Conversation a specialty. Call at the National Hotel." An elderly lady now, sixty-five years of age, she lived with her daughter Josephine. A few pupils, still alive today, remember her as a dull and uninspired teacher who often seemed preoccupied as she read her fortune from a pack of cards.

On a December day in 1890, Caroline, daughter of Joseph Bonaparte, died. Her remains were sent to the little upstate church at Oxbow for burial in the adjoining cemetery. The funeral was held in a North Country blizzard. The old Colonel managed to get out of his backwoods home for it. He and a few friends beat their way through the storm to the grave. After the funeral the mourners stopped at a nearby inn. One of the pallbearers declined whiskey, which by now was the Colonel's favorite drink, and asked for tea. The inn had no tea.

The Colonel put on long cloak and cocked hat. In his most courtly manner he said, "The Bonapartes have always deemed it a privilege to provide their guests with what they may desire." He left the inn and went through the storm to a store down the road to buy some tea.

The Colonel followed Caroline three years later. Their graves, side by side in the decrepit cemetery at Oxbow, are marked only by their names. All that the Colonel could leave of his dreams and hopes for fortune was a mortgaged house and his household goods valued at four hundred and ninety-four dollars. Against that were many unpaid bills, including one for hired help, unpaid for six years, and a bill for two quarts of whiskey.

So far as is known the immediate family died out. The daughters vanish from any record. One son lived in Philadelphia until about 1930; another son lived in Rahway, New Jersey. The eldest son Zebulon, born in 1850, ran through an unhappy career of stock and mine promotion and wound up racing poor horses and selling poorer tips on them. He died in Cleveland in 1938. His most promising horse was one named Old Zeb. The best that horse, the last of the story of Joseph Bonaparte in America, could do was to come in third in one race in New Orleans. A horse who had close ties to Napoleon Bonaparte, even by marriage, should have done better.

John Brown's Body

For years people sang "John Brown's body lies amoulderin' in the grave." Men marched to war singing it, but not all who sang knew where that grave was. It is in the Adirondack country, in as lovely a spot as the land possesses. John Brown chose the place for himself. The high peaks to the south shield it. The winter snows cover it. The Adirondack country is John Brown's shroud.

He was not of it. He lived in it for only a few years, but no other man ever so completely caught in himself the strength and the permanence of the mountains. He came to them by chance. His coming had little effect on the Adirondack story, yet he is more vivid, even today, than most of the people who have moved across many pages of Adirondack history. It is difficult to stand where most of those people stood and to try to imagine their world and them in it. It is easy to stand by John Brown's simple house on the broad plateau south of Lake Placid and see him with his eyes to the hills all around and his thoughts far beyond them.

In the spring of 1848 a huge ox cart, its wheels nearly five feet in diameter, rumbled along the rough road from Lake Champlain west, following the tracks that many another settler heading for the interior had followed. By the wagon walked a gaunt man, not quite six feet, not quite fifty years old. Beside him, matching his stride, was a small boy. The man's wife and three daughters rode on the cart. Three older sons were coming, a day or so behind, driving a herd of fine cattle. Other older children were left in Ohio. The cart rumbled on, past the roadside thickets now white with shadbush bloom. Ten years later, on the bleakest of winter days another wagon followed that same wretched road bearing the gaunt man in his casket.

John Brown came into the Adirondacks for a task that appealed to him. The storms of slavery and abolition that so tore at American life in the middle of the last century missed the Adirondack country except here on the flatland below Lake Placid, land named many a year earlier "the Plains of Abraham" and later called North Elba. On this plain lived a number of runaway slaves and their families. The few white settlers in the neighborhood resented their presence and dubbed the settlement "Timbuctoo." The Negroes were not doing well. Gerrit Smith, a well-known abolitionist in central New York who had offered the Negroes the land, was delighted when Brown agreed to leave his temporary home in Springfield, Massachusetts, and come to the Adirondacks to help them.

At the end of the eighteenth century, Peter Smith, an Indian trader of Dutch descent, had gone into partnership in the fur trade with John Jacob Astor. Smith remained in central New York, bought the furs, and shipped them to Astor in Manhattan. He knew well the unclaimed lands of the state and bought large amounts in areas that promised profit. He became the largest landholder in the state and one of the largest in America, with almost a million acres in his possession, some of which he had bought for three dollars an acre and sold for eight. He was hard, shrewd, and, to a later eye, hypocritical. Whenever he went north to dispossess squatters from his land and squeeze what he could from settlers, he always generously distributed Gospel tracts along the route.

His son Gerrit, who inherited the thousands of acres of land in the Adirondacks and central New York, was a different sort. Always wealthy, he moved through life from one reform to another, from vegetarianism to reforms in women's dress, and on to the abolition of slavery. At his home in central New York he was active in the work of the Underground Railroad in bringing runaway slaves north. In 1846 he offered one hundred and twenty thousand acres of land near Lake Placid to Negroes, particularly fugitive slaves, if they would settle on the land and turn it into farms. Some came, but Smith's kindness could not blunt the sharp Adirondack winter or teach the Negroes Northern farming. By 1848 the Negroes had abandoned their clearings and settled in hovels in a ragged settlement to share their misery and their few possessions. What was needed was someone who could encourage them, teach them, and be an example of independence for them.

Brown, a wool merchant who had had little luck in business, heard of the Smith settlement and offered to help. Slavery had long been a live issue with him. Even as he talked with Smith for the first time and agreed to buy a two hundred and fifty acre farm, he may have thought of the Adirondack country as a part in a greater dream. He moved into a little farmhouse with scarcely enough room for his large family, yet whenever a stranger or wayfaring man entered the gateway, particularly if he were a runaway slave, he was welcome. Brown had barely settled in before he had to leave for England to close up some matters in the wool business, but he was back in the autumn and stayed through two winters. That was the longest time he spent there, but he saw the wild flames of the autumn foliage, the blackening winter hills, and the slow but irrepressible coming of Adirondack spring.

He loved the region because, as his wife said, "he seemed to think there was something romantic in that kind of scenery." He cleared fields, cut trees, picked rock, and pastured his fine herd. Over the years men have tried to guess what was going on in his mind in these days, as he walked the meadows thick with blue grass, red with Indian paintbrush. Ten years before he had begun to say to his wife that he meant to do something about slavery someday. In coming here to the shadow of the Adirondack hills he had implied to friends that he sought some safe refuge for his family when the time came to go out on dangerous missions. What they might be he did not say, but many a time he must have looked at the mountains around and thought of the safety and seclusion they offered.

By 1851 it was obvious that the Negro settlement was a failure. Brown had paid Smith nothing on the farm and he left it to go out to Ohio. He was back again at North Elba with his family in 1855. This time he came to a house a son-in-law had built, a little frame house on a clearing on a gentle northerly slope. From its porch he could look straight to Whiteface Mountain, which at times can appear in its isolation like some sacred peak helping to hold up the sky. He did not stay in the Adirondack country long. He left his wife, daughters, daughters-in-law, and only one son, and he was off to join six other sons in Kansas. There John Brown, his sons, and a few others made life as miserable for slaveholding settlers on the Kansas border as night raid and fire could make it. Brown had passed over now to the conviction that slavery could no longer be fought with words; it needed arms. So fast and ruthlessly did Brown and his band of a score of men move that he was often reported leading "five hundred savage abolitionists."

The fight against slavery, with something more than words, absorbed Brown. He gave no thought to earning a living or to sending money back to the family at North Elba. Friends paid off the farm for him in 1857. He came back home for a short visit in that year and again in 1858 and 1859. He might have come more often but could not afford it. When he did come he usually rode horseback from Westport; once when out of funds he walked the thirty miles in winter cold and almost died. Later his children told of his visits; he was a stern and strict father. One son said, "We were always glad to see the old man come back again, for if we did get more holidays in his absence we always missed him."

In the long absences John Brown's family lived as frugally as any settler in the region had ever done. They had bread and potatoes, pork and mutton. They spun their own clothing. They got enough money to pay postage by picking berries in the summer and selling them. After John Brown's death Mrs. Brown was worried by a "formidable" tax bill. A visitor learned the sum was eight dollars. She could have managed it, she explained, but she had lent the last ten dollars to a "poor black woman with no hope of repayment."

Brown's activities in Kansas had given him some fame and celebrity. On his trips home he often stopped at inns along the way and Adirondack groups gathered to hear him discuss slavery and politics. On his trip in 1857 he brought with him the tombstone from his grandfather's grave in Connecticut and placed it near a large boulder just outside the cabin door. On this trip he spent the precious hours of Adirondack spring afternoons carving his own initials a few inches high on the west side of that boulder. Here, he explained, he wanted to be buried, by this aged rock, beneath the shade of an unmoving white pine.

On a day in June, 1859, when the lilacs in the land were full out and the whole Adirondack country was at its loveliest, with the candles of new growth straight on the tall pines, Brown left his home once more. "My husband always believed he was to be an instrument of Providence and I believe it too," his wife said. John Brown probably looked around the land and to the skyline of the hills with more than usual fondness, for he must have known that he might be leaving for the last time. He had told only a few friends what he planned to do: to wage actual warfare against slavery by establishing a base in the Allegheny mountains from whence he and fugitive slaves might conduct raids into the South and induce slaves to revolt. Arms were needed for that warfare. Arms were stored in the federal arsenal at Harpers Ferry, West Virginia, where a resolute band might take them. Only a few of Brown's friends supported his plan. Others said it was dangerous, an argument that carried no weight with John Brown, and futile as well. If it were futile, Brown answered, it was necessary. In October, 1859, he entered Harpers Ferry with twenty-one men and held the arsenal for a day. Federal troops, led by Robert E. Lee, then a colonel, put down the attempt. Before being taken captive, John Brown watched one son die.

After a trial that aroused feelings in America that would never die, John Brown was hanged on December 2. His wife went south to claim the body. She brought it back to the hills, by the route Brown had often traveled. The funeral party had to spend a night on the way: at Elizabethtown an honor guard of Adirondack men stood by all night. The procession set off for the last miles of winding road in an icy driving December rain, on as mournful a day as the woods could show. John Brown was buried where he had wished.

Today house and grave are state property. Here, with the woods nearby, lies the man whose long stride carried him out of them and into history. Those who fought him, hated him, and decried his faith in the equality of man are gone now: few of their graves are remembered. Here, in Adirondack country, lies John Brown, as everlasting in faith and memory as the everlasting hills around.

Mountain Measurer

Andrew Colvin was a prominent and wealthy lawyer in Albany in the middle of the nineteenth century. He hoped his one son Verplanck, born in 1847, would follow him in the law. The boy read in his father's law library but his eyes were turned outdoors. Whenever possible he was at his favorite hobby, drawing maps of the neighborhood where he lived. At eighteen he was in the Adirondacks, making maps for his own amusement and finding that previous surveyors had made many errors. He finished his law course and started practice but soon abandoned it. Independently wealthy, he gave up the law forever. He climbed Adirondack peaks, then went to the Rockies and was the first to climb some of the high peaks there. He came back to New York and to the Adirondack country, the one love of his life. Thirty-five years later he had tramped every foot of the region. That the Adirondack State Park exists today for the people of New York is due more to this man who began drawing maps as a child than to anyone else.

Verplanck Colvin was a handsome man, built broad and strong like an Adirondack spruce. He never married. He was a brilliant man, in large part self-taught, a man who had little use for fools, less for loafers, and none for politicians. Even before he was twenty-one he saw what was happening to the Adirondacks and he began to lecture without stopping for twenty years on "the need for the creation of an Adirondack Park or Timber Preserve under the charge of a forest warden." A few men had said the same thing earlier, but Colvin said it louder and never stopped saying it. His foresight went beyond that. He foresaw the day when the City of New York would have to reach out far for water, even as it now does, and he wanted the Adirondacks saved unspoiled as a potential source of water supply for the city. That strong argument brought various farsighted New Yorkers to the side of a state park.

What distressed Colvin most was that the Adirondack area was still incompletely explored, scarcely mapped, and inaccurately surveyed. New Jersey and Massachusetts had begun scientific surveys of their land, but New York had none. By 1870 Colvin had done enough surveying to work out a plan for the area. Previous surveyors had used untrustworthy compasses. Colvin's plan, for which he was willing to underwrite all expenses, was to start at a known altitude and baseline with a theodolite and transit, instruments for measuring angles, get a trignometrical reading on a height ahead, climb it and determine its altitude with a barometer, then move on to another point and repeat the same operation. (At times he used level and transit.) In the Adirondack area this would mean thousands upon thousands of observations and calculations, climbing up slopes where no one had climbed before, crossing and crisscrossing the entire area back and forth for years. Colvin was eager to do it.

Because of his connections in Albany and because this earnest young man did little but talk about the Adirondacks as a great and little-known resource of the state, the legislature was impressed by the need to do something about the area. In 1872 the State Park Commission was set up and a complete topographical survey of the region approved. Colvin was appointed superintendent of the state survey, at a salary of twenty-five hundred dollars a year. He commented later that it was six years before he could collect his salary for his first year's work.

No man ever leaped to a job more eagerly. With the best instruments he could buy, out of his own pocket, he was at work in the woods almost as soon as the bill passed. For the next twenty-eight years he was the state surveyor. In that time he published eight reports of his work. Parts of the first three still read like fine travel stories.

The report on the very beginning of his work is typical of much that followed, and shows his impatience with obstacles, his lack of interest in his own comfort. He wrote:

> On July 31st I ascended and barometrically measured Speculator Mountain [in Hamilton County], a prominent summit not to be found on any maps. On August 1st with three guides we left Lake Pleasant for Lewey Lake, an unsettled point, situated further in the forest. Near this lake arises a lofty mountain. The best map hitherto published shows either level ground or slight hills where it really rises to the clouds. Accompanied by two guides I started immediately on the ascent. We made a rapid march and camped that night on a notch below the summit, near the edge of a precipice which dropped sheer downward 100 or 200 feet. Next day, bread without water made our lunch. At dusk we hurried as best we could down from the lonely crag, overtaken by darkness.

From known points Colvin, assistants, and guides moved northeasterly, measuring peak after peak, setting metal reflectors on prominent mountaintops so that readings could be taken from lower ground and preparing, when necessary, to fire rockets from peaks at night. After delays for repairing broken instruments and bringing up supplies he reached the shores of Lake Champlain at the end of August. Here known altitudes gave him a chance to check his work. He then turned west into the mountains of the high-peak country. One hitherto unnamed peak not far from Marcy "the guides in compliment called by my name." It still stands as Mount Colvin, as sturdy and well-named a peak as the Adirondacks has. However, as the same guides came to learn what a slavedriver Colvin was on the job, unsparing of himself but as unsparing of others, they might have changed their minds about paying him any compliment. Over the years he frequently reported many an unhappy incident with them:

> Here the guides, dissatisfied with the severity of the labor, demanded their discharge and asked increased pay: nor could they be persuaded to proceed further, exhibiting their torn clothing and soleless gaping boots as evidence of their inability.

On a September morning Colvin and his party started up Mount Marcy:

> It was later afternoon when, drenched with rain and cloud that despite rubber covering had penetrated our clothing, we stood shivering in the gray icy mist that swept furiously over the summit of Mt. Marcy.

The next day was bright and the party climbed Marcy again. Colvin measured it and found it 5,333 feet high, a figure later to be slightly corrected, as were many of Colvin's determinations. He also found that the outlet of a small pond, Tear-of-the-Clouds, that lay between two peaks near Marcy flowed south and not north. It was therefore the true high-pond source of the Hudson, the summit water of the state.

In the next six years he finished the complete exploration and reconnaissance of the whole region, discovering ponds and peaks never before reported. From time to time he published his reports, racing back to a rabbit warren of an office in Albany or letting the work pile up until winter. The reports appeared, written

> . . . as a labor of difficulty. They have been executed in the midst of routine duties pertaining to the office of chief sur-

veyor; the management of survey parties: the details of field work: the intricacy of trignometrical computations, and the settlement of financial accounts.

The early reports have a continuing theme of adventure — of descending icy cliffs at midnight, the precious surveying instruments made fast to a rope, of being caught on peaks without food. During some years he kept at the job most of the winter, working on snowshoes, in fur-lined moccasins, and with toboggans. He reported on one day's work on some lake island:

> The wild winter gale swept over the rocky isle with such violence as to almost extinguish our fire. A fearful night which none of the party will be able to forget. The men fought the cold by stamping and chopping by turns, snatching some sleep occasionally when the fire could be maintained. Many were the longings expressed for "a comfortable night in the snow".

Even a night like that did not stop Colvin. "In the morning," he continued, "we returned to the baseline and commenced the angular measurements, taking careful repetitions." Nor did scanty diet bother him. "Living on boiled lake trout, without salt, pepper, or fat, or bread or potatoes, or any accompaniment, is a very singular dish for very hungry men."

One of his most dramatic tales is a story of February, 1877:

> Descending the slope of Seventh Lake Mountain, we were startled by the sight of the fresh tracks of a panther which evidently made his home in this abode of plenty: shortly thereafter we found the body of a deer freshly killed. The guides were now all excitement and followed the panther's trails eagerly. In less than thirty minutes a shout announced that he had been encountered and pushing forward to the southern front of the plateau I came upon the monstrous creature, coolly defiant, standing at the brow of a precipice on some dead timber, little more than twenty feet from where I stood. Quickly loading the rifle, I sent a bullet through his brain.

That is presumed to be the last panther killed in the Adirondacks.

After ten years Colvin found the fun gone. The territory had been covered over and over. Under his own eyes Colvin saw the Adirondacks change. He summed it up:

> Viewed from the standpoint of my own exploration, the rapidity with which certain changes take place in the opening up to travel of the wild corners of the wilderness has about it something almost startling. The first romance is gone forever. It is almost as wild and quite as beautiful: but, close behind our exploring footsteps came the blazed line marked with axe upon the trees, the trail soon trodden, the bark shanty, picturesque enough but soon surrounded by a grove of stumps. I find following then the ubiquitous tourist, determined to see all that has been recorded as worth seeing. Where first comes one, the next year there are ten, the year after, fully a hundred. Hotels spring up as though by magic and the air resounds with laughter, fun, and jollity. The wild trails, once jammed with logs, are cut clear by the axes of the guides and ladies clamber to the summits of those once untrodden peaks. [Colvin was a bachelor and had his own ideas of woman's place in the woods.] The genius of change has possession of the land. We cannot control it. When we study the necessities of our people, we would not control it if we could.

Even though he never did get around to the job of making the promised area map and was criticized sharply for it, the data Colvin secured during his years of work was invaluable. He knew the Adirondacks as no other man has ever known them. That knowledge he shared in magazine articles and lectures, always dramatizing the Adirondacks as an area worth saving for future generations. He even held forth a delightful picture of a tax-free New York State, its expenses paid from the mature timber. He was largely responsible for the creation of the Adirondack Forest Preserve in 1885. What he had long taught was quoted in the Constitutional Convention in 1894 that "locked up" the woods.

When the basic survey was done in the eighties, he turned to a duller job, but one he welcomed, for it kept him in the country he loved. It was a no less vital job — of surveying and setting straight all the many boundary lines of state-owned land. In the first surveys a century before, the lines were marked with blazed trees. It sounds unbelievable to any layman but after a century Colvin could come along and, after some ferreting about with the notes of the early surveyors in hand, in many cases find those trees, the blaze long overgrown with bark of a texture different from the rest of the tree and therefore visible to a trained eye. It is more unbelievable that some of those blazes can still be found today; by cutting them out and counting the rings the date of survey that made the blaze can be determined.

The work that Colvin now did for ten more years also helped save the woods. Without definite lines, set once and for all, many a private timber cutter did not know where his land ended and where the state land began. In many cases he did not want to know. At the same time, as Adirondack property began to increase in value, individuals sued the state for return of lands which they claimed had been wrongly taken in tax sales or lands where surveyors' lines overlapped. Colvin set out to put all the lines straight, another job of monstrous detail. He continued on the job until 1900.

Then something happened. Whatever it was — disappointment at not being given some high position, weariness, or personal crisis — he quit as state surveyor. He was angered at something, for he carted off many of the records, which only he could decipher, regarding them as personal property and refusing to leave them to his successor. In the same displeasure he even turned on the Adirondacks and announced himself as president of a proposed railroad that he hoped to build right through the region — the very sort of grab that he would have been the first to protest ten years before. Nothing ever came of the railroad. Colvin slowly passed from idiosyncrasy to delusion. He lived alone and was seen from time to time on Albany streets, muttering as he walked aimlessly along. He died in 1920.

That was a shabby end. It is easily forgotten in the memory of the younger Colvin, who saw even as a youth the meaning and value of the Adirondacks for generations unborn. In an era when men from all sides had designs on the woods for their own profit and devil take the next generation, Colvin's was a voice that could make even legislators hesitate before they voted. It spoke from knowledge tediously gained. More than that, it was a voice that spoke from the deepest love. It is pleasanter to remember Colvin as the man who always got from the Adirondack horizon a sense of exaltation that many have felt, that few have been able to put into words, and even fewer into deeds. It is pleasanter to remember him as the man who could write his triumph, alone on a mountaintop in 1884:

I am left with but one man now. The other could remain no longer. It is almost impossible to get men to encamp upon the mountain tops at this time of the year. The last man has deserted and thus I am alone in camp. Cold and snow were too much for this fellow. Paid him off and was glad to have him go. Got some fine observations although, being alone, I had difficulty in securing the canvas observatory against the high wind which arose at night-fall. Descended, however, at dark to the camp with the work at last accomplished but had to cut wood, cook my own supper (thawing snow for water) and found housework after dark, with my limited knowledge of the location of utensils rather difficult. Put out the lights at 9 pm, wrapping up in soft and comfortable blankets, stretched myself upon a deep couch of evergreens and rested well until morning, regardless of catamount or lynx.

Mountain Climber

A little village in Alaska is a long way from the Adirondack country. Robert Marshall covered the distance, and in only a few short years. Many men who have lived in the Adirondacks, then left never to return, took with them something they prized all their lives. Robert Marshall was one of those men. He died in 1939 at the age of thirty-eight, long before his time. He belongs in the Adirondack record not for what he brought to the area, but for a clear statement of what he learned there and for his desire to share it with others.

Marshall came to the Adirondacks as a small boy for the simplest reason — to spend the summer. His father Louis Marshall was one of the great lawyers of the early twentieth century, a friend of both Theodore Roosevelt and Woodrow Wilson. The Marshall camp on Lower Saranac Lake was a typical Adirondack private camp with many frame buildings, painted green and brown. Almost on its doorstep were some of the lovely wooded islets of the lake. To the south was the friendly peak of Ampersand. Far to the southeast were the high peaks.

As a small boy Robert Marshall looked across the lake to where Ampersand stood green against the blue sky. Mountains fascinated him, and particularly the woods that clothed them. One summer day when Marshall was fifteen, he, his brother George, who shared his love for mountains, and Herb Clark, a guide, set out to climb that peak. As they swung along up the steep sides, young Marshall may well have remembered early boyhood dreams of Lewis and Clark and his sorrow that explorers had been everywhere and left so little unexplored.

Ampersand was the beginning of a career of mountain climbing. Before five years had passed the two boys and the guide had climbed forty of the forty-six Adirondack peaks over four thousand feet, the first people ever to do it. Many of the mountains had probably never been climbed before; only twelve had any sort of trail. The Marshalls' achievement gave a strong impetus to the Adirondack Mountain Club then forming and to the sport of climbing mountains. What young Marshall wrote of the Adirondack peaks brought many to see for themselves.

In boyish manner he classified the various peaks by the excellence of the view from them. He put Haystack first, Santanoni second, and Whiteface, the peak that can now be climbed by automobile, only twenty-ninth. More came out of his exploit than that. From those peaks he saw some virgin forest, much ruined forest, and everywhere solitude. Writing of Haystack, his favorite peak, he put down the first lesson he learned in the Adirondacks: "It's a great thing these days to leave civilization for a while and return to nature."

During sunny afternoons on those Adirondack peaks, Marshall decided how to spend his life. The means were available to him to choose any profession he wished. Instead of law or business he chose forestry, a calling in which no man has ever gotten rich and few have become famous. After four years at the New York State College of Forestry he went into the United States Forest Service, not as a dilettante but a working forester, deeply interested in the science of forestry. He took a master's degree at Harvard and a doctor's degree at Johns Hopkins, writing his theses on technical forest problems.

But beyond the scientific facts and the statistical tables there were always the woods and the wilderness, and they drew him on, the dominant forces in his life. He went into government service as director of forestry of the Office of Indian Affairs, then chief of the Division of Recreation and Lands of the United States Forest Service, the job in which he died. A stocky man with a grin that went from ear to ear, he pushed on from time to time far from a Washington desk into the Great Smokies and to the Rockies. In 1929, he went into the wilderness of Alaska for the first time. During one stay of thirteen months, he wrote a best seller, *Arctic Village,* in which, with all his scientific training and his deep knowledge of nature, plant and human, he offered a superb study of the Eskimo and Alaska sourdoughs.

When he returned from the edges of the earth he restated what he had learned as a boy in the Adirondacks, as he pleaded for the preservation of some wilderness in an encroaching world: "There is just one hope of repulsing the tyrannical ambition of civilization to conquer every niche on the whole earth. That hope is the organization of spirited people who will fight for the freedom of the wilderness." To that end he helped organize the Wilderness Society, one of the most forthright voices today speaking for all that is best in conservation.

Because he had been shocked at waste in the woods, Robert Marshall believed profoundly in state ownership of all forest lands. For that he was attacked as a dreamer, an idealist, and worse, if anything is worse. That point of view may have been extreme and impracticable. In spite of it, many men in the big lumber companies were his friends. His sharp criticism of wasteful procedures in lumbering led to reforms and to broadened programs for reforestation.

Robert Marshall was no book-bound conservationist. His records for hiking have probably been excelled in American history only by Paul Bunyan. By the autumn of 1937 he had gone on more than two hundred walks of thirty miles in a day, fifty-one walks of forty miles, and a number of longer walks, including one of more than seventy-five miles. Any walk or any journey reaffirmed what he had learned atop Haystack: "It's a great thing these days to leave civilization for a while." He was a twentieth-century Thoreau, a peripatetic one to be sure, for he could never have stayed by the shore of one lake for long. He would have laughed at that comparison as being farfetched, yet it was Thoreau who wrote, "In wildness is the preservation of the world."

Robert Marshall died of a heart attack before he reached what most men consider the most useful years. Once he found Alaska he was rarely back in the Adirondacks. What he wrote, and his words are still widely read today, underlined two lessons he had learned in his life. The first was scorn for those in government who believe that the only proper treatment for the natural resources of state or nation is to turn them over as quickly as possible to friends or to private interests who know the right people in the right places. The second was that the right to preserve the woods for the sake of humanity against misuse and commercial encroachment is as sturdy and fundamental a right as the right of other men to destroy them in the name of progress or profit.

Those lessons Robert Marshall first learned in the Adirondack country.

❧ VI ❧

Adirondack Battle

Wilderness Locked Up

At the end of the 1870's an old lumberman who loved the woods watched a lumbering operation of the sort that was becoming increasingly common. As he saw a team loaded with spruce logs four inches and less in diameter he said, "They're cutting straws. And there go the Adirondacks!"

The twenty years after 1870 may have been part of the Gilded Years but they were also the Age of Alarm. The few isolated voices that cried out "Save the woods!" before 1870 won few converts. The issues involved were complex. Large industries and the economics of much of the area, along with many a livelihood, depended on the woods. Big money was at stake. One lumberman who cut surreptitiously on state land in the early seventies was estimated to have made fifty thousand dollars in five years. Hitherto the woods had been considered a source of valuable lumber. The idea that in themselves they had a value in their natural form, untouched by saw or ax, was a new concept. To many men it seemed opposed to the real prosperity of the area.

The State Park Commission, formed in 1872, continued to "inquire" about broader state ownership of timber lands; Colvin was a vociferous member of that commission. From the beginning its members were divided on the meaning of the word "park." To some it implied an area where the state would buy and own all the land and hold it for recreation. To others that sounded too much like the creation of a giant private estate. That difference of opinion did not matter. For years the legislature cheerfully ignored the reports the commission made.

Each year after 1870 saw more paper mills built. By 1900, of the one hundred in the state, sixty-four were getting all their wood from the Adirondacks; New York State led in the production of paper. For a time large spruce continued to go into lumber, but in a few years all sizes of spruce went to the pulp vats and even the smallest trees could be used. Lumbering methods had changed. Instead of taking only large trees as in the past, the land was now stripped, often without leaving one seed tree. At the same time new lumbermen came to add their cut to the annual figures. One of the most striking was a Connecticut Yankee, "Uncle John" Hurd, who bought sixty thousand acres in the northwest quarter in 1882 and even built a railroad into the woods from the north to get out his wood. That railroad, eventually extended to Ottawa, began at Tupper Lake. It had little population to tap, yet for many years, as the Northern and Adirondack Railroad, it ran one train each week day and none on Sundays. Hurd was responsible for the rise of the lumber town of Tupper Lake and for the heavy cutting of the woods of the northwest quarter.

Spruce climbed in value. State land was eagerly bought, stripped, then once again allowed to revert to the state for taxes. Timber stealing from state lands became more profitable. Many cutters disregarded the lines that marked the seven hundred thousand acres of state land. The legislature passed a law in 1876 setting up a twenty-five-dollar fine for each tree cut from state land. Few among the Adirondack people would testify to the identity of timber thieves. At the same time the state lost land, as the woods became more valuable. By claiming some use or residence on lands that had reverted to the state for nonpayment of taxes, a man might have the courts order the lands returned to him. The courts often sided with the plaintiff, who might have lived on a few acres and thereby claimed thousands.

As they saw the condition of state and even private lands grow worse in the 1870's and early 1880's, those who loved the woods felt helpless against the lack of interest in Albany and against the power of the lumber companies. Piles of debris left by the lumbermen wherever they walked were natural fire hazards. Fires increased as the mileage of railroads increased. In 1880 almost one hundred and fifty thousand acres of woods burned, the fires started by farmers clearing land, by sportsmen and their campfires, and by locomotives. No force was at hand to fight the fires. "In over at least one-half the area lumbered fire follows the axe," a state report said. "A large area utterly unadapted to agriculture is being made desolate and nearly valueless and its streams become every year more slender and fitful."

Before any forest conservation movement could gain a following, a new attitude toward natural resources had to develop. That new attitude grew every time a fisherman in the Adirondacks returned to his hotel at night and cursed his luck. His question was, "Why doesn't somebody do something?" In time the answer was obvious: Only the state could do anything. The hotelkeepers became concerned; fewer fish meant fewer fishermen. Several hotels even stocked lakes for their guests. The New York Association for the Protection of Game, formed in the 1860's, now added its voice to the protests of the many who wanted something done. Very slowly a new idea spread — that the state should hatch trout and plant them; in fact, that it was the proper function of the state to aid in the preservation and restoration of natural resources. That idea is almost an axiom today. In the seventies it was new. The first New York State hatchery was opened in 1870 and a second, in the Adirondacks, in 1885. Slowly the state began to stock lakes and ponds; more important, the public approved.

At the same time, in the late 1870's sportsmen concerned about the future of hunting urged that something be done to cut down the unrestricted game slaughter, to make laws tougher and have them enforced. These reformers were usually outsiders; not for years did the local people take kindly to attempts to stiffen the game laws. The first wardens ever appointed, eight of them in 1880, had no easy time for a decade.

Speaking chiefly through *Forest and Stream,* the reformers urged the elimination of the use of dogs in deer hunting. A roar of protest, flanked by some extraordinary arguments, rose at the very thought of eliminating this favorite sport. "Hounding improves the health of the deer by speeding their heart beat and increasing their circulation," one defender said. Another said, "How is the consumptive to console himself for his last days if he is not permitted to hound deer?" The arguments failed. Hounding was abolished in 1885, thanks largely to the agitation of *Forest and Stream.* That magazine could now comment: "There will be wailing in camp. The Wall Street broker whose annual custom it has been to hire a gang of guides and a big pack of hounds and waterkill his deer is not particularly delighted to lose his gory recreation."

Restrictions against hounding deer were removed the following year, but a pattern had been set for stricter game laws and for their enforcement. When guides and hotelkeepers saw that fewer deer meant less business they began to support stricter measures. In the nineties even Paul Smith himself went to Albany to testify on behalf of tighter laws. One newspaper summed up that journey and its startling significance in one line: "Paul saw a great light!"

In the next years the number of deer a hunter could kill was reduced, the season shortened, and the killing of fawns and does prohibited. Hunting licenses were first required in 1908. In 1920 the season was shortened to one month, and it remains so today. At various times the game protective force has been enlarged and improved, to a point where today there is no finer corps of uniformed career men in state service, and more important, none more respected.

The tourists of the 1870's knew personally the damage done to fish and game and cried "Help!" They were less conscious of the damage to the woods. Yet help for those who hoped to save the woods came from unexpected places. Various New York City organizations, concerned about the possible effect of the denuded Adirondacks on the Hudson watershed, began to take an interest in Adirondack preservation in the eighties, particularly the New York Board of Trade and Transportation. Its interest made clear that the future of the Adirondacks was not a local problem but one of state-wide concern. This group became the most staunch defenders of the woods, thereby emphasizing a truth that has appeared often in Adirondack history: The most vigorous defenders of the Adirondacks have been people outside the area, often people of wealth and influence with no particular personal stake in the area. That did not make their work easier. At the thought of any organization's trying to put restrictions on lumbering, many Adirondack people felt that this was an attempt of rich downstaters to lock up the area and so keep it from sharing in the spread of industry or in American prosperity. The few newspapers in the region in one voice opposed any attempt to regulate the woods. Down in New York, the *Times* and the *Tribune* thundered again and again, "Save the Adirondacks!"

In 1883 those who raised that cry won a first small victory when the legislature passed a law withdrawing all state land from further sale and even appropriated a small amount to buy additional land. Public opinion was moving to the side of conservation in the Adirondacks. The legislature moved with public opinion. In 1885 it approved the creation of a forest preserve and a commission to manage it and added:

> . . . the lands now or hereafter constituting the Forest Preserve shall be kept forever as wild forest lands. They shall not be sold nor shall they be leased or taken by any person or corporation, public or private.

That was the first step in the interest of "saving the Adirondacks," but it had a hole a mile wide in it.

That law was fundamental. In spite of its shortcomings, and although three state-forest agencies had been created earlier in California, Colorado, and Ohio, the New York Forest Preserve Act was the foundation of American forestry. It preceded the federal law creating the national forests by six years.

Under the law the Forest Commission, appointed by the governor to serve without pay, was to plan forest replanting and to organize fire prevention by forming a corps of wardens and ordering railroads to put screens over the stacks of locomotives. The state further agreed to pay those counties in which state land lay annual sums equal to the local taxes they might have had were the land owned privately, a system which continues to this day. The commission was ordered to attempt to awaken an interest in forestry in schools and colleges, out of which came the first school of forestry in America at Cornell.

The forest preserve lands were now protected by law. They could never be sold. To many people the Adirondacks seemed saved at last. Saved they were for eight years, but the law of 1885 said nothing about selling, leasing, or taking the trees that stood on those wild forest lands. It was not long before lumbermen, legislators, and even a governor discovered that hole.

In 1892 the old idea of a state park came into legislative being. The confusion between "park" and "forest preserve" has always been a real one. Obviously, if the forest preserve was to be distinguished it could be done either by setting up each small scattered piece or drawing one wide line that would include much private property and call that the boundary of a "park." The 1892 bill did not affect private property in the Adirondacks in any way. The old hope of one hundred per cent state ownership in the Adirondacks had been abandoned. When the Blue Line was first drawn it surrounded an estimated 3,588,000 acres, of which the state owned only one quarter. (All that is said here about the Adirondacks applies, of course, to the Catskills, where much of the balance of the state forest preserve is concentrated — all within its own "Blue Line.") The act setting up the park said nothing about its specific use. Its chief function was, in time, a psychological one. Park was a more comprehensible term than forest preserve, and more easily dramatized.

In 1893 the legislature, acting under the influence of some group or other, found the hole in the 1885 law. The legislature granted the Forest Commission permission to sell the right to cut trees on the forest preserve, particularly spruce over twelve inches; for a commission supposed to guard the woods, the members seemed mighty eager to sell. Against a loud roar of protest, Governor Flower signed the bill. The lumbermen won that round, but it did them little good. More and more people were convinced now that the forest preserve had to be put into the state constitution, beyond the reach of the vagaries of changing state officials.

A constitutional convention happened to be due in the summer of 1894. Various conservation groups presented to that convention an amendment to the state constitution to read:

> The lands of the State, now owned or hereafter acquired, constituting the forest preserve as fixed by law shall be forever kept as wild forest lands. They shall not be leased, sold, or exchanged, or be taken by any corporation, public or private, nor shall the timber thereupon be sold or removed.

At the last minute the words "or destroyed" were added, to block any flooding of state land that would ruin the trees.

The convention submitted the amendment as Section 7, Article VII of the state constitution. In the autumn of 1894 the voters of the state approved it: Nothing in the "forever wild" clause could henceforth be changed without approval of a majority of all the voters of the state. No tree could be cut nor windfall removed, no mature timber could be harvested nor roads built through the woods, without amending the amendment.

The amendment stopped any possible chance of forest management, of forest cultivation as practiced in Europe, or of using forest products as a source of revenue for buying more land. Those were not the pressing problems in 1894. The problem was to stop thieves. The amendment stopped them, and in that sense "locked up" the woods. The urgency appeared just a few days before the amendment went into effect, on January 1, 1895, when some Albany officials tried to grant hurried permission for a projected railroad to cross state lands from North Creek to Long Lake. They were stopped by injunction.

The size of the Adirondack Forest Preserve has grown, largely by purchase, from 676,000 acres in 1894 to 2,179,556 acres today, 40 per cent of the area of the park. For some of that land the state has paid as much as fourteen dollars an acre. Several substantial gifts of land have added valuable property to the state holdings. In 1895 the Forest Commission was combined with the Fisheries Commission, to deal with the problems of the forest preserve and the fish and game. After several changes, the Department of Conservation under one commissioner was created in 1928.

The 1894 amendment affirmed the future of the Adirondack country. Henceforth the real industry of the Adirondack country would be recreation. What that decision has meant to the Adirondack people and to all the people of the Eastern seaboard was expressed in 1918 by Frederick A. Seaver, a North

Country journalist who fought the idea of a park in his Malone
paper:

> It was believed that the park plan must proscribe industrial
> operations, prevent the development of natural resources, and
> shut out hopes for future growth. We must admit that the park
> plan was wise, evils were not suffered and more money and
> larger benefits for the county came in the preservation of the
> forests than through their destruction for lumber, charcoal,
> and pulp.

Trees Lumberjacks Moose

The story of the Adirondack woods after 1894 to 1950 is a
happier one. Slowly but steadily state officials have worked for
their restoration and preservation. To restore the woods seedling trees had to be grown; before 1900 there was no sure way
of producing them cheaply. Clifford R. Pettis, one of the first
graduates of the School of Forestry at Cornell and later Superintendent of the Woods, finally devised methods for cheap and
sure production which were later copied by the Federal government and by every state government. The first tree nursery was
established in 1902. Trees began to move out to the waste
places by the thousand, then by the hundred thousand — larch,
Scotch pine, Norway spruce, white pine, and other trees. As
many as five hundred thousand trees were put out in one
planting.

In 1908 the state agreed to supply trees at cost to private owners. They set out three million seedlings in 1910. The reforestation of the Adirondacks, both on private and state land, had
really begun. Today most of the state's trees, still supplied to
the private owner at cost through a free management plan, are
produced at two nurseries, Saratoga and Lowville. The number
of seedlings supplied to private owners or set out by the state

is tremendous. In 1951 more than thirty million baby trees were planted; the total number of state seedlings set out in the forty years between 1910 and 1950, most of them in the Adirondacks, is the huge total of three quarters of a billion. They show up today in many fine stretches of reclaimed clearings and in plantings along the highways.

Reforestation was not the only problem in the early twentieth century. In the dry spring of 1903 many forest fires broke out, set in almost all cases by sparks from railroad locomotives. Fires raged in many parts of the woods for six weeks. Before a heavy June rain ended the miserable dry spell, more than 464,000 acres of the Adirondack woods had been burned; to this day thousands of those acres will not grow a decent tree.

That should have been lesson enough on the need for better fire fighting measures, but it was not. Fires again broke out in 1908; before they were extinguished, another 368,000 acres were gone. Improved methods of fire prevention followed, with the emphasis on detection and early alarm. Watchers were stationed on mountain peaks, where fire towers were built; fifteen stations were erected in the first year, increased in time to the hundred of today. Railroads were ordered to burn oil during dangerous seasons. A vital law was passed ordering lumbermen to chop into smaller pieces the downed tops of coniferous trees, even on private lands, so as not to leave high piles of debris. As a result of the measures of 1909 there have been no really bad fires in the Adirondack woods since.

The worst injury the woods has had in a century, since a tornado in 1845, came not from fire but from a windstorm. On November 25 and 26, 1950, the wind came up from the southeast, an unusual direction for an Adirondack storm. It increased in velocity until it reached one hundred miles an hour at some places. One tree after another went down in the north, central, and western parts of the woods. Before the wind had blown itself out, thousands of acres of private land lay in ruin, as well as two hundred and fifty thousand acres of state woods, including some of the choicest timberlands. Some have been cleared away but many still lie where they fell, now dry, to make a monstrous tinderbox.

A third problem faced early by the state was the extension of the forest preserve by purchase. Between 1894 and 1916 land was steadily added to the state holdings. Large additions came after 1916 when seven million five hundred thousand dollars was made available for land purchase, largely for Adirondack land. Another five million dollars was appropriated in 1924 for the same purpose. In addition to the land in the Adirondack and Catskill parks, the state owns more than five hundred and twenty small parcels of forest preserve land, a total of 32,692 acres, outside all Blue Lines. Most of these bits had to be acquired by law for unpaid taxes and are an administrative headache for the Department of Conservation.

The defense of the forest preserve against attempts to change its definition in the constitution has been up to the voters of the state. Scarcely a session of the legislature has been held since 1896 without the introduction of some proposed change. The first, to permit the leasing of small private camp sites, was quickly defeated.

Early in this century power companies, wanting to build dams for water power, succeeded the timber groups as those most interested in changing the "forever wild" provision. Donaldson called them "a new breed of grabbers." The objection to the use by power companies of Adirondack rivers is the real fear that their dams will flood and destroy hundreds of acres of woods. That agitation, which began forty years ago, is not dead today.

In sixty years only six changes to the amendment have been approved by the voters: permission to set aside 3 per cent of the forest preserve for water storage facilities; the building of three different highways, one in 1927, to the summit of Whiteface

Mountain; permission to build a ski run on state land on the side of Whiteface Mountain. In 1953 the automatic 3 per cent water storage facility allotment was withdrawn. Henceforth each dam project will have to be submitted separately to the voters.

More changes might have been effected had it not been for the formation of various organizations dedicated to the defense of the Adirondack woods. The New York Board of Trade, mentioned earlier, continued its work. It was joined in 1902 by the Association for the Protection of the Adirondacks. Since the latter's membership was drawn largely from various clubs and private preserve owners, it was open to the charge that it was moved only by the selfish interests of rich men. Other conservation groups have been formed in later years and are always ready to protest any threatened encroachment on the Adirondack Forest Preserve. In 1922 the Adirondack Mountain Club was formed, supplying another very loud voice when needed.

In 1896 the many lumbermen were the villains of the Adirondack story. The few lumbermen today may disagree with the "forever wild" provision and believe the woods would be better cared for under another policy, but that is their privilege. They moved in fast after the November, 1950, storm when the state asked for help, to try to cut down the fire risk in the downed timber by removing salable trees, and not always at a profit to themselves.

By 1900, New York had fallen from the leading wood-producing state in 1850 to the seventeenth largest. Yet more than sixty paper companies were cutting pulpwood from private lands in the Adirondacks. Other companies were cutting for lath and lumber. Today less than a half-dozen paper companies and perhaps twenty other operators, of varying size, cut some thousands of cords of pulpwood and some millions of board feet of lumber, petty figures compared to the hundreds of thousands and the billions of the Pacific Northwest. Today New York ranks in the upper thirties among lumber-producing states.

Today's pulp cutters take what spruce they can find, but also cut balsam, hemlock, poplar, and even some white pine. In addition to these pulp men and the lumber producers, several woodworking mills in Tupper Lake, making bobbins, toothpicks, and ice-cream spoons, use all the hardwood maple and birch they can get. Those mills give that Adirondack town the appearance of a small industrial center, yet their owners are concerned about the shrinking supply of wood for the years ahead as they search the countryside a hundred miles around for the wood they need.

The lumber industry in the Adirondacks has little national importance now, but it is still an important part of the area's economy. It works on private preserves and holdings deep in the woods. The companies in the lumber business have expert foresters on their staffs and some replant the land they have cut. Some do not and trust in Nature. Their workings are open to regular inspection by conservation officers, who check on "top lopping" and other fire-prevention measures.

Adirondack lumbering today, as everywhere else, is an industry as mechanized as possible, with mechanical log loaders, bulldozers and tractors to move logs and make roads, cranes to lift hardwoods, and huge trucks to get the cut out. Adirondack people may do the trucking and supervising, but many of the lumberjacks today are French Canadians, in on bond for the period from early autumn to early spring.

A half-dozen small camps, in appearance much like the camps of fifty years ago, can be found deep in the woods in winter. Few have as many as fifty employees. The long, low bunkhouse still has one end filled with double bunks for the lumberjacks and a kitchen and dining room at the other end. Over the beams of the bunkhouse still hang the extra shirts and socks of the workmen. Today the whole place is lit with bottled gas. Hot water comes from a gas heater. Cutting by the cord or by the thousand feet, the lumberjacks do well. They work from dawn till dark. After supper they sharpen their saws — power saws that whine far through the woods. Then sleep, breakfast, and back to the woods.

One thing has not changed; the lumberjacks will not stay if the food is poor. North Country couples are often the cooks, their sleeping quarters curtained off the kitchen. They turn out food in large quantities. Three or four big pots of baked beans vanish at breakfast, along with bacon, eggs, and toast. The noonday meal, with silence as the fixed rule at the table, offers enough meat pie or pot roast to serve three times the number of ordinary men. The bread is baked right in camp, of a sort not found in a village bakery. The evening meal has more meat, more potatoes, more hungry men. Although the number of lumberjacks in the winter woods may be much smaller than in years past, and although every precaution is taken, it is still dangerous work. Branches fall and kill men, machines slip. There are few winters when some sturdy young lumberman is not carried mute from the woods.

One other thing is unchanged. Every camp still has its horses stabled in a warm building near the bunkhouse and cared for as carefully as the lumberjacks and usually with more affection. Once all the timber that came out of the woods was horse-drawn, if only to a stream, with teams of thousand-pound animals hauling bobs fitted with heavy bunks, five cords of logs in each one, each cord weighing about three thousand pounds.

The tractor came into the woods after 1918 and then the heavy trucks. They move the logs to the mills today. Yet the lumber-camp horses still do one job that neither truck nor tractor can do as well. When a tree is down and cut into sections, the teamster hitches his horse to the log and draws it to the skidway, where the logs are piled. If the logs are heavy hardwood, a team may be needed to move the burden. Not only can the horses pull on steep slopes where neither truck nor tractor can work, but the horses have a way of avoiding snow-covered rocks and other hindrances. Many need little driving. Once the log is hitched on, they move by themselves without an order, head down, their breath frosty on the winter air, their chest muscles bulging if the log is heavy or the going tough, as perfect a living machine as moves.

When lumbering ends, just before the spring thaw that softens the roads, the horses are trucked out of the woods to summer pasture. They do have one day of labor during their summer. Every year in August the Adirondack lumberjacks hold a field day at Tupper Lake. It is a lumberjack's Olympic Games with the implements he uses in the woods where no out-siders can marvel at his skills. There are contests between giants using hand saws, power saws, and axes. The place to find the old woodsmen, however, is around the horse-pulling contest, where the horses of the various companies are matched and set to pulling weighted stoneboats. Whips snap, drivers shout, and the mammoth loads move down the field. A tractor can do that more easily, but no tractor ever brought out the affection and pride that goes with the lumber-camp teams.

It was not only the trees of the woods that concerned state officials after 1900, but restoration and protection of the wildlife in the woods. One of the most successful of restoration proj-ects was the stocking of beavers in the back corners of the Adi-rondacks. They were brought from the West in 1902 and re-leased in likely places. They did so well, although only a dozen pairs were liberated, that the beaver catch today adds much to the income of the trapper in the Adirondack winter.

One of the most tragicomic stories in Adirondack history was the conscientious attempt to restock the area with moose. At the end of the nineties a small but excellent magazine on the Adirondacks, *Woods and Water,* appeared in New York. It attracted little attention until it was learned that it was being published by a seventeen-year-old boy, Harry Radford, a New York college student who knew and loved the Adirondacks. The most ardent of conservationists, concerned about the woods and the life in them, he sat down one day to muse on the missing moose. Thereupon he decided that singlehandedly he would induce the state to reintroduce the moose. He went to Albany and pestered all sorts of individuals about the moose, even up to Governor Odell. Then he organized the Association for Restoring the Moose to the Adirondacks — membership fee one dollar. With great foresight Radford appointed eighteen men vicepresidents for his association, not one of whom had ever met moose loose or en masse, but all influential politicians. In 1901 the New York Legislature, eager to find any excuse for a truce on moose, appropriated five thousand dollars for the purchase and liberation of moose. Radford declared triumphantly that, thanks to this victory, New York State would soon have a mass of moose. The skeptical Forest, Fish, and Game Commission that had to do the work felt the matter was moot.

The only problem remaining was to produce the moose. That took two years. In the summer of 1902 fifteen scared and thoroughly traduced moose, uproosted from the Northwest, arrived in the Adirondacks. They were loosed or unloosed — whatever it is that is done to a moose. Most refused to leave civilization and had to be driven into the woods. Within a year they had either been shot or had become recluse moose. None were ever seen again. A few years ago, however, the Conservation Department reported that a hunter near Lake Placid had shot something big, something mighty like a moose. If so, he had probably come down from Canada sightseeing to view ancestral mews.

The story of fish stocking by the state is happier. Over the years more hatcheries have been built — their cost defrayed in part by the license fee the fisherman pays. Various new species have been tried, from salmon to rainbow trout, and fish are dumped in Adirondack streams and lakes by the million.

The cost of raising the fish for stocking purposes runs high. Nursery trout cost one dollar and more per pound by the brookside. Less than 50 per cent survive. Some salmon that have been stocked in a few deep lakes have cost as much as eleven dollars a pound. The state likewise stocks game birds in various parts of the Adirondacks, but the continuing increase in the number of hunters and fishermen never produces enough to satisfy everyone. Deer have needed no restocking. A large group of wardens, uniformed and proud of their service, make violations of the game law risky. Killing one deer out of season can bring as much as two years in prison and a five hundred dollar fine. Now and then a warden happens on a group of friends out trout fishing and armed with frying pan and salt pork to cook the "short trout," undersize, right on the spot. Those meals can cost twenty-five dollars in fines and are expensive eating.

Times do change. Twenty-five dollars once paid for a week at a fancy Adirondack hotel, with "short trout" served three times a day.

❦ VII ❦

Adirondack
Problem

Change Change Change

In 1906 a party of brave men left Williamstown, Massachusetts, by automobile for Blue Mountain Lake. In his book *Township 34*, Harold K. Hochschild published the log of the journey:

> We left early in the morning. All went well until we were entering Saratoga Springs where we broke a spring. The delay in repairing this forced us to stay in Warrensburg over night. The next day went smoothly until we got to the hills beyond North River. On the first hill, the road was so bad that we had to take everything out of the car. . . . On another hill we had to back the car to the top. The gasoline tank, which was under the front seat, fed gasoline to the carburetor by gravity. The grade was so steep that the tank could not feed while the car was going forward.
> . . . We had five flat tires on the trip. The trip was made in a 1905 Winton car.

That may have been the first automobile trip ever made into the Adirondacks. Less than fifty years later the state police poured onto the roads around the hamlet of Wilmington to handle traffic where cars were blocked for eight miles with people coming to see North Pole, a tourist attraction on the side of Whiteface Mountain. That is one measure of the change in the Adirondack country in a half century.

The automobile changed all of American life, but nowhere more completely than in the Adirondacks. It led to the building of roads, to making inaccessible places accessible. It led to hard times for the railroads. Once welcomed so eagerly, the D. and H. pulled up its Adirondack tracks and moved out of the central region in 1942. The New York Central, which claims it loses forty thousand dollars a year on its Adirondack division, has been trying for some years to eliminate one of the two daily trains between New York City and Lake Placid. Bus lines cover Adirondack roads as in every other area in the country.

Most of all the automobile changed the vacation habits of the American people and the use they made of the Adirondack country. The fifty years after 1900 were a period of decline of private camps, hotels, and particularly of the reputation of fashionableness. That reputation is often based largely on exclusiveness, and the automobile meant that each year less and less of the area was exclusive. Those years were also a period of growth. The changes that took place can be studied from various viewpoints — of transportation and roads, of facilities offered, of government organization and control of the woods. All point to two things: the broader use of those woods and the tremendous increase in the number of people who come to them — numbers that not even Murray's contemporaries could foresee. The woods locked up against the few meant the woods opened up for the many.

After 1910 more and more people ventured on the Adirondack roads in their Chandlers, Pierce Arrows, Franklins, and Marmons. The automobiles came from all over. In them came more vacationers. Having heard about "their park" and the attraction of life close to nature, they could find no place to stay in the woods. On state land there were more than four hundred miles of possible camp sites on lake fronts, but unless people were willing to rough it in what was really the rough, they had to turn to hotels and boarding houses. Even the people of the Adirondack villages who might have planned to pitch a camp in the woods had to take a tent out and dismantle it after each week end. It became clear that the state would have to make provisions for people using the woods. The first step came in 1912, when campers were permitted to build simple tent platforms on state land, and let them remain throughout the year. It was clearly stated that such sites, along with the platforms, were state property.

That ruling satisfied the villagers but not the itinerants. For them the important change came in 1920, when the state built the first of the large camp sites, complete with necessary facilities, and made available for many city people a place by the lakes in the woods. Those camp sites in every part of the woods have increased in number over the years. In the summer of 1952 137,091 persons spent 647,020 camper days on the thirty-four camp sites and their 3088 separate camping places. More than a half-million other people came as picnickers or sightseers. The existence of the state sites has been criticized by some, who feel that the state's relatively inexpensive facilities compete with tourist cabins and motels. What additional number of people the camps have brought into the area to patronize stores and services is beyond counting. Each year the demand for camp sites grows.

After 1920 the authorities acted again to make the mountains and the woods even more accessible. With the help of the newly organized Adirondack Mountain Club, state employees began to cut the well-marked climbing trails over the high peaks. Camp building and trail cutting both seem to violate the "forever wild" amendment that forbids cutting a single tree. The legal basis for such activities came in a court decision which agreed that the state has the duty of preventing fires in the Adirondack woods and that trails serve as fire paths and therefore

may be built. The decision further held that it was in the best
interests of fire prevention to have thousands of campers gathered at recognized sites, under control, as it were, instead of
having thousands of separate campfires burning brightly
throughout all the woods. The same decision justified the use
of private lumbermen to remove and buy timber after the
1950 blowdown.

One by one the older forms of Adirondack summerings gave
way to the new. Big private camps were hit by the shortage of
labor in the First World War and by the slow rise in income
taxes. The generation of men who had built them, loved them,
and poured money into them died off. Their children either
lost interest or could no longer afford them. The fondness of
local politicians for raising taxes until their golden geese were
killed or walked off, together with the growing impossibility
of staffing the camps, closed more in the thirties. They were put
on the market.

Their owners then learned a sad truth: There was no market
for them at more than a fraction of their cost of construction.
A large camp on the east shore of Upper Saranac Lake that had
cost two hundred thousand dollars to build and equip went
for seventy-five hundred dollars in 1938, with the new owner in
for forty thousand dollars of repairs at once if he wanted to save
his investment. After doing that, he still had the problem of
finding a staff; it had taken thirty-eight men to run the place.
Other large camps were sold for whatever they would bring.
Some were just abandoned and have not been occupied for
twenty years, although heirs still pay taxes on them. Some camp
owners found philanthropic or educational organizations willing to take the camps as gifts. One New York insurance company purchased a big estate which it now uses as a vacation
headquarters for its employees. The Seligman camp on Upper
Saranac Lake became a hotel. The Blagden camp on the

same lake was turned into the Deerwood-Adirondack Music School, where a symphony orchestra plays beneath the pines on summer afternoons. Perhaps twenty large camps still remain in private hands today.

What have remained more or less intact over the years are the colonies of "camps" — summer homes, each on its few acres, on the shores of Lake George, Upper Saint Regis, Blue Mountain Lake, and Lake Placid. Many have new owners. Kate Smith, with a camp on Lake Placid, has become an Adirondack native. Unlike the big camps, the smaller camps are bought eagerly whenever they come on the market.

The old hotels passed on. The old race of innkeepers died out. Their heirs tore down the old wooden buildings that had really been frames for colorful men. Those hotels that fire spared were run much as they had been in the nineties, except for the stables in the rear now converted to garages. Each year more gave up as the first of the tourist cabins were built along the highways and the homes in the villages put out signs, "Tourists — Two Dollars a Night." Other hotels were turned into "lodging for a night" stands, with the hot dog replacing home cooking. A few were bought by out of the area people and have become lavish country-club-style hotels, complete with rhumba teachers. A very small number of old-fashioned summer hotels survive at Lake Clear and elsewhere and the rockers rock on the porches. The rockers will outlast the hotels and will certainly outlast the aging guests. There are probably more accommodations for the vacationer today in the Adirondacks than ever before, as one cluster of tourist cabins after another dots the roads and as more motels appear on roadsides.

A new sort of summering appeared in the Adirondacks in 1905 when the first private children's camp opened; eventually the idea developed into camps for adults, of which there are a few. The children's camps, scores of them, are on many of the lakes, and thousands of children come to them each summer.

In recent years the camp populations have changed; they now attract younger boys. In the country behind Lake George on the road to Lake Luzerne, a string of dude ranches do a big summer business. They are complete with corrals, cowboys from Albany, and mounted cowgirls who, in Levi's that are a little bit too tight around the seat, yippee their way 'neath the unmoving white pines.

In the 1930's the Adirondacks saw another change. The publicity accorded the 1932 winter Olympics held at Lake Placid brought winter tourists in number. They have come ever since. The little villages of Old Forge, Lake George, and even Lake Placid, which used to close up in October and sleep until May found an industry for their winter months. The steeper and more accessible hills in Vermont and New Hampshire offer serious competition to the Adirondack area but the winter tourist is an important part of Adirondack economics.

The tourist trade, increasing from year to year, is wonderful while it lasts, but it is seasonal. That means lean months for the villages. As a result the small villages still yearn for small industry and for steady payrolls the year around. Industry, large or small, has not stampeded for the woods. Transportation, power, and tax problems, as well as the distance from raw material, has kept them away. Yet there is room for laboratories and similar organizations that want quiet and seclusion for their work. One new "industry" has come: a New York storage firm that has built bomb-proof vaults in Saranac Lake and offers to store valuable papers and documents on the well-reasoned assumption that the Adirondacks, of all areas in America, is the one least likely to attract an atom bomb.

The various mines in the area are open and working. The discovery of ways to work titanium, now useful in making the "white" of white-wall tires, as a pigment in white paint, and a heat-resistant metal of military use, along with the blocking of imports of ore from India during the war, led to the reopening of the mines at Tahawus. The National Lead Company grinds out two thousand tons of ore a day there and operates a complete town in this remote Adirondack valley, providing the four hundred employees with school, homes, store, and movies. The iron mines at Port Henry, now operated by Republic Steel, work thirty-three hundred feet under the surface on an incline of eight thousand feet and ship out four thousand tons a day of 66 per cent ore concentrate. The iron mines at Star Lake, owned by Jones and Laughlin, and the mines at Lyon Mountain, operated by Republic Steel, carry on the traditions of Adirondack mining.

An Adirondack restaurant keeper described a new species of tourist who has appeared in recent summers. "They're 'hamburger tourists,' " he said. "They want to drive and drive from one place to the other. They never have time to even eat a regular meal — just hot dogs and hamburgers. 'Can't be bothered,' they say. 'Have to drive another two hundred and fifty miles before evening.' "

Many people come to the Adirondacks today to spend every day of a precious vacation in the woods or by a lake but, as in every other resort area, the quick-traveling tourist has become more numerous each year. His coming is good for motels, tourist cabins, and quick-lunch stands, which thrive and multiply on Adirondack roads. For him, the natural assets of a given area are not enough; the roadsides must sprout attractions and there must be "things" the tourist can do or places other than mountains and lakes he can see. A number of these attractions may be far out of Adirondack spirit, but they do prosper and they bring people from all over America.

The most successful is the North Pole, opened in 1949, complete with animals, Santa Claus, and toy stores on the side of Whiteface. It has drawn ten thousand people in one day, from every state in the Union. An old guide might be astounded to see elves and gnomes in costume running around under the pines but he would also be astounded to see the prices of land in the little town of Wilmington, at the base of Whiteface, once a sleepy Adirondack village and now a metropolis of motels. He would be astonished to find similar attractions, successful if not as well advertised on many other roads — from Frontier Village to MacDonald's Farm at Lake Placid — "See chickens hatching. Enjoy a chicken dinner and hay ride. Barn dancing every Saturday night." Tourists come from everywhere, then go their way with the proper stickers and bumper cards as proof that they too have been where other tourists have been before them. Certainly the Adirondack country prospers thereby.

The problem of the care of the Adirondack woods, discussed a few pages on, has been widely publicized. Little is said about what is happening today to many Adirondack roadsides, village approaches, and lake shores that are privately owned. More and more the quick-buck fever takes over — anything that gets the tourist's dollar is fine — to create what one visitor called in disgust, "Honky-tonks with trees." To see clearly what is happening a man need only look at the cheapening of the village of Lake George and of the shores of Mirror Lake in Lake Placid.

Such criticism might seem to be small-souled, carping, and selfish. Both Lake George and Lake Placid have attracted tourists in larger numbers than ever in recent summers. The spirit of the day is, "Whatever brings the tourist is good." If that means more roads to open more lakes to frozen custard stands and charcoal hots, good! If, when all private land on roadsides is lined with shacks and neon lights, there's pressure to build commercial facilities on state land by the roads, good!

An Adirondack politician can get to his feet in open meeting and say, "I wish we had more Lake George developments everywhere in the Adirondacks. I'd like to see a road built to every Adirondack lake so the 'poor people' can enjoy it." Too often, those "poor people" turn out to be the ones who can afford twelve and fifteen dollars for a night in a gaudy motel. The politician is applauded and re-elected without any thought that what he advocates may in no distant time so change the Adirondack country as to ruin its summer business.

It is fair to ask, "When some roadsides and lakesides are cheapened to the ultimate, what tourists are going to bother to drive three hundred miles to enjoy the country that lies behind them?" Competition for summer visitors among the many vacation areas in America is tough today. Those areas which manage to stay different are the ones which, in the long run, will prosper. Others ask, "What matter what is built along the roads as long as a man can get into the woods and away from it?" It matters much.

The automobile tourist today does not start out for a specific place. He says, "Let's drive to the Adirondacks." Behind the garish fronts and the neon, the woods and lakes may lie untouched, but the motorist is not going to bother to look for them. He will drop his dollar or so, spend his night, and race on.

The quick-buck commercialization of part of the Adirondacks is sometimes defended: "That's really democracy at work." To see democracy at work, visit the state lakeside camps, with rich and poor side by side. The careful way the camp builders have preserved the sense of the woods and their beauty is the best argument for building more of those camps. Other tourists want private accommodations and more such are needed. Motels and cabins would do the area better service if they too tried to preserve some sense of the woods, instead of breaking out in jade, flamingo, and orchid replicas of haciendas, adobes, and sheepfolds, bedecked with neon and chrome. As the gross commercialization spreads, a far more substantial tourist trade will be lost, of those people who might have found the most precious asset of the Adirondack country — the remoteness and charm of lakes and woods, without electric signs and pseudo patios, less than 300 miles from the large cities of the land. Once that

charm is nibbled away, and the little foxes are always experienced nibblers, the thousands who might have come to seek
that charm will not bother.

Perhaps intelligent planning and foresight can prevail. After
all, Paul Smith, a man who knew more about the Adirondacks
than any present-day politician or chamber of commerce, once
felt that the sooner some Adirondack assets were spent, in fish
and game, the richer he would be. Then he changed and wanted
restrictions.

And the newspapers said, "Paul saw a great light!"

Forever Wild — Forever?

The Adirondack woods may seem peaceful to the visitor, but
a stormy debate has raged over them for sixty years. Ever since
the words "forever wild" went into the state constitution men
have asked whether that was really the best policy for forest
care.

Even in 1903 the Forest Commission itself had doubted the
wisdom of the "forever wild" policy. What many say today an
official report said then:

> Our foresters are debarred from doing any work that would
> increase the productivity of these forests by cutting of diseased
> or decaying trees, or by the substitution of merchantable spe-
> cies for worthless ones. Matured trees must be left to fall and
> become breeding places for destructive insects, while under
> the clearly expressed mandate of the law no timber can be re-
> moved and converted into money, even when it is killed by
> fire or where, still green and injured, it covers the ground for
> a thousand acres or more in some windfall.

Today's well-heated version of the continuing debate came
after the great November storm of 1950. Critics of the "forever
wild" policy had a chance to point out that much of the timber

that fell like jackstraws in that storm was long past mature, a pushover for a strong wind, and on any private lands would have been cut long before. The resulting downed and dried treetops made a dreadful fire hazard. It will last a decade.

After a survey of that storm damage, the *Conservationist,* the publication of the New York State Conservation Department, asked in print whether the 60-year-old policy was really the best way to care for the woods. The Commissioner of Conservation, Perry B. Duryea, and other heads of the department admitted that they felt the policy fell far short of present-day needs and called for a re-examination. That the Conservation Department heads should propose this infuriated many people who felt that the department's job was management according to the state constitution and that they should not question the constitution itself.

In every battle over "forever wild" each side has always accused the other of selfishness. Selfish men there may be on both sides, but that accusation from either side should not hide the fact that a real and complex issue is involved on which experts differ, and that each side has people who believe genuinely, deeply, and beyond any selfish interest that their point of view is the better one for the woods.

Sharp name-calling has always marked every argument over the Adirondack Forest Preserve. Those who would change the "forever wild" provision in any way or even examine its continuing wisdom are, according to their opponents, "despoilers of nature," "political termites," "wielders of the opening wedge," and "starved timber thieves." Among the supporters of a new policy today are the heads of the Department of Conservation, a number of the faculty at the Cornell School of Forestry, the chancellor of Syracuse University, and many forest experts. Some wood-products manufacturers, although not all, are on this side. These people believe, as reported in the *Conservationist:*

. . . that the Forest Preserve, although very good, could be made much better. We believe that its forests could be made and kept healthier, and that in doing this a modest income might be realized that could be flowed back into our property and that wildlife could be made more abundant than it is now.

Because they believe that much of the forest preserve is slowly deteriorating, they propose that the whole area first be zoned. "Wilderness areas" in the high peak country, by many lakes, streams, and where the forest protects critical watersheds, would remain untouched and forever wild, no matter what their condition. "Management," by cutting, clearing, and re-planting — not for profit but for improvement — should be applied to other areas where such work might improve the timber stand. Land for recreation areas along highways and some lakes should be set aside and more facilities for the public constructed on it.

The management group has its arguments. In fact, they say, a forest is not best preserved by leaving it alone. Are old spruces to stand only to fall victim to spruce beetles? Shall other mature trees be left for the first heavy wind? A forest full of such trees is not well preserved. Timber is a crop and should be harvested like any other crop. Private landowners in the area who follow such practices find their woods in fine shape. Much of the United States National Forest is operated and flourishes on a "managed cutting" basis. The wealthy private clubs that own thousands of acres of Adirondack land often oppose "managed cutting" and support the "forever wild" policy on state lands, yet practice careful cutting on their own lands. Their woods are improved by it. Thick old woods are not the best shelter for birds and animals; if increasing wild-life is a prime end of conservation, a forest policy that produces mixed hardwoods and coniferous cover, of uneven ages and with many edges and open glades, is preferable.

The critics hold that the chief use of the woods is for recreation. A "forever wild" policy limits that use. What recreation for any but a few hardy citizens do remote areas offer if they are impossible to reach except by the toughest going? What is a state forest for, if not to be used, and if its recreational possibilities are not broadened for a greatly increased population? Furthermore, a "managed" forest will bring in some income. That money can be used to buy more lands for the forest preserve. Finally, what few industries the Adirondacks have, offering year-round jobs and helping pay taxes, are chiefly woodworking industries. Those now there could remain if they had some assurance of raw material from a managed forest. And more such industries might come.

The group who would keep the woods forever wild not only have their arguments. They also have many questions. These groups are described by their opponents as "starry-eyed idealists," "impractical big city folk," "millionaire camp owners," "two-week vacationists," and "sloppy sentimentalists." Among the leaders of this group are the popular conservation organizations, including the Adirondack Mountain Club, the Association for the Preservation of the Adirondacks, the Wilderness Society, and many others, including expert foresters.

The forest preserve, they say, was set aside as a natural forest, to be kept forever as a historical sample, as it were, of something now almost completely gone from the Atlantic seaboard. Lumbering of any sort is incompatible with that objective. In a natural forest old trees die. They fall, rot, and provide the food for the next generation of trees. A natural forest that is a wilderness has its own unique educational values, not to be obtained by the sort of neat cutting and prettifying done in the forests of Europe. Comparison with the national forests and their methods is beside the point; the national forests are eighty-five times the size of the Adirondacks and have no similar population stress on them. Even at that, seven million two hundred thousand acres in various states are set aside as the New York Forest Preserve is set aside.

It was never intended, they continue, that the forest preserve should be a source of lumber for any industry, or a source of income. With as unique a possession as the forest preserve forever wild, the legislature can appropriate money to buy new land. The state can build more camps but only along roadsides; no one disputes the need for more. Other recreational facilities can be built on the tremendous amount of Adirondack land now in private hands. As for game, the number of deer certainly do not decrease under the present policy. Why drag them in as an argument for "managed cutting?" As for industry, the chief industry in the area is the care and feeding of tourists, most of whom come because the woods are as they are. "Manage" them, and the real industry of the Adirondacks will be seriously affected. As for opening up remote areas, they quote from Robert Marshall:

> For thousands the most important passion of life is the overpowering desire to escape periodically from the strangling clutch of a mechanistic civilization. To us the enjoyment of solitude, complete independence, and the beauty of undefiled panoramas is absolutely essential to happiness.

That type of recreation is unique, and cannot be supplied by a woods largely "managed," which really means "timbered," or by conventional tourist facilities.

The protectionists ask: Just what does "managed cutting" mean? Does it mean taking all the trees over a given diameter in the main body of the woods, to leave a forest filled with piddling poles? Who is to decide what areas would be managed? The Conservation Department today may be staffed with sincere and devoted public servants, but who knows what sort of men will be in it tomorrow? What guarantee is there that, once the "forever wild" provision is relaxed, the political finaglers, a breed not unknown in Albany, won't march in?

One of the finest men ever to walk the woods, William F. Fox, Superintendent of the Woods, wrote in 1903:

> It is difficult for a forester to see a good reason for the constitutional clause which prohibits State land from being used to provide the people with wood. Its advocates cry, "The Forest must be preserved." But this law compels conditions under which the forest may be destroyed by fire, insects, fungi, and by the annual decay and loss of unharvested materials. "But we are afraid of collusion between the lumbermen and the State officials and we think it better to endure the ills we have, than to fly to others we know not of." This is an unjust and unnecessary arraignment of the officials who have been appointed to look after the forest. If the people of New York are so degenerate that they cannot find men of integrity to take care of their public affairs, it is immaterial whether the forests are preserved or not.

Superintendent Fox was an honest, unselfish man who believed what he wrote. Two years after he wrote that, his superior, the head of the Forest, Fish, and Game Commission, was forced to resign because it was discovered that fifteen million feet or more of timber had been stolen from state lands with the connivance of someone in his office.

This is not meant as a reflection on Conservation Department officials today. Since 1910 a magnificent corps of career men, secure in civil service, has been developed. Many are among the most fanatical defenders of the "forever wild" provision. It does explain the reason for the fear among many citizens of letting one ax loose in the woods to "manage" them. It is a fear that overrides even the most unshakable confidence in the continued rightness of all decisions of the Albany officials, who, by the way, are by no means unanimously agreed on any one forest policy. Today's worry is not the chance of timber theft.

It is the well-grounded concern that if the "forever wild" provision is relaxed in any way whatsoever, the smart boys will come running with their axes and dance halls. Nothing said in Albany, even by the most sincere and dedicated officials, can entirely remove that fear.

The proposed suggestion to zone the woods and to apply different policies to different areas might seem to be a sensible solution, in so far as it protects the high-peak area and the river sources. However, the entire Adirondack area and not just one part serves as watershed for northern New York. Any considerable cutting of woods anywhere in the area will decrease the volume of the rivers.

In 1952 the Joint Legislative Committee on Natural Resources, under Senator Wheeler Milmoe, began a study of a proper policy for the forest preserve. A group of citizens, from professional conservationists to paper manufactures, was appointed to study and advise the committee. At the end of 1953 Senator Milmoe issued a progress report which may indicate the type of suggestions to be made to the legislature at a later date.

To Senator Milmoe, "the State Forest Policy ['forever wild'] as now constituted and administered, does not seem to be fully serving the best interests of most of the people of the state." He criticizes that policy because it interferes seriously with the development of the state highway system, with the development of telephone and power transmission lines, and hinders the building of "essential" access roads. In addition, Senator Milmoe would revise the policy to improve recreational opportunities, wildlife habitat, forest-fire and forest-pest control, and details of forest-land ownership.

With some of the latter suggestions few could quarrel. It is fair to ask, however, what sort of Adirondack country Senator Milmoe foresees, with more power lines running where they choose, with access roads built wherever it strikes the fancy of some local politician to demand them, and with more highways cutting up the region into even smaller pieces. If the senator's proposals were adopted, little of the relative wilderness charm of the region, now its greatest asset, would be left.

That report is just one indication of the mounting pressure from many sides to change the character of the Adirondack country. Another is a current proposal to build a Thruway from Albany to Montreal, part of which would cross forest-preserve land, and thus permit a highballing truck to reach Manhattan an hour sooner — or permit Americans to drive even more quickly to the Canadian woods, where there is still untouched wilderness. When the Saint Lawrence Seaway is built, just northwest of the area, it will greatly increase population in that region and indirectly put added pressures on the Adirondack country for more recreation facilities. The total sum of these pressures could mean the end of "forever wild" in much of the woods.

Between those who would cut trees for "management" or "improvement" and those who would let Nature and time repair the woods, while letting them stay wild, there is no easy compromise. Those who would keep the woods forever wild realize that they are taking a gamble on Nature and know that fire and disease can in the meantime be serious.

Those who advise a new forest policy, of an open Adirondacks and a managed woods, are also taking a serious gamble. They are gambling that their changes will not so spoil the Adirondacks as to ruin the present thriving tourist trade built on people who come only because the area is "different." They are gambling on the effect of the possible loss to New York State and to all the Eastern seaboard of a unique wilderness area, of unbroken stretches of forest in which millions today find satisfying recreation without benefit of a more elaborate system of highways, timbered woods, more power transmission lines, or even a Thruway. Coming generations may not look back with fondness on those who took that gamble and lost, those men who had some of the last wilderness in their keeping but agreed to let all except the small high-peak area be cut up into woodland lots, picnic grounds, and tree nurseries, in the name of improvement.

No one should object to increasing greatly the number of state-owned facilities and camp grounds along existing highways, to continued tree planting on private and public land, to adding to the forest preserve by the purchase of any private land within the Blue Line that comes on the market. Beyond that, keeping the Adirondack woods wild forever is the lesser of two gambles.

So long as the forest preserve is in the constitution, safe against the vagaries and ambitions of local politicians, any change will have to be voted on by all the citizens of the state. It is their woods. It should remain so.

When the people are told clearly the rarity they possess they will keep it the way it is, with "new woods permitted to supply the place of the old so long as the earth remains."

VIII

Adirondack
Year

. . . So the Adirondack country was discovered, explored and developed.

Hitherto this book has dealt with the changes that centuries and decades have worked in the land and in the woods that cover it. People as well as time helped bring some of those changes.

Another time cycle, in which human beings have no part except as watchers, works in the woods. It brings changes that come season by season, week by week, day by day, often hour by hour. From year to year, as the earth turns, the woods stay the same. Yet from day to day and month to month they do change, as surely as the earth does turn.

Here is the story of the Adirondack country, as each new month brings its wonder and magic in the woods.

April

The Adirondack year starts with the spring.

Because a fusty Roman consul in 153 B.C. decreed that a year should begin on January 1, the day he happened to take office, our world has followed the custom of starting a new year with that date. It would be better to commemorate the coming of the sun to the north after many months, the promise of green life in the land.

For the farmer sharpening his plowshare and fingering the moist earth, the gardener who has had packets of seeds waiting for weeks, the fisherman who has admired his trout flies daily for what has been an eternity, the first day of spring is a real New Year's Day.

The Adirondack spring brings not only the quicker pulse of new life but the feeling and fact of freedom, almost forgotten during the winter. It is the freedom of the earth from the blanket of snow, of the lakes from the shackles of ice, of the motorist from slippery hills, of man from heavy boots and clothes.

By early April snowdrops are out. Snow is off lawns and gardens and lies clotted and dirty in the shady places in the woods. A few nights are frost-free. Rains beat back the snow and make the earth a wet and heavy place, with the sound of running water everywhere. Hillsides sprout waterfalls. A cascade falls into another. A sudden cold day will freeze the falling water; where roads cut through sheer rock they are lined with thick ice. Roads everywhere are in poor shape. Sand put on during the winter still coats them. Repair crews get out and fix the holes. Many a bump repairs itself as soon as the frost is fully out of the ground.

On the lakes the ice, once transparent and brilliant-clear, turns dark and dirty. For a day or so, as moisture on the surface sinks into the mass, soft crystals show on top. Under the warming sun, the ice becomes porous, loses its buoyancy, and sinks to the water level. Its whiteness gone, it is dirty black even under bright sun. Long cracks show. The wind opens fissures and clear water appears. One April morning, usually after the fifteenth, the ice begins to move off in floes, no longer a solid but a mass of parallel crystals that tinkle on the shore as the southwest wind drives them. In less than a week the lakes are free.

Lumberjacks are out of the woods and the horses with them. Tote roads are a mass of mud that can sink heavy lumber trucks to their axles. The last flapjack is flipped, the last doughnut cooked, and the camp shanties are locked up. Deer, never far away, come close without concern. Out of the woods in forest-beaten clothes come the bearded men who have been running trap lines. Their catch of beavers piles up on the floors of the fur stores. Weary and worn, the trappers walk the streets with cash in their pockets. In bars they tell of the "blankets" — the big ones — they did get, and how the biggest beaver of all slipped away.

The Adirondack housewife starts housecleaning. Storm windows come down. Flower seeds are started on the window sills in the warm kitchens. Pigs farrow; if the nights are cold that means extra work to keep out drafts and chill. Baby chicks are under the brooder and crowd in close on a cold night. Garbage cans rattle behind the house as raccoons and porcupines look for their first full meal in months. Caretakers get out to the remote camps and survey the winter damage.

Trout season opens in mid-April. Men who may not fish the rest of the year make a rite of getting out once during the first week or so. Ice may still cover a shady place on a favorite stream, but that does not matter. Every stream has fast-rushing water, even those that will be dry pebble beds by July. Garage mechanics, doctors, and clergymen rush out on afternoon appointments that require rubber waders and fly rods. The members of the various Trout-Count and Literary societies get out to the brookside. They go as on safari, armed with totable stoves, potable soups, and a large stock of remedies for snake bite and for protection against sunstroke and Gila monsters. Sometimes they see a trout. More often they report only that the yellow perch are thriving and have lived happily the winter. That always raises the question as to whether they would be able to recognize a trout if they saw one.

A few fly fishermen show up in the first days. These are the purists who bring along thermometers to test the temperature of the water. The device is tossed out on the stream. If it breaks on the ice the water is obviously too cold for fishing. These fly fishermen can get much practice casting. They have been reading about it all winter. They have checked all the new books published on the sport, envied all the stories of the speckled monsters in the New Zealand rivers and in remote streams in deep Africa and the Andes. With all that knowledge stowed away, they are set for the opening of the Adirondack trout season, except for one demeaning detail. If they want any trout they must dig a mess of worms.

The fishermen, worm or fly, return at evening. Their story is the same as last year and the year before: few trout. The water was too cold. The water was too high. The perch have eaten all the trout. The beaver have eaten all the trout. The trout have eaten all the trout. Some Adirondack people have eaten all the trout; too many of them followed a half mile behind the hatchery trucks last autumn and took out the planted fish as fast as the hatchery men put them in.

Fish or no fish, the first April days by a trout stream are memorable. The color of washed blue sky overhead, the cry of the jay in the bare trees, the smell of wet earth, the rush of high water, the sight of a beaver diving by his dam, the rarer sight of fawn and doe nosing the wet earth, go home with the fisherman, even when he takes home no fish. As soon as the ice is off the lakes other fishermen troll by the shores for lake trout. It is slow fishing and cold when the wind has a bite, but it can produce big fish. A mess of big rainbows or brown trout may also show up in a store window, but the rumor goes around at once that so-and-so sneaked in on a private preserve and caught them when the caretaker wasn't looking.

By mid-April the wet world dries. It dries astonishingly fast. If no rains fall the woods can soon be like tinder. The threat of fires in the woods, so wet a few weeks before, is real until the trees leaf out. If no rain falls the rangers hurry to the fire towers on the hills.

What happens in these days happens so slowly and by such minute stages that the wonder works almost without being seen. The woods are bare and barren, without a leaf anywhere except on the witchhobble in the thickets, but the days before leafing out add their own colors to the woods. Except for the new ruddy tone on the white birches they show up only at a distance. They are not the garish colors of autumn. What covers the woods on the horizon hills is a wash of pastel shades, of pink and lilac, lavender and rose, from the swelling maple and birch buds and the new life in their bark. The mistiness of those pastel colorings joins with the mists that rise from the earth, almost like the mists of creation.

On the floor of the woods, the shift from the browns and the blacks of winter to the full green of spring is just as slow. Moss clumps on the rocks green as soon as the snow has gone. Lichens on the trunks of old trees lighten. The earth is brown with dried leaves, but whenever a wind lifts them the live green underneath flashes in the morning sun. Partridge berry and ground pine are freshening even as the giant white pine above them. The first spears of trillium and of jack-in-the-pulpit pierce the surface. The clumps of fern still seem dead and droop with the broken bracken of last year's growth. These leaf out late. In the sunnier places arbutus is ready to flower and lady-slipper shoots begin to push aside the leaves.

Snow and even a wintry day or so may turn up at any time, but they are futile gestures. Although the ground may whiten, the strengthening sun soon takes care of that. On rare days in the past fifty years the temperature has fallen to minus 10. An occasional day of 75 degrees foretells heat, forgotten since last October.

Plows appear in the fields and crows cry loud over the brown furrows. The first hawks come near the barns. Over the song of the newly come hermit thrush, the vireo, and the call of the phoebe, is the cry of the jay and the hammering of woodpeckers. The first wild bees cruise the fresh frosty air. Swamps and watery places are loud with peepers at night. Robins, chickadees, and nuthatches are up with dawn. The sound of a cold wind in the frozen trees is gone. The fresh warm wind bears live sounds now and the lake laps at the rocky shores.

May

In earliest May the Adirondack world is one of delicate color. Maples show a pale red-scarlet, birches a light green. Tamarack are palest yellow. At a distance the woods seem washed with lilac in some lights, with rose-pink and mauve in others. Even the sunsets take on a fresh brightness. Leafing-out is slow, although warm rain and hot sun can hurry it so that in some years it seems to happen overnight. Places that were sunny in the winter have fresh new shade. Long vistas in the woods are closed off by bright green walls. With the first leaves the fear of fire is gone; it will not return until a July drought dries the woods.

The poplar tree now has its one moment. The rest of the year it is the weed of the woods, and Adirondack people say, "Popple ain't much." It is brittle and not good for much. Despised, deemed fit only to drop, rot, and provide a more fertile ground for its betters, the poplar has one bit of glory, and that is now. For a few days it is the loveliest thing in the woods, particularly when seen at a distance. As it puts out its fringed catkins, its gold-green and yellow-green fuzzy "flowers," the poplar brings the first strong color to the hillsides. When the sun is full on them, the hills shine with the poplar's green and yellow light, the freshest tone of spring. In no time at all birches and maples leaf out and the poplar's brief glory is gone. In its moment it is alive and dominant on the hills in sheets of transient beauty. As it shines in spring sunlight a man can forget that neither house nor wagon, box, fish pole, or decent kindling can be made of this tree.

On some days summer seems to have come for good: the next day is chill and the night brings frost. Snow can fall, more fleeting than the snow of April, a last flutter of a season dead and gone. A few days may be below freezing: others can be above 80 yet drop to 35 at night. On the distant hills the summits stay snow-capped until well on in the month. Fresh green on the hillsides and blue over the white peaks give the Adirondack country a vivid horizon.

Blossoms break in a shower in the woods, in meadows and along the roads. The shadbush is the first to flower, in such abundance as to recall the snowdrifts so recently gone. This is its short glory; the remainder of the year it is just one of the tangled shrubs of roadside and thicket. The white of wild cherry follows soon after. Spruce buds and tamarack take on their new blue-green. On the pines, particularly on the Scotch pine by the roadsides, new growth stands like Christmas candles. On the high peaks dwarfed trees try for new growth and little Alpine flowers bloom at the edge of the snow.

Open places and deep woods are alive with birds, with wood pewees and black-poll warblers the last to arrive. Gulls come over from Lake Champlain, floating patches of white against the green pines and spruce that line the shores. They are the ordinary herring gulls, the species common in the big city harbors. They come in twos and threes. They will ride the wavelets for hours, then rise gently into the air, see a lake nearby that looks more comfortable and go to it, or return almost to the exact spot they just left. Their cries blend with the call of the crow, the boast of the phoebe, and the rain song of the robins. The loon's cry is again heard on the lakes. A few ducks may pause in northward flight. A few black ducks may even decide to stay the summer on some back pond.

Perch move about in the lakes and sunfish start scraping circles by the shore for their nests. Small boys go worm digging. Toward the end of the month when the water reaches 60 degrees bass move into the shoals and swim close by, guarding their newly laid eggs. For the next few weeks a man can see the fish that he will seek and not find after July first.

Boats, so industriously painted and repaired during the winter, are brought to water's edge. On a quiet May afternoon a man comes gladly to a lakeside and sees his boat take to water once again; once again he is free from his earth roots and is waterborne on a beloved Adirondack lake. Those whose boats are tied at the docks on a little mountain lake are forever prisoners of the enclosed shore. Not for them, ever, are the distant horizons, the new seascapes, and the mystery of strange landings. For those who do their boating in the Adirondacks it's always round and round the same old lake, always to come to rest at the same old dock. These men may never face peril on strange waters but they have their own pleasures.

When a man comes to know one little lake well, every feature has some worth and meaning. At a spot in the west bay he once saw a deer come down to the rocky edge; he never passes that point without looking to see if that deer might be back, even though it was twenty years ago that he saw it. He remembers the spot where the mink used to slip into the shallows and cut their nightly furrow. They are long gone now, but the man remembers as he passes by and looks for them. Each year he sees the broad float of lily pads return in the south cove, in the same-shaped float each year, with the same channels. He can take his boat through with no less pride than a skipper bringing his Diesel yacht into a Caribbean harbor.

It takes a small lake to develop this sort of intimate knowledge, and with it the close affection. That is the return paid to those whose only boating is around and around the same familiar shores. That makes it his lake, by love if not by law. The lake may be shared by other people in other boats, particularly on a sunny May afternoon. No matter. For a man who loves it, it is his. Even if its name on the map is just Mud Pond.

With mid-May come black flies, the flaw in the Adirondack spring. The wetter the spring, the worse the invasion. As they hatch in running water they are fine food for trout, but thinking of that does not shrink the swelling of their bite. They are worst at dawn and at dusk and hover in a thick cloud over the head of the fisherman standing in the rushing trout brook. Mosquitoes and punkies soon follow. They can be so numerous that deer are driven in torment from slopes and thickets and plunge neck-high into river and lake at dusk to escape the pests.

Farmers plant potatoes and oats. Gardeners watch the thermometer and wonder when they dare plant corn and set out tomatoes. The first small boys show up at swimming places and do more shrieking about the cold water than swimming. The first family picnics turn up in the woods. The first trailers bearing Florida licenses arrive. People who run tourist camps in the North in summer and in the South in winter are back. Roadside cabins are refurbished and the first help arrive to open the summer hotels. New building and new painting start along every road. Out-of-state cars begin to fill the parking places.

By the end of May the flowers of spring are at their height. The lilac is their greatest glory. The Adirondack lilacs are not the expensive sorts with double blossoms and fancy names. They are the common lilac, not the least demeaned by the botanical tag of *vulgaris*. They stand in front of almost every Adirondack farmhouse. Some are broad mountains of bloom twenty feet wide. How they came into the region no one knows. Early settlers may have brought them from Vermont. They thrived. They stand out now in the open sunny places as the one certain show of exotic spring color. They bloom mad and wild, as if Nature would compensate for the dour northland winter and the lateness of spring warmth.

When Walt Whitman wanted to pay one great-worded tribute to Lincoln he wrote:

> When lilacs last in the dooryard bloomed,
> And the great star drooped in the western sky . . .

and

> Passing, I leave thee lilac with heart-shaped leaves,
> I leave thee there in the dooryard . . .

In the lilac Whitman chose the perfect tribute to one common man. In the Adirondacks the lilac is the common man's flower. Often, the more bleak and weatherbeaten the house, the more glorious the flowering lilacs by the unpainted gate or the broken fence. The house may have no color in front of it for the rest of the year, but during a few short weeks in spring it has the windblown loveliness of its lilacs, a month after they have bloomed in the South. On a fair spring wind the lilac odor is one with the fresh smell of pine from the woods.

The lilac is the house cat of flowers. It rarely wanders far from where men are or where men have been. Its seeds are not carried off by birds to sprout in mountain glens and wild places. No matter in what unlikely spot a lilac appears, some man once lived there and planted it. That weights with grave memory many a lovely lilac bush now growing by an empty roadside in some out of the way place.

Life in the Adirondacks is tough. Many a man has faced it and been beaten by it. He lies now in one of the little country cemeteries, a lovelier place for the lilacs at its gates. His children have moved away. His house has fallen with time; not even the foundations remain. Yet the lilac bush he once planted grows on, standing where it stood when a housewife could glance at it now and then from the kitchen window as she went on with her endless chores. Today, even when the lilac stands in the midst of second-growth pine woods, it is a last and lasting proof that once a man had been here and had tried for a short moment to gain a living from the shallow topsoil and the hardpan underneath.

By the end of May the Adirondack world is a green world. It took long to come about. For a few days it seems as if it would never pass. No one need mourn that neither he nor it will last forever. The Adirondack spring is rich enough, and it is pointless to try to live beyond it into springs yet to come. A man can wander through meadows where the blueberries are in blossom and their little pink bells move in the wind. He can sit by a lake and see the wind whip it white. He can watch the kids chasing a ball or catching their breath as they try the shining waters. He can be content in the beauty spread so lavishly roundabout. Many a man will call these days the best in the whole year.

June

Yet there is June. As everywhere else in the land, it goes too fast.

The greens of June have no precise naming. The buttery green of new spruce shoots, the blackened green of old spruce, the silvered green of the undersides of poplar leaves in a June breeze are one with the ruddy green of maples, the metallic green of raspberry leaves, and the sunlit green of new cedar. With them is the gray-bearded green of young poppy leaves, the feathery green of young tamarack, the waxed green of young pea shoots and the whitened green of young iris, the translucent green of a lawn after a June shower and the feathered green of a young hayfield under the first hot sun. Nearby are the leathery green of primrose leaves and the white-green of the new fern fronds. And what are the precise names for the velvet green of fresh moss beneath the hemlocks, the paper green of young birch leaves, the purpled green of asparagus as it comes from the earth, the rubbery green of tulip foliage, and the dusted green of Indian paintbrush now flourishing in the meadows?

Looking at the heat haze over the hills on this solid green world, it is difficult to believe that four months ago the woods were gaunt and black, the hills snow-covered. The change to the rich maturity of June is always a surprise. From one year to the next a man forgets how thick the green carpet grows on the floor of the world and how bright with flowers, how avidly the maple saplings reach for the sky, how daintily the foam flower floats in the slightest wind. Yet as June races by, the signs of spring recede with it. Already the spring fullness of the brooks and lakes has gone. Rocks show in stream bottoms and the lake levels fall to their summer mark.

As a man stands and looks at the woods in blossom and at his young garden he feels that the frost must be past, but Adirondack people always expect a frost in early June. It may come but it is rarely harsh. More likely are occasional days with downstate heat and the first of the few breathless hot nights when the lake lies still under the moonlight, the water beetles skate about in silly circles, and a battery of insects storms the window screens.

The fresh-washed sense of spring is still in the air. The alders bud late in the brookside thickets, a kingfisher darts and poses over the water, and a woodpecker hammers its own rhythm on a distant apple tree. The first of the mountain thunderstorms comes swift and hard in its impact; Adirondack lakes blow up to whitecaps and spume in a moment. Mosquitoes grow smarter and find the slightest chink in the screen. The tent caterpillars do their miserable job on wild cherry and apple trees. Markers are put atop roadside trees to guide airplanes spraying against assorted insect invasions.

Daisies plate the open places. The ruddy orange of Indian paintbrush colors the meadows. Hay grows fast. Potatoes are well up and the farmer wonders what their price will be at harvest. Blueberries start to fill out and raspberries are in flower in the woods. Deer come down to the gardens by night. Grackles nest near the house and evening grosbeaks come now and then from their hidden nests to the feeding places. The woods are alive with warblers, kinglets, thrushes, and juncoes. Fishing slows down as June dries the trout streams.

The coming of people that began at the end of May is full flood by the end of June. Businessmen begin to ask the vital Adirondack question: "Will this summer be ahead of last year?" The first climbers try the high peaks. The first canoers appear on the lakes and rangers have the overnight lean-tos ready for them. Every week end the townspeople are out at their camps by the lake shores on state land. The first city cowgirls sit shakily on dude-ranch horses. State camps are open. The first campers pitch their tents and build their smudges at night to keep away the punkies and the no-see-ums. The last days of school drag as slowly as anywhere else, but in the afternoons the kids are at the beaches and do not seem to notice that the water is still too cold for comfortable swimming.

At children's summer camps painters, carpenters, and caretakers work long days. They patch holes in roofs that were hit by falling branches in a winter wind and rebuild the corner of the dock that the winter ice wrecked. They haul off fallen trees. They paint boats, put out the safety floats at the swimming place, set up new diving boards, clean up the tennis courts, and repair tables, chairs, and bunks. The many jobs all have a sense of things-about-to-happen. Lake shores that have long been silent will soon echo the calls of a hundred kids. Lake waters, unbroken by a diving body or a canoe paddle, will foam and splash. A familiar cry will sound in the brush: "Johnny, the mail's in!"

As the caretaker finishes a last paint job he talks to his helpers about the kids of last year. "Remember the boy who learned to hoot like an owl and used to wake up the whole camp at two every morning? And that one from New York who ate enough for six men — I remember he used to put maple syrup and sugar on his baked beans. And the girl who got a rope around a porcupine and wanted to take it home for her baby brother? And the one who put water in the truck's gas tank on the last day because he didn't want to be driven to the railroad station? Oh, brother, were they something! I wonder if they'll all be back this summer?"

He puts his paintbrush down for a moment and looks across the empty lake. "Things have been peaceful around here for ten months now and that's long enough."

July

Now summer is full-grown. New cones shine on the tops of the tall white pines. Ghostly Indian pipe appears on the floor of the woods. All the summer flowers are out — twinflower, oxalis, wild clematis, and many more. Sheep laurel shows its pink blossoms in swampy and desolate places and hangs over the old rocks by the lake shore. The smell of fresh pine is strong.

Usually July is warm, although temperatures have gone below freezing in rare years and snow has fallen on one July 4. A heat wave in the cities to the south can mean a heat wave only slightly less oppressive in the Adirondacks, but hot nights are followed by nights when a log fire is comfortable. Rain comes irregularly; bad July droughts are not rare.

Many birds start a second set of eggs. Others have raised their families and have already left for the South. Loons still cry from the lakes. Foxes bark on distant shores. The house dog returns from a run in the woods with a nose full of porcupine barbs. A bobcat scream can wreck the quiet night.

The bass season opens. In no time the perennial cry goes up: "Where are the bass?" At dawn on July 1 and every hour thereafter the pools and rocky coves on a thousand lakes and rivers are whipped white by fishermen who dreamed the winter through of the pulsing smack of a three-pound bass at the end of light tackle. A month later many are still dreaming. The bass, so plentiful on the nests by the shore in June, are gone. Often they will bite after dark one day and not at all the next. They turn up in the shallows, then disappear into the deep for the next month. They will not bite on moonlight nights except on those moonlight nights when they do bite. Some men can go out and get a mess of them almost at will. Others can fish all season long and catch only perch.

Bass fishing is not a simple thing of bent pin and worm, although that system can produce as many fish as five hundred dollars' worth of tackle. The two schools of bass fishing usually scorn and revile each other. The first school uses live bait, worms, frogs, and grasshoppers. A fisherman so baited heads for a quiet pool in a lake, drops his line, and waits. If any bass are around he may get them. That technique is too infantile for the school of the artificial lure. Some of these fishermen use bass flies and fly rods, fewer use spinning reels. The majority are plug casters, armed with short rods and, as lures, things made of wood, plastic, or metal that are supposed to represent fish, frogs, or just some oddity that the inventor, although never having been a bass himself, imagines bass might like.

So fisherman and his boat go out at dusk. The sunset dapples the still water as a wisp of evening breeze rustles in the pines. Like a barbed taunt, a fish jumps in the distance. The circle of his splash is living gold. Ever hopeful, the fisherman clips a plug resembling a gray mouse on his line and whams away at a sunken log by the shore. Nothing now breaks the silence of the evening but the measured splash of that plug. At dark the mosquitoes join the fisherman, plaguing him. He casts on and on, changing his lure a dozen times. Late in the evening he turns homeward from the silent water, without cheerful whistle or happy word. No bass. Weary and frustrated, he ties up his boat at the dock. Just then he stops, as he hears a noise out in the center of the lake. Out there in the quiet of the night, the bass are jumping like mad.

The stream of people into the Adirondacks is now full flood. People in the private camps are "in residence," as their servants say. Every road is crowded. "No Vacancy" signs glow at the roadside tourist camps. Souvenir stands are busy. Village soda fountains and restaurants are jammed. Women's costumes that are mostly scanty shorts and scantier halters make Adirondack streets look like roads to a Florida beach. Kids from camps, hotel guests, and mountain-climbing enthusiasts climb the high peaks, up and down in a day; others go into the high-peak country and come out a week later, miles from where they entered. Observers on the fire towers on the mountaintops have no time to be lonely; hikers and trampers come up in droves. Canoers travel the lakes and over the carries, stopping for the night at state-built lean-tos. Water skiers cut sharp corners behind speedboats. A few sails appear on a few lakes. Dude ranches are packed. Big summer hotels import one floor show after another from the cities.

The population in the Adirondacks now increases by the hundred thousand. People are everywhere. Particularly are they at every front door, guests invited and friends just driving through. A carful from Rochester: three for dinner. A carful from Albany: four for dinner. On the assumption that Adirondack people must lead lonely lives and are glad to see any friendly face, people turn up without bothering to write or phone. "And how do you spend the summer?" one gentle housewife was asked. "Buying food and cooking it in a hurry," she said. As she saw another car come into the drive, she hurried off again to the supermarket. These days Adirondack people see little of one another. They are too busy with relatives and guests from elsewhere.

The state camps, with hundreds of camp sites, are packed tight. A thirty-thousand-dollar trailer is parked next to two boys who cycled up from Syracuse with a pup tent, fishing tackle, and ten dollars to last two weeks. A place like Fish Creek Camp, with four hundred fireplaces alight at night around seven miles of lake shore, is one of the exciting sights of the Adirondack summer.

Yet so large and spacious is the region that in almost no time a man can be in the woods without track or tread and even by lakes where he finds no sign of human being. There are many lakes where men do not come, and not all are too remote. On such a lake only the marks on the old rocks by the edge show that four months ago the water was blanketed by heavy ice. The wall of woods that edges the lake is deepest green. Deer can stand just a foot back from the water's edge and be unseen. The woods and the lake are as they have been for centuries, ever since some ancient glacier gouged out a hole between two hills or dammed a ravine. A tree may fall by winter's storm but another takes its place. Whatever man may have done here in the past with saw and ax does not show.

In the early morning the lake lies quiet without a ripple. A noon breeze starts it shimmering, a full southwest wind in the afternoon sends little waves tumbling against the rocky shores. At twilight the water is quiet again. Moonlight burnishes it and deepens the shadows. At one end yellow water lilies bloom. Blue pickerel weed waves over them. Bluing huckleberries on trim bushes hang down on the rocks. In shadowed places the new moss is fresh and green. Warblers and redstarts flash by in the thick woods, their nesting finished. Over the water, swallows dip and glide. A kingfisher flies low. A blue heron patrols one swampy spot, watching for careless frogs. Now and then a loon comes from some hidden nest and cries a bitter sarcastic cry. Little fish idle by the shore. A school of golden shiners moves by, popping at throngs of insects skating the surface. Newly born bass, an inch long, skitter in the shallows. Without noise a mink or muskrat heads to the opposite shore on some urgent business.

When men do come to the lake they feel at once the distance from the troubling front page of the world's newspapers. As a man stands by a deserted Adirondack lake on a July day he can feel more than that; everything is as it was last year, the year before that, as it was a century ago. The sense of timelessness is real. That timelessness also is in a museum, in inanimate objects that time cannot change. The lake and the woods are alive and filled with life, yet they too are beyond time.

They do change, but only with the seasons. Nothing in or around them tells one year from another. One summer on the lake is like any other, like summers long past and summers still to be. By the lake, apart for a few moments from a worrisome world, a man shares in that timelessness just by noting it. For those few moments he can know it and be part of it, as he can never be in his own world where man-marked months and minutes count his years.

As a man tramps the woods to the lake he knows he will find pines and lilies, blue heron and golden shiners, shadows on the rocks and the glint of light on the wavelets, just as they were in the summer of 1354, as they will be in 2054 and beyond. He can stand on a rock by the shore and be in a past he could not have known, in a future he will never see. He can be part of time that was and time yet to come.

That, too, is the Adirondacks in July. Many a man wonders whether these are not the best days in the year.

August

Raspberries are ripe. They grow in wild sunlit meadows where deer and even bear may come after them. They grow in open places in the woods, one with the ferns and the fragrant balsam. They grow in the sandy soil of deserted railroad tracks where the sun's heat for a few short weeks beats down and where cedar waxwings fly primly to a tree nearby. They grow among downed timber and often by a lake where the soft wind over the water shows the silver under the leaves. Wild raspberries are not like blueberries which seem to pick the most accessible open places by the roadsides to bear their fruit. Going for them needs tough shirts, trousers, and boots. It needs some sense of woodcraft. In moving eagerly from one clump to another, deeper and deeper into the woods, the berry picker may have quite a job finding his way out when the pail is full and the sun a long way farther across the sky.

It may be difficult to understand why anyone should be willing to wade through brier and bramble just for a pail of wild berries. The answer lies in part in the odor that comes on the air when the berry is picked, the deeper odor that comes from a filled pail. More of the answer lies in what happens to the berries once they are safely borne home. In a little while a few jars of jelly stand on the window sill to cool, a red jelly shot through with living light.

That jelly is for the days that are hard to recall or imagine on a hot August morning — days when the morning sun has no heat in it, when the thermometer is far below zero when January binds the land. It is then that the jelly from the wild berries turns back time. A glass is opened at breakfast on a January morning, and the unforgettable odor that was in the summer woods returns at once. With it comes the memory of wild and sunlit meadows, the open places in the woods, the ferns, the memory of sun heat, of soft wind over the water, and of cedar waxwings flying primly close by. With that odor summer comes back.

August is also the time for the annual meeting of the Society to Encourage the Use of Blueberries in Blueberry Pie. The berries grow freely everywhere. Many farmers' wives will do nothing else but gather them until they have enough jars put away in the cellar. Blueberry pie turns up on every hotel menu. The true Adirondack cook puts in blueberries, lemon juice, and sugar. Scoundrels and counterfeiters use assorted pastes, gums, and fillers.

Blueberry picking brings its own certain reward, that is, if the berry picker is not overcome by the loveliness of the day and the sky overhead. It is a fine occupation for restless weekend guests from the city. They can usually be sold the job by the promise of fresh blueberry pie. If they really pick and not merely roam the hillsides, they can bring home a big harvest, although a sharp watch must be kept for those berry-blind urbanites who blithely pick spikenard berries for blueberries or turn up with a kettle full of unripe red chokecherries.

On August nights bonfires burn by the shore of many lakes. They are not built for warmth but because men discovered long ago that firelight seems to attract bullheads into shallower water. This is the ideal time for lazy fishing for bullheads, known in some parts as catfish. Many a father and son or husband and wife set out for an evening at a favorite spot. They can be pretty sure that where bullheads have once been caught bullheads will be found again. The bullhead is no beauty, but it is sweet and almost boneless. No one argues that bullhead fishing is sporting or adventurous in the sense of the whip of a bass leaping in fresh water, but it has something completely satisfying in it. At least, it almost always produces fish. And on a warm August night who wants to fight a fish, anyway?

August days can be warm, but killing frosts have come even

in the first week. By all available records and memories this is the one month in which no snow has fallen. The chill and frost can pass in a day and intense heat settle again over the woods.

While July has the air of being able to last forever, sooner or later August brings a day that shows that summer is mortal. The day may come early in the month or late. It may follow high heat. Suddenly the wind shifts. The night wind over the woods has in it a first chill. By morning a branch of maple at the woods' edge shows scarlet. The great chemistry of autumn has begun. Crickets take up the chorus that marks the coming end of summer. One may ride into the house and chirp from the hearth whenever a pile of firewood is brought in for a chilly evening. Those piles come in more frequently.

By late August the woods begin to look tired and dusty. Hills on the horizon have a rosy wash over them. The last flowers of the year are out, equal in number, if not in delicacy, to the flowers of spring. Fields and roads are covered with goldenrod, Queen Anne's lace, joe-pye weed, mullein, and bergamot. Wild asters open. Phlox blankets the garden, but the afternoon wind shows the dried edges of the leaves beneath the flowers. In the vegetable patch raccoons come nightly to the ripening corn. Purple finches and juncos come to the birdhouses in small flocks, like travelers making ready for a long journey. Now and then a flash of yellow streaks by the pines as a belated warbler looks for his fellows already gone.

The children's camps are closed. Trainloads of sunburned kids have gone back to the cities. The woods and beaches where they shouted and ran are quiet again. In the summer homes on the lakes the owners think about storing camp equipment which they uncrated only a few weeks before. Hotels are still crowded and porch rockers rock just as fast. The help are moved now not by the happy prospect of a prosperous summer ahead but by the uncertainty of finding new jobs for autumn.

In the villages, where parking places are as crowded as ever, the shopkeepers and tourist-cabin owners are up a little earlier to work a little harder. They are tired but try not to show it. Business may have been good generally, but they know that what they don't make in the next few days they won't have a chance to make again until next June. That knowledge adds its own sense of hurry and strain.

A new crop of tourists has come for these last August weeks. Those on short vacations have an extra eagerness to take in all they looked forward to through the hot July days in the city. Those who have been around all summer are now conscious of the many things planned for what, just eight weeks ago, seemed like such a long time but which just never did get done. A faster tempo marks all activity, as if to crowd every last thing into every late moment. More steaks than ever are put on out-door fires, more swimmers splash in the colder waters. Boats seem to move faster up and down the lakes. The fishing parties come out earlier, stay longer, and more regretfully leave the coves in the back lakes and the shady spots on the rivers. What seemed infinite just eight weeks ago is measured, and the measure is short. As a boat slips away from the dock or as hikers head into the woods for the hills once more they know that it is not just one more ride or one more hike but one of the last rides, one of the last hikes. For the summer people their Adirondack days are numbered, and the number is small.

By the lakes the night fires of the camps shine in the water. The sunsets add copper, bronze, and even brown to their colors. The lakes pick up those tones and look utterly unreal under a gun-metal sheathing. Overhead the ruddy moonlight falls on the haze over the distant mountains. A light evening breeze ripples the lakes and waves lap lightly at the moored boats. Crickets chirp in the darkness. These are the bittersweet days and nights, and many a man will say they are the best of the year.

September

The flickers now gather in flocks on the lawn and the swallows by the roadside. In the morning they are gone. It is like that with the summer people. On one day lakes are alive and noisy, camps are filled, and every tourist cabin taken. A day or so after Labor Day and most people are gone. Some private camps may stay open for hunting season. Some hotels keep open for another month. Yet two of the best Adirondack months are ahead. As the Adirondack people say, on a hot September afternoon with a warm wind raising whitecaps on the lakes, "We keep the best weather for ourselves."

As the old-timers leave they wonder if there will be another summer in the Adirondacks for them. As the hotel help and even many of the visitors leave they say regretfully, "If only there were some way to make a living up here the year around." For the first time in months empty parking places appear on village streets.

All the house guests are gone. For the first time in months no one needs to apologize for the bad weather or to answer a guest's question, "Does it always rain?" Neighbors drop in and talk leisurely. They entertain one another as they had no time to do in summer. By midwinter only pleasant memories about last summer's guests will be left. In no time a man will be saying to his wife, "It's pretty quiet, isn't it? June will be here before we know it and we ought to start asking a few people up for their vacations before they make other plans."

At the state camp sites, trailers are again hitched to cars. Gear is stowed and good-bys said, with promises to return the next year or to meet in Florida in the next month. By mid-September the last of the trailers is gone. Porcupines that have sniffed at the salty smell of trailers, based the previous winter by the Florida sea and now headed back to it, move about the camp sites without concern. Nosy deer come from the woods and take over the lake shore once more. The camp caretaker puts up the bars on the entrance road and heads off to a village for the winter. His hard work now begins: figuring how to get even more camp sites for next year around the rigid border of a lake that is already plotted out to the last inch.

Many odd-shaped crates arrive at the express offices. They are filled with little trees, sent out for reforesting purposes by the Conservation Department from the state nurseries. They cost a small sum plus transportation. On some of these September days many men walk, if they walk at all, with backs like ironing boards. Setting out baby trees may be setting out roots to the future, but only those who have put in a thousand trees six feet apart each way know that the forests of the future are started not only with seedlings but with grunts and backaches. The trees won't amount to much for some years. The man who plants them on a sunny September day may never live to see their glory. But he plants today with a calm assurance that trees will still be growing in the land twenty-five years from now. His children may walk the woods he has made.

Farmers are busy in September. Potato vines have browned and the crop must be dug. Most Adirondack farmers use mechanical diggers, but picking potatoes still needs hand labor. Many a farmer's wife makes spare money now by working in the fields for the large growers, bending over a thousand times a day and following down the field after the digger. Winter preparations begin. Wood must be cut, screens removed, the last house repairs made before the first cold wind comes.

In the store windows hunting equipment replaces fishing gear. Conservation trucks drive back roads and stock streams with fish. Men walk the woods to look hopefully for deer tracks and to make a mental note of where to hunt in a few more weeks.

On the lakes a stronger wind streaks foam across the water.

Algae, working since the end of August, fill some lakes with a gray cloudiness that soon passes. Maple seeds spiral down on the lakes and the waves wash them into scaly piles on the sandy shores. The lakes, so busy just a few weeks before, are empty, except for a loafing loon and a few sheldrake ducks that are chasing whatever it is that lures a sheldrake. On the rocks in the middle of some lakes young gulls try their wings. In back streams beavers labor fast against the approaching cold. Their dams are repaired. Every animal in the colony works harder to get in the winter's food supply of poplar logs and to anchor them firmly at the bottom of the water beyond the reach of ice.

Meadows and pastures are rusty, marked with the seed heads of golden rod and fireweed. In open places in the woods ladies' tresses and rattlesnake plantain are among the last flowers to bloom. Day by day more single maple branches turn color, then suddenly an entire tree. It may be a small one by a road or a large one in the meadow that goes first; there is no order to it except that the same early tree is usually early each autumn. Against the reddening of the woods, particularly noticeable at a distance, the spruces begin to darken. Birches fade and give a springlike yellow-greenness to the hillsides. The unobtrusive English ivy over the rocks, unnoticed all summer, turns a flaming red. Pine needles begin to brown and fall, showering down to provide slippery walking in smooth places. Lilac leaves crisp at the edges. Fat bear, their cubs gone their own way long ago, may come through the rusty bracken of a deserted farm to search out the old apple trees and a last meal of the year.

As days stay warm, nights grow chilly. A few maple leaves begin to fall; that, the Adirondack people say, means frost within a week. The first frost usually holds off until about September 15. The day of the first frost commences bright and clear. The heat of summer is gone but its sparkle remains. A breeze rises in late morning. The afternoon has a close warmth that makes any thought of approaching frost almost ridiculous.

By evening the sunset fills the sky. The temperature falls from the sixties to the low forties, almost as fast as a leaf twirls down from a tree. At dusk, mist comes off the land in wisps of thin batting and the temperature continues to drop. At night everything is very still and the long leaves of the late corn are quiet. By bedtime the temperature is in the thirties, the stars are as bright as in deep winter, and the night air has a fresh crackle. The gardener lies abed, remembering the crops still out in the garden, and he hopes. The chill of the night air through the window cuts sharply through those hopes.

Next morning tells the story, but not at once. A heavy dew can mask for a little while any damage done. By mid-morning cucumber and squash leaves are up at the edges, wrinkled and black. Tomato leaves are shriveled. Only the root crops are left untouched, and all in one night. The gardener turns to the garden to clear up the debris. The day after the first frost is even clearer, more sparkling, almost springlike. The next ten days and nights may even be hot. As a gardener pulls up the blackened squash vine he has a chance to think of next year's garden. Next year, maybe, the frost will hold off until October.

As the month ends the woods race to their climax of color. Another heavy frost sets the distant mountain peaks shining white against the high blue sky. At sunset they turn lilac. The reds on the hillsides below deepen under the violet of the early twilight. The evening wind carries more chill in the earlier darkness. But the days come warm and clear, in a world where the mounting color on the hills spreads like fire.

October

The Adirondack country, so green a few months before, now has little green. On highland and lowland the world is red, with all the reds from maroon to madder and vermilion flaring in the sun. A hillside of maples will have fifty different shades. The contrasting swatches of green pine and blackening spruce are subdued by the reds that flame among them. At dusk the sunset shows violet and purple against the gold of the sky and the red of the hills. Sunrises are drenched and splattered with crimson. When the October moon comes early it shines down on a world sometimes whitened by frost, rarely whitened by snow. It shines on a world in which the only life is color, but that in abundance.

The climax comes about the first week in this month. During these days hillsides are covered by an intricately woven Oriental rug, lavish in red, brown, orange, and yellow. Sunlight on the slopes is deepened and enriched. People come from miles around to stand on some height where they can look down on a valley and mark the brighter red of the soft maples by a river's edge. Painters come and photographers, but none catch fully the radiance of a bright afternoon.

A better way to see autumn close is to walk in the woods on the few rare October days before the first leaf falls, when the sun is bright and the color still holds. On these days sunlight comes filtered through the leaves and picks up yellow tones overhead. It is not the red of the thick maple leaves that colors the light but the gold of the translucent leaves of birches and beech. They pick up that light and reflect it so that it seems to come not only from overhead but from all sides and even from deep within the woods. Any leafy hardwood place on these days is like a golden room, lit from within.

The golden light shows the weariness of the woods, but it so gilds them that they do not seem forlorn as they will in a few weeks when the last leaf has fallen and the woods are naked to the grim November sky. In this soft October light the stalks of goldenrod stand in the open spaces, their seeds gone, their heads gray-bearded. Fireweed long ago threw its seeds to sprout next year, no one knows where, and the stalks hang with a crest of fine shavings. Fern fronds are a dead brown, wind-broken, but a few still stand and rustle in the air.

The new growth on the little evergreens looks dusty now but is already tipped with buds for next year. On the forest floor the leaf-fall of last autumn is almost gone into compost and duff. On it lie the pine cones that fell last spring, gray-tipped with resin. Wild asters that sprout wherever sunlight falls look frowsy, yet they still can toss in the breeze as the last flowers in the autumn world. In shady corners late mushrooms are a spot of white. Only where the clumps of moss and chains of partridge berry grow is there any show of defiant green.

Golden light burnishes the coppery sides of the yellow birches. It picks up pink tones in the white birch bark. It even softens the dead brown on the cedars. It deepens the mahogany color of raspberry leaves. It tips the blueberry bushes, their last berries gone with the frost, but with their leaves afire in a scarlet that outflames the maples.

All the autumn glory of the maples is not in the great trees overhead. Every small sapling in the woods, even one a foot high, has its own scarlet and crimson flare. The long sprouts that have come in one summer from a maple stump flash their own color so that the tawny red and the flaming red that show over the woods when seen at a distance are inside the woods as well. And all under a golden light.

These golden days in the woods are few. They do not last long. They last only until the first birch leaf floats slowly, gracefully, inexorably to the ground. As the color fades in the maples, the leaves fall first from the tops of the trees. They fall slowly, then swirl down in torrents. Black branches now show gaunt against the bright sky. The woods turn brown and green again.

On Adirondack farms the sound of the ax and saw in the wood lot echoes all day. Night frosts settle on the roofs and drip off in the morning sun. A mist comes from the lake and mornings are gray until the sun cuts through. A few camps and hotels stay open for the hunting season, now close at hand. A bright week end may send people out to the woods and the lakes for a last picnic but they are home long before the dusk. On the lake shore boats are hauled out for the winter or hung from boathouse roofs. Snow fences go up on open roads. Highway crews stick red flags in roadside ditches to mark them for the snowplows that will be out on many a coming winter dawn.

The last of the migrant birds leave. The Adirondacks are not a major flyway, but flocks of geese and ducks can be heard over the river valleys. At times loud quacking resounds at dusk on the back ponds. Before sunup the birds are gone again and no one knows precisely what species the itinerants were. Some of the days, golden on the lake, tempt fishermen. The bass season is still open but the bass are no more obliging than in summer. Bird hunters search for grouse and woodcocks. The woodcocks are found in old pasture land and a dog is a necessity. Grouse can be found in thick woods, particularly if the woods are second growth by an old apple orchard. A hunter can come on eight or ten birds feeding around one old apple tree, now and then.

On some early October day a man appears on the street in a pair of red and black checked pants and a scarlet jacket; he is like the first branch of the maple that turned in August and signaled the change to come. In no time the villages are full of men in similar costumes. While the hunting season does not open until late October, hunters dress up for it days in advance. In bars around town the talk is of rifle bores, bullet velocities, and of how the big buck got away last year. To hear the talk a stranger would think that every man in town means to be out in the woods every possible day. Many are, even if employers complain. A man can work eleven months in the year. He can hunt only for one month.

Rifles are cleaned and oiled a dozen times. Sights are adjusted, readjusted, then adjusted again until they can draw a bead on a mosquito at a hundred yards. Cartridges are bought and put carefully in a locked closet. The hunting knife is sharpened ten times. The proper costume is refurbished, or, more likely, bought afresh, for styles in hunting clothes change each year as manufacturers discover newer and redder dyes. Licenses are bought, topographical maps studied. Visiting hunters pour in from downstate. Everything is ready for the synchronized leap of thousands of men from thousands of beds at dawn on the opening morning.

Hunters aren't the only ones to know the precise date the deer season begins. All spring and summer the deer may have browsed in the prize strawberry beds near the house or come into the garden and cleared off the lettuce in one night. Through the first days of autumn they even appear in clearings on the out-skirts of villages. They come down early to the farmhouse to race the farmer for his apple crop. They move with disdain of the human race in every proud step they take. Even late on the afternoon of the day before deer season opens they may be working down in the nearby balsam swamp. But come 11:59 P.M. on that day and no magician with a giant wand could make them vanish faster than they take themselves off. Runs in the woods where deer tracks were thick all summer are bare now. All the while, thousands of men in the wildest costumes are all over the woods, many in places where no self-respecting deer would ever be found, out of breath, climbing slopes, trampling swamps, and asking the same question, "Where did they go this year?"

The state keeps a record of all deer taken. More to the point would be a record of the miles the thousands of hunters walk, the number of times they take the twist of silvery poplar leaves falling earthward for the flash of a whitetail, and the number of days spent in the woods when a man never even sees the track of a deer. That discourages none of those who wait for the opening of deer season. Among them are men and women who have gone out on every possible hunting day for the previous ten years and have yet to get a deer. They do not complain. Anyone who has walked the Adirondack hills during the late October days, through air that sparkles, and seen the higher peaks white with snow, reflected in the blue of a mountain lake, knows that it isn't the hunted that matters but the hunting.

The local "biggest buck" contest has its rack along the village street; a dozen dead deer hang stiff in the chill air. A few huntters bring back bear and perhaps even an occasional bobcat. The hunters hope for snow: tracking will be easier and the dry woods less noisy. Many hunt in groups, on drives. Deer come to the swamps and lower places at night to feed. With the first light they head up toward the ridges. Hunters do likewise, watching for the runways the deer have made, posting some of the group by them while the others swing around to windward. These men come through the woods barking like dogs and driving the deer ahead to where the waiting hunters can get their shot. It is always a shock to meet some distinguished Adirondack doctor or scientist and to be told by one of his friends that he is one of the best dog-barkers in the business.

Other men prefer still hunting, going out alone and climbing the ridges. If they see no deer, at least they see other things in the woods that now appear so dead and empty. They see the old pines, still sturdy no matter how the wind has whipped them. They see the loose bark flapping on a nearby birch and the new bark underneath. They see bluejays gathering weed seeds and nuthatches in their headlong rush down the side of the trees. They see brown buds on the spruce, shielded for the winter but full of confident promise that a spring will come someday. They get a sense of being firmly rooted in a sure world, in a world that is always full of the promise of life, even in the midst of seeming desolation, if only a man would look. And many a man will say that these are the best days in the year.

As for the deer, wherever they may be during the season, one thing is sure: Come 12:01 A.M. the day after the season ends and the hunter who may have walked hundreds of miles for weeks without sight of one can see one plainly now. He need only look right there in his own garden where a ten-point buck is busily rooting off the straw mulch so carefully placed around the strawberries.

Not all hunting is sport. Each season brings its grim stories of men killed in careless accident, by a trigger-happy idiot, and then the miserable business of toting the corpse of a full-grown man out from the deep woods. In hunting season Adirondack parents lay down a strict law for their children: no hiking, no playing in the woods. Many people will not drive along woodland roads until hunting season is past. The Boy Scouts stay out of the woods these days.

By the end of the month the world is a tired and tattered one, with the debris of autumn on all sides. It awaits the snow that will bind mountain, woods, roadside, fields, and town into one. There may be snow flurries. With the first one small boys hurry to the attic for skis and skates. Wood fires now burn nightly in the fireplaces and a wood stove in the kitchen feels comfortable. If the woods are not too dry, brush fires burn outdoors but a permit is needed for them. A distant forest fire, even one in Canada, can fill the air with smoky haze and dim the sun.

In the small Adirondack village the late afternoon sunlight comes golden through the bare branches of the tall maples along the street. An errant wind stirs up the leaves in the gutters. On the lawns small boys finish their football games and move slowly to their homes. A few babies in carriages are hurried indoors. The gardeners turn from their tidied beds and take their tools to the shed. A grocery truck finishes last-minute deliveries. A belated paper boy, his bag empty, pushes his bike up the hill to home. The fainter smell of burning leaves blends with wood smoke from the chimneys.

By five the men downtown are leaving their work and heading home. For just a little while the streets are full of cars. The cars turn quickly into their separate driveways. Most garage doors are closed after them for the night. A mother's voice calls for some tardy child, loath to get home to the schoolwork that waits. Even the house pets are called indoors. By late twilight nothing moves on the streets but the leaves in the gutters.

The lights go on, first in the homes, upstairs and down, then along the streets. The window curtains are drawn. From a great distance comes the sound of a child at his piano practice. Nowhere is there sound of human voice or human laughter. In the early evening a few cars are again on the streets. People are going to the movies, to lodges, to church services, to committee meetings. For the most part the streets are deserted, and if any one is out he is not there aimlessly but hurrying to a definite destination. The lights in the shop windows downtown shine on the sidewalks but few passers-by are there to be attracted.

Nothing breaks the mid-evening quiet. The lights in the houses shine brightly on the dew on the lawns. No children call and no voices sound from the lawns or gardens. The back streets are totally empty except perhaps for a pair of raccoons strolling down the sidewalk from out of the hills.

When the moviegoers come home the last cars are off the streets. Any car thereafter is probably that of a doctor on some emergency call. From house after house comes the sound of the locking of front door. In house after house the lights go out. Thin moonlight shines on pockets of mist that hang low over the dips in the roads. It puts color back into the dark trees. The wind dies away by late evening and even the rustle of leaves is gone. The night brings every sound closer. The village clock strikes the hour and seems nearby. If a dog howls in the distance his cry seems to come from just down the street. Everything is wrapped up and put away. Each separate family seems to have gone its own way, to have entered its own four-walled world, closed tight the door and cut all contact with the world around or outside. On the farms on the edge of town the farmers follow this great law of autumn: the gathering-in. In the town the same autumn law holds. There, it is in the secure gathering-in of people, of family, and of the little houses under the misty October moon.

If a man stays up late and looks to the east, he will see new constellations. Orion is low on the horizon, its bright points sharp in the autumn sky. There is further proof, along with the quietness and the oneness of the little town, that the earth has again swung its course and that another October can be added to the tens, the hundreds, the millions of Octobers that have gone before over the Adirondack country.

November

Snow may come now but only in flurries. The old days when winter arrived at the start of the month and blanketed the earth until late April seem gone.

Like October days, these are days of worry in Adirondack towns. The woods are still full of hunters, not all of them alert to the danger of fire. Forest rangers do not rest this month. If no rain falls and the November woods stay dry, they are troubled days, for people know how a fire can sweep faster than a flaming broom. The fire towers on the hilltops are manned each clear day. If a drought persists, the woods are ordered closed. State police and Conservation Department men then work hard and late to get the hunting parties out of the woods.

On those rare days when a sudden thin column of smoke does rise from the woods, the observer spots it, gets a map reading, and phones a central office. Other towers in the area take a bearing. In five minutes, the central office will have the fire pinpointed; in ten minutes, Conservation trucks are sent on their way. From his tower the observer advises on the progress of the fire and may suggest other ways to tackle it.

The fine autumn weather that seemed measureless a little while ago is gone. Typical autumn days do turn up but the growing grayness brings more darkness and chill. The lakes are dirty gray under the gray clouds. At night thin ice forms on the lake edges. November can be lovely at times but it can also be a mean month of which as little good can be said as of March. No longer autumn, it is not yet winter. In the change back and forth the weather can be awful. Toward the end of the month a first snowfall may come and the Adirondack farmer says, "The first coat of snow is as good as a coat of manure." A warmer day follows and the snow disappears.

Under the heavy frosts that whiten the peaks the mountains seem to come closer. Their ridges and folds are better marked. The lilac tone on them at dusk changes to amethyst. By some optical trick the opposite shore line of the lake comes nearer. Vistas are open through the woods. Where green walls were solid a few months before, alleys are now open to the sunset.

Adirondack homes are ready for the winter. Storm windows are up. Woodpiles are stacked high. At the first prolonged cold spell farmers kill their hogs. Some still smoke their own meat but most take it to professionals for easier commercial curing. Favorite Adirondack meals appear on the table — salt pork first soaked in water to "freshen" it, fried crisp and served with cream gravy and boiled potatoes, or flapjacks with country sausage, the "country" being Chicago until the home-cured meat is in.

Cold rains and freezing spells make the roads treacherous. Some people put on snow tires, others put on "tractionized" snow tires. A few use chains. Village taximen, who drive in any sort of weather, go on using their regular tires. In any case, the motorist puts a sack of gravel in his luggage carrier and an old shovel. He may need both before the winter is over.

Except for an occasional flock of belated geese, all migrant birds are gone. Chickadees, nuthatches, an occasional jay, and downy woodpeckers, the regular winter visitors to the feeding stations, turn up every morning. The first of the evening grosbeaks come erratically. The crows still call from the tall pines. In the woods the crossbills, siskins, and brown creepers that do not come to the feeding stations live on pine cones and seeds. A ruffled grouse may start up from under an old spruce. Late in the month a flock of snow buntings, down from the Arctic for the warmer Adirondack winter, may wheel and flash in the fading sun by the roadside.

The hunting season comes to a close. Everyone has tales of deer gotten and deer missed. In the lucky homes, venison pot roasts, venison chops, and even venison sausage come on the table. Some housewives will can the meat for later use. Wardens patrolling the woods come on dead does shot by mistake and left to rot. At least once during the month some hunter may be lost in the woods. Townspeople turn out gladly for the search, hoping they will never need one themselves. If the weather stays open and fair the lost man may be found in a day or so. Others have been found only the following spring lying under some old spruce where they crawled in exhaustion and died.

By the end of the month the thermometer is below freezing every night. The kids stand around and say, "When will it snow?" Their skis are waxed and ready and their skates are sharpened. They are in winter clothes — mackinaws, galoshes, ski boots and ski pants, although many Adirondack children go through winter in jeans. A school corridor is a noisy place now with the shuffling of heavy-clad feet. Now and then the temperature may reach several degrees below zero, just as an occasional day of belated Indian summer may turn up. The mean temperature for the month is about 30 degrees. The road crews have their plows ready and watch the weather closely for a call that can send them out on a cold Adirondack dawn.

The lumbermen are working hard in the woods. This is the best of lumbering seasons. The whirr of the power saw in the woods today is louder than the crack of the ax. When the ground is frozen solid the trucks get in and bring the logs out. The cook-shanty stove is always smoking and in the remote clearing the odor of doughnuts frying is strong on the cold air.

The Christmas-tree choppers now come into the spruce groves and balsam swamps on private land and harvest the ten- and fifteen-year-old evergreens. The cutters blow on their nipped fingers and warm themselves now and then at the roaring fire which has been built safely beyond the reaches of the trees. Most of the trees come from "tree farms," where they were set out specially to be cut for the children of a Christmas a decade away.

Many of the old-fashioned housewives now busy themselves making Christmas pine pillows for their less fortunate friends who have to live in cities or far from the pine woods. They are filled with fresh-cut evergreen needles in lavishly decorated or utterly simple cloth cases. One whiff from the box when it is opened in a city and the breeze that furrows an evergreen mountainside or ruffles a mountain lake comes softly into the room.

They may be called pine pillows, but the housewife who is particular about her handiwork raises Cain if the men dare bring in anything from the woods but balsam. Pine needles make second-rate stuffing; their odor disappears too fast. Some stores used to offer pillows that had neither balsam nor pine in them but sawdust impregnated with synthetic oil of pine. In the Adirondacks they always figured those were made by a bankrupt nutmeg maker from Connecticut. To an Adirondack housewife, if it isn't balsam, paradoxically, it isn't a pine pillow. Once a housewife starts to make pine pillows for her city friends the men around the house know what they'll be doing. The amount of needles needed to fill one small pillow is surprisingly large. A man can work in the woods for a morning, clipping balsam branches and at noon be sure he has enough to last the season. The housewife scissors the broad green needles into a container. In no time, surrounded by shorn branches, she is calling, "More balsam!"

When the last load has come to the house and all the pillows are stuffed they are put out into the damp air to pick up added moisture. The fragrance of balsam hangs in the house for a week thereafter. In a little while the pillows will be boxed and mailed and the housewife's Christmas snipping is over. She has sent off a rare present — a breath of mountain air.

November dwindles away, in cold rain or wet snow. No one is sorry to see it go. It may end with one of the deeply dramatic events of the Adirondack year — the freezing of the lakes. In some years they are frozen tight before December; in other years they still show open water at Christmas. Whenever the freeze comes it has its own grim beauty.

For some time, even though the temperature stands below freezing by day and night, the gray water of the lakes swirls free and beats on the rocks by the shore. A few cold nights may ice the edges in the sheltered coves. That first ice may look solid to impatient small boys and curious puppies but one step in it and off they dash to the nearest fire. Under the day's light and wind that ice moves quickly away.

Snow may make the broad world around a white world save for the black blot of the lake, blacker for the solid white roundabout. At night the winter sounds of the wind and the swaying pines have with them the unseasonable sound of open lake water still free. The lake water itself may still be alive but it has no life in it or on it. In late November one last gull may settle on it for a morning and then circle slowly into the gray above and off to the South. The fish have long since left the shallows and are in deep water where it stays a steady 38 degrees above zero throughout the winter.

Then one day the wind comes up as usual with the morning. For once a bright sun appears. During that short morning the lake is almost as blue as it was in summer. By early afternoon the wind is down and gone. Not even the smallest breeze ruffles the water. Through the short afternoon the temperature falls; by dark it is close to zero and going lower. The early sunset sends lilac over the hills and sheathes the lake with bronze.

The new moon in the west is too puny to outdo the stars. By hundreds they come to watch the quiet world below and to set the still water with their points. In early evening the lake far out still reflects the starlight but it is gone from the water near the shore. With dusk a thin film of fine ice crystals has formed at the edges and is spreading out across the water. Long ice fingers skirt the places where deep springs offshore are still too active to freeze. Sometime during the night ice covers the whole surface. It is not done soundlessly. At times, as if in protest, imprisoned air breaks the night silence with rasping cries like a bound child's. When early morning comes the life of the lake is gone. Ice an inch thick has planked it down from shore to shore. At last the lake is one with the wide white world.

So it will stay until April. The winter sun may beat on it, the wind ruffle it, the snow will blanket it as it blankets the land, but it is not altered. The ice will grow thicker, perhaps to twenty inches. The surface will pick up the pink and gold of January sunsets and redden in the dawn. High winter days, with the sun, blue sky, and deep cold will make it a field of crystals. On many a morning small tracks will run out from shore over it and run back as mink or muskrat ventures to see what new wonder the winter has brought. In later winter cold the air under the thick ice will snap and boom and send long cracks running from shore to shore, to tear the night until a man wakens nervously and wonders what hellish misery is loose out there on the lake. But the silence that is winter in the woods is unbroken now. The last freedom on winter's earth is fettered, and November ends.

December

The Adirondack winter puts on its grip not in one sudden tight clasp but in a series of increasingly severe embraces. Snow may fall, a little at a time, and the weak sun cannot melt it. A leaden day may bring heavy snow that falls slowly, steadily, implacably, to twelve or fifteen inches, covering rock and fallen tree, field, woods, and lake, and making one world of white from the peak of Marcy to the front door of a man's house. Rarely do high winds come to drift it. This first heavy snow is welcome. It is winter. The kids are out at once with their sleds, but the skiers wait until the first fall packs and makes a base. Plows and school busses get through, no matter what the snow. The horse-drawn sleigh, however, is gone from the Adirondacks except for a few kept as curiosities for rides on holiday parties.

Or the first storm of winter may come instead in a dramatic and deadly sleet storm. On such a December day the sun doesn't rise cheerless over the hills of gray; it doesn't rise at all. In its place comes rain, then with a sudden chill, rain changed to snow. The wet snow sticks to everything. In an hour it turns a variegated world into one solid world of white. Every tree becomes a priestly figure in flowing white vestments.

Soon the storm pushes modern man back a century. The first modern convenience to go is the automobile. Gentle rises in the roads suddenly become slippery mountains that cars cannot climb. Snow tires and chains are valueless; the foresighted who have them are blocked in front and behind by those who have them not. Even the heavy school busses stall. Many a child learns what his forefathers knew — that legs can also be used to get home from school.

As heavy tree branches fall and take down wires, the electricity goes next. With it goes oil heater, electric clock, radio, kitchen mixer, electric stove, and water pump. Kerosene lamps stand on the back shelves but no one in this modern world has remembered to stock up on kerosene. Out comes one of the great unsung inventions of man, the simple wax candle. The telephone is next. This has its own concern in it — no calls to neighbors to see how they are faring, no calls, if need be, to doctors. As the evening goes on, its peace unbroken by the demanding ring, someone wonders if the most valuable invention since the telephone is not the "no telephone."

Night settles close and still the snow comes down. In a thousand isolated homes, the sense of being walled against the world is real, with every family for itself. Whatever help may be needed in the night ahead will have to come from within. No one says that, but it is apparent in the general restlessness and in the unspoken knowledge that it is a long time until morning. Even the house pets cannot settle down. With that new slight anxiety comes a staunch, forefatherly feeling that has its own quaintness and even novel charm. It is fun to live of a sudden in another age, even as the chill from the idle central heating grows real. Fireplaces warm up the nearby air but the house temperature falls steadily. An old wood stove in the kitchen means hot meals now and bottled gas is a godsend. In the flickering candle light the walls of the room show strange shadows. Doorways and even steps seem to have shifted in the darkness and cannot be taken for granted.

Man against Nature on a snowbound night, with enough

candles and woodfires, isn't very serious. Outdoors it is Nature against Nature. The first crack of a huge pine branch weighted with snow and brought to earth is like the crack of a murder pistol. The moan of a tall cedar as it topples and sinks is a cry of barren despair. All night the crack and crackle of the agony of the woods breaks the quiet. Now and then, with the roar of a small avalanche, the wet snow thuds off the roof and breaks a troubled sleep.

The morning comes back gray. Light snow falls as if trying to shroud torn tree limbs and fallen trees. Even a lonely birdhouse on a pole wears a silly white cap eighteen inches high. The house dog is the first to inspect the peaceful world outside and promptly vanishes in snow well over his head; that kills off his exploring spirit. A man tries to get a car from the garage and is stuck before going fifteen feet. All that pleasant warming quaintness of being one with our forefathers, so real the night before, is gone. The world of today is out there beyond all that white and where is that snowplow, anyway, and the power crews and the phone repairmen?

The first heavy snow may melt and bring that Adirondack abomination, a green Christmas, death to the winter sports season and to the hopes of hotels, tourist cabins, and creditors. As of 1953, three of the last six Christmases have been green or at least lacking in more than an inch of snow. Snow is a valuable commodity today. Snow on the hills means skiers and skiers mean "outside dollars" in backwoods towns. When a heavy snowstorm hit New York City right after Christmas in 1949, the Adirondacks saw none of it. The hills were bare, with open rifts on the lakes. An experience like that brings up the perennial winter topic: "What has happened to the old-fashioned Adirondack winter?"

There is reason to believe that complaining about the passing of the old-fashioned winter has been a favorite occupation in northern New York for many years. The number of light winters that have turned up in recent years is cited as proof of the changing of the climate. But a record kept a century and a half ago in northern New York, on the edge of the Adirondacks, shows: "1799 — Slight frost in September. No hard frost until December. Open winter with snow of moderate depth. 1801 — Winter was memorable as warm and open. No heavy snow until February 24th. 1824 — Winter open and not two weeks of sleighing." Even in 1813 one writer said of all of New York State: "It is a common observation that the seasons are not so clearly defined as formerly. A general modification has taken place in the last ten or fifteen years."

In normal years the snow comes early and stays. The average mean temperature for the month is about 20 degrees with drops to 20 below and even lower in transient cold spells. Different types of days turn up. Some are the rare, clear, white-gold days, following a spell of intense cold at night, with the temperature at 25 below. The snow crackles and the cold prickles like needles in the nostrils, but people call them "real Adirondack days," the more precious for being rare. They end with a majestic sunset, a blend of magenta and turquoise against the mother-of-pearl on the eastern hills and gold and purple in the western sky. Rarely do more than two or three of these days come in succession. More common is the gray day, in all its variations, with dripping snow or rain.

The Adirondack motorist is now in for his worst time. Some people refuse to drive again until April. Snow alone is little trouble; the plows get out before the late dawn and clear everything but the small side roads. In no time the combination of freezing and thawing which marks so much of the month lays ice on the roads which the plows cannot remove. What is a pleasant and easy drive in summer to a neighboring town thirty miles off may be something not to be undertaken. A man may start for his destination and reach it with as little trouble as in July. On his return he may run into the sort of weather that means doing thirty miles in seven hours, and that right out on the slippery edge of danger.

Before the end of the month ski tows are open and hills are in use. Some are municipally owned or rented and give the kids a chance to learn to ski free of charge. Winter vacationers begin to show up on Adirondack streets. Almost every village provides a municipal skating rink. At many country schools the janitors flood the playgrounds. Strings of colored electric bulbs make them a gay place at night.

In some years one small snowfall follows another so that the ground stays covered. The snow begins to pile up in the shady woods, a foot, two feet, three feet deep. The bird feeders outside the kitchen door are well patronized now. White-breasted nuthatches and chickadees are always around. Jays call in the woods and may come to the stations in twos and threes; one can take on as many as a hundred sunflower seeds before leaving. Grouse and a rare pheasant may come near the poultry yards if the snow is deep and the seeds in the woods hard to find. Hunters are out, trekking over empty fields after the snowshoe rabbit; unlike the deer hunters, they rarely return empty-handed. At night, foxes may bark at the moon. The sound of dogs chasing deer is not as rare as it ought to be. Trappers are busy, setting traps by the water for mink.

The end of the month brings Christmas. No holiday better fits the Adirondacks, the land of living Christmas trees. Those who try to cut trees from the plantings on state lands may find a forest ranger waiting down the road. The ten-dollar fine for that one tree off state lands makes it an expensive Christmas. Many a village sets up a municipal tree, hangs out lights and the little streets are gay. The pork slaughtered just before the holidays provides extra meat on the farms. Some farmers have tried raising turkeys in the Adirondacks and a few have succeeded. Whatever the Christmas dish, no one seems to go without.

The young people come back to the hills for the holidays. Village streets are alive, more so than they will be at any time until far-off June. Ski trains from the cities, a few out-of-state cars, bring visitors. Someone may even have found an old horse-drawn sled for a party, and sleigh bells echo on back roads. Houses are decorated with homemade wreaths, ground pine or balsam, and the odor of balsam is in every home. There is no native holly, but partridge berries are just as bright. The less tough souls who fled the Adirondacks in October for the South sometimes now write back plaintively, "Send me an Adirondack wreath." For those for whom the Adirondack country is year-round home, it is a good season. With a crystal day that brings the distant snow-capped peaks clear, with a dry cold air that never seems as cold as the thermometer shows, with the ski tows busy, the rinks crowded, and the laughter of children all around, many a man will say that these are the best days of the year.

At the end of the month winter is firm on the land. For some, the woods are never more inviting, given, that is, the proper pair of high boots and a sturdy heart. The going can be rough in spots. Some people get out for the annual Christmas bird count; careful spotting shows about twenty species, including redpolls, crossbills, brown creepers, tree sparrows, and red-winged blackbirds. Others go into the woods for the sheer joy of walking. They cannot be traveled on skis or snowshoes; too many broken branches and trees lie just under the snow. They must be tramped on foot. That needs a sunny day, with the air as bright as the sunlight on the snow. The sunny day is important. On a gray day that threatens and often brings snow a man can easily wander aside, miss a turn or two, and come from the woods no more.

The winter woods, even the familiar parts, are a different world from the woods in summer. Landmarks are often gone. The stump where a turn to the right leads down to the lake is now snow-covered and is only one of the other snowy humps roundabout. The young birch thicket, a green wall in summer, is a spidery lattice across the sunset. The great spruces hang heavy with the snow on their limbs. Under them is perfect shelter, almost free of snow.

To the hiker plodding along it seems a deserted world, but whenever he comes to a clearing or upland meadow he sees at once that others have walked the same way and not long before. The precise, unhurried tracks of a fox cross the ridge, the footprints of someone who knew exactly where he was going and on what quiet murder. Near a raspberry copse a mingling of tracks can finally be read as those of two deer who pawed around for a time without concern as they nibbled at the tops of the briars. On the heavily crusted snow to one side are what seem to be large tracks of a huge animal, tracks a full twelve inches across. At first glance and at a second and third slightly more nervous glance, they could be bear tracks except that the bear must have been featherweight; nowhere have those fuzzy tracks broken through the crusted snow. The odd round tracks end suddenly; from them go the loping marks of a rabbit. Before he began to run he moved a jump at a time and his whole furry body, resting warm on the snow, made the large round marks. Deeper in the woods the neat clawed tracks of a bobcat end at a pine. Its trunk shows the fresh scratches of one who climbed to find shelter for the night. All too near, by a balsam, are the marks of a grouse. They end suddenly at a spot just below the cat's resting place. The snow is badly scarred, and dotted with a few feathers.

Although a man may walk miles through the winter woods and not see one moving thing, he leaves feeling that the woods are keenly alive. As he sees the tracks that cross and recross the cleared places, as he hears grouse rise from a thicket to one side, he comes to feel that there, under the pine, or there, under the low hemlocks, eyes are watching him. They watch on all sides, safe in the brush. They wait for the interloper to pass. They wait for winter silence to settle again over the solitude and the snow in their world wherein they can live a winter and a man cannot live a night.

Some people climb the mountains in winter. To those who like level ground and get slightly out of breath climbing out of an armchair, mountain climbing is something to read about, not to do. They will concede that on a summer day when the earth in its lower altitudes is hot and the peaks that reach into the cool blue promise a sure escape from a sultry world, climbing mountains may be attractive. It is something else again to sit down deliberately, plan, and gather equipment for climbing those same peaks in winter.

Each winter it is done by younger men from the Adirondack villages and by members of various college mountain-climbing clubs. On many a New Year's Eve a group spends the night atop Marcy in 35-below cold with its own unique New Year's party, which would seem a long way to go just to avoid wearing a paper hat in a more accessible night club.

For any who have climbed Adirondack peaks in summer, along well-marked trails, the winter world is a new one. A stand of young six-foot pines in summer may be an empty snow-covered flat in winter with the trees buried eight feet under. Summer waterfalls are winter ice walls. A fire must be built to melt snow for drinking water. Firewood may be hard to find if there is need or desire to stop overnight. A compass is a necessity; old trails and lumber roads may have vanished in snow-banks. The climbers move on skis with rawhide creepers or fur treads to prevent slipping. Some may use snowshoes. All wear snow goggles. The three- and four-hour ascents of summer now become six and eight, but the tedious descent is now only an hour and a half slide. On some of the climbs the Conservation Department keeps lean-tos stocked with food, blankets and, as an ominous note, toboggans to bring down any accidents. In summer the traffic up and down the peaks may be like a big city street. In winter nothing else alive appears except perhaps an astounded snowshoe rabbit.

Yet the reward of the climb must be great, for some people return to it each winter. What the winter world below looks like from atop that peak is something that only those hardy enough to make the climb ever know.

Verplanck Colvin once climbed Marcy on a winter day. He left a description of what he saw for those who will never see it. Now and then his ink got slightly purple. Of a winter afternoon on Marcy he wrote:

> We stand upon the highest land in New York. Frozen clouds drift slowly and wearily below. Away to the south and east in billows and billows of dappling silver, they extend to where the horizon joins with them in mingled brilliancy. The sun sinks slowly westward. Behind us, on each mountain side, are the deepening shadows of other mountains. The gorges begin to fill with unutterable gloom; now the sinking sun shakes from itself for one moment the haze and mist and covers our mountain with a burst of glory that makes it seem transfigured. All the frost-wreathed forest on the sun-side slopes bursts into sparkling light, each tree a weird Christmas tree, adorned with wondrous fantastic frost work. The sun descends amidst the clouds. Each white mountain peak gleams with faintest crimson. Then all is gray and chill and night.

As the old year ends in the Adirondack country the fields and slopes are white under the December moon and the world is still. Shining hillsides wall out the clatter of the world beyond.

January

In early January it snows. The nights are starlit, with the temperature well below zero. The climate may be changing but no Adirondack January has ever passed without sharp subzero temperatures. Some Adirondack villages almost take pride in being able to report bitter low temperatures; for years Owls Head, on the northern Blue Line, guarded jealously its reputation of being the icebox of the state. Boasting about how cold it was last night is an Adirondack winter sport. Let a man admit it was 15 degrees below on his back porch and his neighbor, a hundred yards away, reports a temperature of 20 below. A man really does not need a thermometer to be able to boast that he lives in the coldest place of all: he just needs a little advance notice of temperature reported from other places.

Cold as they may be, these are busy days for the lumbermen. Their trucks move back and forth along the narrow roads into the woods and bring out the winter's cut. These are idle days for the farmer, once the cows in the steaming barn have been milked; he may even turn to trapping or to working with the snowplows on the roads. In these days icicles hang long on the eaves. The snow may thaw a bit by day and free water drip, but at night everything is again frozen tight. In the woods deer begin to yard up in the balsam swamps. A hard winter and heavy snow, with an icy crust on top, can be brutal. Many an Adirondack farmer will put out a pile of hay in a back field for them.

These are the days when the evening grosbeaks begin to appear in large flocks at the feeding stations. They are the result of one of the most singular events in American ornithology, a widespread migration of a new species into a new habitat. All over the Northeastern states, on January mornings in 1890, various bird watchers glanced at the snowy world outside, looked again more closely, then rushed off to their bird books. They saw a new bird, seven to eight inches long, with a thick, parrotlike yellow-green beak. The male was most striking — a flying burst of yellow-gold and black with white patches in the wings. The female was grayer and less brightly colored. The birds traveled in blocks of ten and twenty, appearing usually only in the mornings. One of the very first reported was noticed at Lake George. They have been a common Adirondack winter visitor ever since, with more appearing one winter than another.

Against the Northern winter nothing seems quite so out of place. The jays and the woodpeckers, around all the time, belong with the landscape. But it is startling to see a flock of flying flaming gold come through the snow-crusted pines, seeming to wing their way between the small branches with marvelous skill as they scent from afar a feeding station that has sunflower seeds. They do not winter in the desolate woods but only around habitations that have feeding stations. With their heavy beaks, their tropical color, and their continuous chatter, quarrel, and argument over which bird was the first on the perch, they seem like a flock of jungle parrots that has lost its way, as out of place on snow and ice as orchids abloom of a sudden on the leafless birches.

The wary birds watch and wait in the trees near the feeder. When things seem safe one adventurous bird planes gracefully down to the food. In a few moments others follow, arguing like a convention of fishwives. When they stand quiet, which is not often, they have the grace of a great beauty dressed in cloth of gold. To some they are the best-named of birds — a living epitome of evening with the gold of sunset on their breasts and the dark of night in their wings. With spring they usually disappear, although a pair may stay around until July. They are particularly welcome on a cold January morning and many an Adirondack resident watches for them as for the coming of old and cherished friends. On a gray winter day no one could ask for greater beauty, whenever it comes, than the sudden flash of the winged gold against the snow.

In early January trailers pass along the roads, not the plush-lined ones of the summer campers, but shacks of wood or sheet metal, scarcely large enough to hold one man standing upright. They are on runners; sometimes they are drawn on them, at

other times on a frame and a pair of wheels. They are fishermen's shacks and they are headed out to various lakes, among
them the Saranacs and Champlain, to be put in place on the ice.
The smelt season is open and the most frostproof race of men
in the world is out after them.

The smelt is a native of some Adirondack waters; where it is
not a native it has gotten in by some sly maneuver, so that many
lakes now have them. It is a shiny silver fish, sometimes a foot
long, usually shorter. It is a company-loving fish. Where one is,
a hundred gather, as any ice fisher soon learns. It can be caught
without stealth or skill by simple hook and a bit of fish as bait.
Ice fishing is not the pleasant relaxed sport of summer. When
the shack is out on the frozen lake surface, the smelt fisher cuts
two holes in the ice, one on each side of the box or seat he will
use. He baits his hooks, lowers his lines, and starts jigging them
up and down.

If smelt are around the fisherman can fill a bag with large
frozen splinters. The fisherman is about as frozen as his catch.
A north wind on an Adirondack lake is something that nothing
can temper, whether the something is an oil heater, a more
prosaic wad of newspapers tucked inside the shirt, or the fluid
in a bottle. Some men sell their catch and pick up a little winter
cash, but the catch has fallen off in recent years and few are in
the business. Most fishermen are amateurs and lug the smelt
home to be fried whole, if at all.

Anyone who prefers a fireplace in winter to a shack on a lake
wonders why men will rise at dawn and go forth to freeze all
day, no matter whether the catch is one or a hundred smelt.
Winter fishing is scarcely a test of man's brain against fish brain,
as is the case with trout, for the smelt's brain probably does not
function in winter or he would be asleep in some deep hole like
any of the more intelligent fish. It is no test of brawn to yank
up a nine-inch smelt or even two at a time. One smelt fisherman,
sitting in a warm parlor while the odor of frying flapjacks and

ham came from the kitchen, explained it. "Smelt?" he said. "I don't know whether they taste different or not. You wouldn't ever catch me eating them. The finest thing about smelt fishing is the appetite it gives you for flapjacks. If I don't eat 'em, why do I go fishing? Mister, I like fishing. What else is there to catch up here in the Adirondacks this time of the year?"

Another winter activity on the lakes, ice cutting, is almost gone from the Adirondacks. It used to start toward the end of January. When the lake ice was fourteen inches thick or better, men with saws or long sharp pikes over their shoulders, and with teams of horses moved out of the lakes. Today the ice cutters have gone the way of the blacksmiths, the livery stables, and the sleigh-bell makers. It is cheaper now to bring ice up to the Adirondacks by freight car from the artificial ice makers downstate.

In a usual year the zero cold breaks without notice in mid-January. It is even warm. The sun is bright and the wind is from the south. The snow on the ground may be a foot deep, but by the end of the day it has shrunk. Rosebushes buried for weeks stick out like stiff prongs from the white surface of the garden. The high mounds of white in the woods turn back to gray rock. That night it rains and the snow slides off the roofs in jolting thunderclaps.

It is a new world in the morning and a wet one, with water running down every hillside, water in the road ruts, black water on the ice of the lakes. Patches of brown are in the meadows. The pile of dried fern fronds, the whole debris of autumn and of the death of the year is shamelessly exposed. The ski slopes are rocky hillsides; skis stand in the corner as useless as in July. More rain follows. The whole ground is brown, with only a rare patch of white at the edge of the woods.

This is the January thaw, as much a part of the cycle of the year as the seasons. It is regularly expected and even welcomed as a breathing space in the middle of a long winter. Thaws come in other months but go unnoticed. Rather than missing a year, thaws have been turning up twice in January in recent years and in all the other winter months as well. The thaw may hang around for a few days or even a week.

After a few days, the south wind veers to the north. A first few flakes of snow fly in the air. In an hour the earth is white again. Gone are rocks, fern fronds, plants, patches in the woods and open garden. Once again the temperature falls. The sun can do little in the chilly air. The thaw has been and gone but from it a man can take hope. It shows that, in spite of the way he feels at the end of January in the Adirondacks, the snow and the winter are not eternal. The garden and woods are not to be forever buried. The winter can be licked for good. All it takes is a few warm nights, a warm wind, a warm rain. And April.

February

It snows and snows, perhaps no great quantity at any time but always enough to keep the ground white with six inches to a foot of snow. Back in the woods the snow is piled four to five feet deep. February is the coldest month of the year, with the lowest temperatures. Mornings with 25 below are not scarce.

The deep cold of the nights sets the trees to cracking, to break the winter quiet. As the ice on the lakes reaches its greatest thickness the air trapped underneath will sometimes boom in the night. On the hills skiers are out early and late. Icicles lengthen. Static electricity inside the house crackles whenever metal is touched. Days may be a bit brighter, the sky bluer, the sunsets more purple. An occasional belated "January thaw" may turn up. Yet change comes steadily, if only in the earlier dawn, the later sunset. Lumbermen stop cutting. All effort is spent now on getting the logs out of the woods before the roads turn soft in March. Young fawns are born in the deep woods. Young bears are born but the mother goes right back to sleep. The sap begins to run in the maples. The branches of the blueberry bushes are a deep crimson against the white snow. People eager for a touch of spring go to the woods and bring in twisted branches of witchhobble, heavy with buds. Its odd white blossoms soon open in the heat of the house. If a chance rain washes the snow from a bit of the garden, iris shoots, primrose shoots, and the pale sheaths of daffodils show beneath the dead wreckage of last year's flowering. Snow soon hides them.

In mid-February some people go outdoors on a restless quest to seek some living proof that winter is not forever. It is not on the lake, where the unchanging ice thickens with each cold night. It is not in the drab and dirty woods, where wind-ripped branches lie at the base of the trees. As a man walks across the green meadow he finds no sign on the horizon or on the hills. Then, on the ground, the sign he seeks appears.

On the field, where clumps of grass stick awkwardly from the snow, a flock of birds walks about nervously, as preoccupied as a group of ladies late for a matinee. They are chocolate-brown birds, a little larger than sparrows, gray-white on the breast with a white bar above the eyes. Most surprising, although they can be seen only close up, are two black tufts like horns on their heads. A close look shows a long straight claw protruding on the back of each leg, the "larkspurs." The birds fuss about in the meadow looking for seeds. If a man comes too close they will take off in a flock, fly a short way, and quickly settle down to more important things. They are always on the ground or on the wing, never on trees or on bushes.

They are the prairie horned larks, the first of the migrant birds to return. They come North long before the snow has gone. After a winter in Louisiana, Georgia, and Florida, they beat the bluebirds by a few weeks and the human birds in trailers by two months. They come with the air of having work to do and wanting to be at it. Once North, they ignore the snow and get right to nest building. They pick some spot where the snow has melted and build their nests on the ground. If new snow comes before the mother has started to sit on the eggs and buries the nest, the birds wait a few days and start a new nest. There is an unholy haste about these birds; before they head South in autumn they may raise three and perhaps four broods of young. They seem dedicated to one end, to try to populate the earth with prairie horned larks.

A lucky man who happens on the breeding ground of a pair of larks may see them at their avocation, of carrying their song to the skies. As music it doesn't amount to much, but the manner of singing is something to make anyone forget that some weeks of winter and perhaps hard winter are still left in the land. The song may be sung on fence post or rock. More often, the horned lark, like the European skylark, must take his song skyward, rising high overhead, singing the while, higher and higher, like a rocket filled with song that mounts to burst at the apex of its flight. Faster than sound, the birds drop swift and silent to earth, to gain strength for another flight and another shower of music on the air.

So the winter-wearied man finds his sign as the larks rise high in the Adirondack sky and cry to the waxing sun that winter is not forever, either in the world of man or in the world of busy birds. And people say, as they see their woodpile almost empty, as they weary of bundling up, as they see the woods still dead and little life anywhere, "It can't be long now."

March

But it is. March means a dozen promises of warmth, and winter's end betrayed by nightfall as the temperature sinks low again. How so much mischief and disappointment and general orneriness can be put into thirty-one days is hard to understand.

March days get into men's moods. If political scraps have

been simmering in the villages, and most villages have them, they boil in March. Neighborhood quarrels, parental arguments, schoolroom spats turn up more frequently. If young married couples have been running into squalls, this is the month they can break into tempest. This is the month farmers walk restlessly a dozen times a day to the barn to check on what they checked on an hour before and spend more than one evening figuring if it wouldn't be smart to sell the farm. Nothing's really wrong with politician, family, parent, child, bride, farmer, or farm. It's only March. This is the month when the smart people, at least those who are solvent, try to get out of town to the South and meet the spring coming North.

In March a man congratulates himself on having come through the winter without a cold and thereupon comes down with the worst in three years. March is the month when a man figures he can get by without another tank of fuel oil and thus spare the budget. Along comes subzero cold and here's the fuel-oil truck and there goes the budget. As lovely a morning as the year brings can turn up, with a soft south wind, with the sound and sign of moist earth and of frost leaving the ground. By noon it has become a howling winter day, with snow flying, cars skidding, and drifts piled up in the garden where just four hours before flower shoots were showing a first fresh green.

By day the roads run water but at night are frozen hard again. The back roads have icy ruts that can slip a car over to the ditch in a twinkling. Mud covers sidewalks and street. A driver, innocent of the rides of March, can go along happily with his window open, to get a tidal wave in his face from a passing car. The mud is tracked into the house by small fry and onto living-room rugs. The children mill around, their skis and skates useless in the mud; every indoor activity has been tried a hundred times and all are boring.

The sun comes out bright again. Temperatures stay above freezing for a night and a man asks hopefully, "Now?" He need not ask. The next day everything is frozen tight again. New icicles form on the roof, new snow falls. Again the cry of March in the Adirondacks rises: "How long, how long?"

Village unemployment rolls are now at their highest. The number of visitors on the streets is zero. Heavily loaded lumber trucks come highballing along the roads, bringing the winter cut out as fast as possible, sometimes driving around the clock, coming through lonely back roads at 3 A.M., skidding down ice-covered hills with ten tons of big logs aboard. A skid and an overturned truck and all the work of loading has to be done again, to say nothing of an injured driver in the hospital.

If the Conservation Department has declared an open season beaver trappers head for the dams in the backwoods. Rabbit season has closed. Winter fishing is over as the lake ice becomes treacherous in the succession of warm and cold days. Fishermen bring out their trout equipment, clean it, repair it, clean it again. A bright afternoon may even lure them outdoors to practice a few casts, but a shift in the clouds can bring sudden snow and they retreat to the fire indoors, asking, "How long?" Frost leaves the ground, but nothing can be done in the resulting mud in farm land or garden. Tomatoes are started in seed flats near the kitchen stove. On a rare warm day, with the temperature near fifty, house plants may be set outdoors for a few hours. The wind shifts, plants come indoors, the sky darkens, and it snows, and all that is left is to cry "How long?"

March brings one new activity and one cheerful note. Adirondack people watch the weather closely in the first weeks, or even at the end of February, waiting for the first sign of "sugar weather," bright sunny days to set the sap running fast in the maples, and cold crisp nights. Most years have them, but sugaring has been spoiled or shortened many a time by a March that stays cold, sleety, and sunless until it is too late to make decent syrup.

The Adirondack country has a large lore about maple tapping. The first hole each year should be breast-high on the south side of the tree, and if a second hole is made later in the season that goes on the north. The largest flow is obtained by tapping on the side bearing the most branches or over the largest root. The richest sap comes from the layer near the bark; deeper bores give less syrup and of darker color and less value.

When sugaring time comes, from Deer River to Chateaugay, from Poke O'Moonshine to the Kayaderosseras, men work fast. A few people make sugaring a big business; they may have as many as three thousand trees in their sugar bush, pipes to run the sap down from the grove to the evaporators, and gauges and gadgets to tell just when the sap has boiled down enough and is fit for syrup and for sugar. The average Adirondack farmer who has a few trees knows little of this industry. He looks on them not as a source for profit but for pleasure. As long as he has the strength to carry the sap buckets to the boiler he knows that he will not have to eat "pancake syrup" that is 99 per cent cane sugar or glucose with a touch of artificial maple flavor added. He usually makes enough syrup for his own family, but if the sap runs well he may have a few gallons to give to friends.

His is hand labor. By hand he bores the holes in the trees, inserts the metal spouts, and hangs the buckets. Twice a day he collects the thin, watery sap, and, in pails that hang over a yoke on his shoulders, he lugs it to a shallow pan over a wood fire. There it boils and the room fills with a steam that has a cottony flavor. Never must that fire go out, day or night, as it boils down the forty gallons of sap for every gallon of syrup. The farmer knows when the syrup is thick enough, not by gauge or gadget, but by holding it to the light as his grandfather did, by testing it on snow where the thin liquid crackles gold, or, if he has a real genius for sugar making, just by the way it smells.

Once sugaring time was a time for celebration. The last day

of sugaring saw dancing and singing at the sugar house and, of course, sampling of the newly made sugar. Now and then "snow parties" do take place these days, with singing and dancing in the kitchen by the stove and the chief point of the party, eating "wax on snow." A snow party needs only neighbors, a Sunday-school class, or a class from a rural school, some pails and buckets filled with snow, and a kettle of thickening sap boiling on the kitchen range. The routine is simple. The guests take a soup plate filled with snow, pour a few tablespoons of hot syrup over it, and watch it cool and harden to taffy. Then the mass is rolled up on a fork and eaten. That is a sweet dish. The Adirondack people — and nothing better proves their hardiness — add two unchanging items to a snow party: salted crackers and sour pickles. A party of twenty can put away a couple of gallons of syrup, a gallon of pickles, and pound after pound of crackers in one evening.

Sugaring time is usually over by March 20 and still the winter may hold. If a man looks to the hills he will see the first of a pink film spreading over the distant ones. The maple branches, seen against the sky, show swelling buds. The first robins are on the soggy lawns, the first crows are calling over the sodden fields. Rain water stands in puddles on the lake ice. Slogging along in mud, in the stronger sunlight, a man asks as he looks up in the clear-washed sky, "How long?" Then it snows. Standing at his window and considering a winter world from which all promise of freedom has been snatched away, a man can wish desperately, "If only the wind would shift to the south!"

Another cold day rises. Noon is bright but frosty. The sunset is muted and gray and heavy clouds roll in from the west. The thermometer starts down. At dusk it stops well above zero. The barometer falls slowly. Suddenly the windows on the south side of the house begin to rattle in a fresh breeze. Over the woods comes the quiet sigh of freshening wind. Rain begins to trickle on the window panes. If a man goes outdoors for a moment he can feel something new, fresh, and alive in the washed air. Through the night comes a new sound, of water dripping from the eaves, water running over the icebound land. For the first time in weeks the night promises a temperature above freezing and rain that will not slacken. As a man opens the windows and feels a touch of comparative warmth in the air he can say triumphantly, "South wind!" He may even feel he's helped to bring it, just by watching and hoping.

In a day or so the sheet of snow in the woods and the remnants in the fields begin to shrink, first over the banks and slopes, then under the heavy trees and finally in the open places. The hummock of snow on the ridge turns out to be a forgotten stump, a rock, or a large pine downed by the winter wind. The woods look messy and untidy, full of the raw scars of winter. The leaves of last season still hang on the beech. The tips of the cedars are brown with winterkill, but a May breeze will brush that off. Although the world around is a drab world, on the distant mountain slopes the winter black of the spruces and pines lighten into a first green, and over the stand of birch and alder thickets there is the first misty pink of life in the branches. The spruce buds, ready since last August, are fat and their sheaths are almost broken through. Over the whole land is new odor, the clean fresh smell of raw earth.

The snow is off the lake ice and rain ripples the puddles. In a few places the lakes are "making water" — rifts show in the ice where there is current underneath. The open water flashes in the sun and the colder water sinks to the bottom. The brooks are broken loose again and the water rushes by the ice that may still overhang the banks.

The silence of winter is gone. There is sound everywhere, wet gurgling sound, of water running from field and woods, in roadway gutters, from every slope, down every hill. Water gushes from fields, from woods, and from springs that will be dry long before June. Water oozes from the ground as the frost comes out, and the earth is a muddy place. One sound is still missing, of the lakes lapping at their shores, but that will soon be heard. More sun and more rain, and lake ice, slowly thinning, will darken to a dirty gray then change to a thin skin of long ice crystals that will rise and fall on the windswept water like a rubber boat. The sharp wind of a late April day will finish the job and free the water. Patches of ice will break off and move fast across the lake, to end on the shore in a continuous tinkle of breaking crystals. The lakes will be blue and windtossed once again.

No people walk the woods these days. The lumbermen are gone, their tote roads a mass of mud. In the remote hills the bears waken from sleep and move out to the open glades with their cubs, nuzzling in the brown grass for a trace of anything fresh and green. Deer began to move from the balsam swamps up the slopes, nibbling at the hemlocks as they pass. The fawns that floundered in a snowy world can move free now — those that survived February — and bound ahead through the leafless brush and the stands of maple whips. The sounds of the lonely world are wet sounds, of soggy squashy mud, but high overhead the crows cry and the blue jays call from the old maples. Only on the distant shining peaks is the world unchanged. The snow and ice will stay there through May.

So, hour by hour, the woods come again to life. The change is not a sudden one, worked overnight as by the rise of one great curtain. Rather, a hundred voile curtains mask what is to be and rise one at a time to reveal just a bit more of what is to come. What they reveal is the coming of one of the miracles of the land — an Adirondack spring.

And many a man will say, gratefully, that these are the best days of the Adirondack year.

►§ *Afterword*

Thirteen years have passed since *Adirondack Country* was first published, an interval that has not essentially altered the quality of life in the Adirondacks as described by William Chapman White. Yet these years have brought inevitable change to the Adirondack community. Trudeau Sanatorium has closed. An entire Adirondack town has been moved to a new location. The 1967 New York State Constitutional Convention has intensified the age-old debate over two of the topics my husband selected as the running themes of his book. One is "the ever widening use of the region as a vacation area." The other concerns "the acute problems that have arisen in considering the future of the woods" that he loved so dearly and wrote of with such beauty.

My husband would surely have wanted to incorporate such changes in a new edition, but they posed a problem during the planning of this republication. Should we violate the integrity of his text by adding facts and figures he could not have known? Or might there be some other way of including this new information? After much thought, we decided on this afterword in hopes that it would inform the reader and at the same time disarm the critic, by preserving intact a text that many have come to love.

This section, then, will present summaries of new material—

additions I believe my husband would have made himself. Some will be brief, others longer, as dictated by context. Some will convey certain of his opinions that bear as directly on the present and the future as on the past of more than a decade ago, when he expressed them himself.

ADIRONDACK STATE PARK

The present acreage in the park (first mentioned on page 8) is 5,693,500. Of this, 3,450,330 acres are privately owned and surround in a freeform patchwork the 2,243,170 acres of the forest preserve that are owned by the people of New York State. Over the years $17,000,000 (page 222) has been made available, either by bond issue or legislative appropriation, for the land added to the state holdings.

ADIRONDACK CAMPS AND HOTELS

Although the members of many of the same families still return annually to the same summer camps, almost every year since 1954 has seen the closing of one or more of the Adirondack landmarks. Nehasane (page 146), the camp first owned by Dr. Seward Webb, has been inherited and is occupied by a grandson. But its unusual arrangement with the New York Central was terminated and its unique railroad station made obsolete when all passenger service on the Adirondack Division was discontinued in 1965. Access now is only by road out of Long Lake. Following the death in 1958 of its founder, Sherwood Kains, Deerwood-Adirondack Music School (page 233) was purchased by George Bissell to be added to the woodland of his neighboring estate.

Sagamore Lodge (page 146) was given to Syracuse University, which uses it as a student-faculty center and a site for national and international conferences. Junior and senior reading courses are also conducted at Sagamore with the purpose of improving the study skills of potential college students. The university also owns and in the same manner operates other gift properties, among them Pine Brook, on Eagle Island, and Meadowbrook, on Blue Mountain Lake. Probably the most substantial of the acquisitions has been 12,000 acres of Brandreth's 22,000-acre tract. The Brandreth heirs have retained 10,000 acres, including hunting lodges maintained on the lake shore by the individual families, and have reserved hunting and fishing privileges for themselves and their guests. Syracuse University timbers the rest for the benefit of its endowment fund. The university also owns Limekiln at Inlet, a timbered 2,000-acre tract given by the Finch Pruyn Lumber Company of Glens Falls. The university is holding this tract until the regrowth of timber can produce another crop.

Camp Intermission on Lake Colby, originally the property of the late William and Emma Morris (page 180), was bought by the State of New York in 1961 and is now the Conservation Education Camp and Conference Center. The acquisition of Camp Intermission served a threefold purpose: it provided public access from a highway to a large tract of adjoining state land along the shore of a lovely, unspoiled lake (pages 263–4); the main building is used by the Conservation Department as a conference center; and over a span of ten weeks every summer, it accommodates, in giant lean-tos built by the state, a total of four hundred boys. Sponsored by their home communities, they take part in outdoor recreation and study the ecology of the Adirondack region.

The era of the great Adirondack hotels (page 233) closed officially in 1962 when Saranac Inn went under the auctioneer's hammer, despite several attempts at restoring it in previous years. The best-preserved of the lake-shore cottages instantly sold at excellent prices, but the main building, a sprawling, white-shingled structure, has reverted to the auctioneer and survives as a shabby reminder of the glamorous past. Splendid white pines that graced the ground have been timbered. The inn's famous golf course was reprieved from dissection into building lots by Harry S. Littman, the owner of a summer cottage on Upper Saranac Lake, who bought it and now operates it as a golf course.

Lake Clear Inn (page 233), where the porch rockers rocked, in 1963 met a fate similar to Saranac Inn's, but, being on a more modest scale, it shows greater promise of becoming a permanent cottage colony.

ADIRONDACK AMUSEMENT CENTERS, MUSEUMS, GUIDE BOATS

Although Old MacDonald's Farm (described on page 236) has withered, Santa's Workshop at North Pole in Wilmington and Frontier Town north of Schroon Lake continue to be hardy perennials in the North Country's amusement garden. Others have sprung up and flourished: Land of Make Believe at Upper Jay; Story Town at Lake George; Enchanted Forest at Old Forge. Northwest of Lake Placid, the Home of 1,000 Animals imposes an enlarged, gaudily decorated façade across one of the otherwise most inspiring approaches to Whiteface Mountain.

Among this miscellany the unpretentious charm of the Adirondack Center Museum at Elizabethtown and the flawless, colorful authenticity of the Adirondack Museum at Blue Mountain Lake are pure gems. Noteworthy too is the fact that the Adirondack Museum, opened in 1956, has been obliged to enlarge parking facilities in two successive years without feeling the need of distributing stickers and bumper cards. The museum is sponsored by the Adirondack Historical Society and is also guided by the society's president, Harold K. Hochschild (page 229). As part of an ever expanding and imaginative program, a new boat building was erected on the museum's splendid site overlooking Blue Mountain Lake. Famous old crafts of the Adirondack waterways are now on display, including several variations of the celebrated Adirondack guide boat (page 158). Purists may differ over who created the first guide boat, but certainly the Hanmer model as developed by Theodore Hanmer and his son Willard has gone into Adirondack history. Theodore died in 1957 at the brisk old age of ninety-seven. With the death of the son in 1963, Hanmer guide boats became collector's items. At a recent auction of one of the old camps, a Hanmer boat went to Thomas I. Parks, a summer resident of Rainbow Lake—who was delighted with his "bargain"—for $1,500.

The Hanmer boat shop on Algonquin Avenue in Saranac Lake was sold in 1964 to Carl Hathaway, who plans eventually to specialize in Adirondack guide boats but for the present engages largely in boat repair.

LUMBERING AND TUPPER LAKE

Except on small jobs, tractors have totally displaced the valiant lumber-camp horse teams (page 225). Loggers no longer, they nevertheless still compete in stoneboat-pulling contests at Woodsman's Field Day, now held alternately at Tupper Lake and Boonville (page 226). This spectacular annual competition is just about all that persists from the colorful days; the mechanized machinery that retired the camp horses also made the lumber camps obsolete. Today's lumberjack usually commutes to his job in his own automobile over roads gutted out of privately owned tracts by bulldozers less heroic but mightier than Paul Bunyan.

Although Tupper Lake has lost the lusty, payday atmosphere of a lumberjack town, its factories still turn out plentiful supplies of bobbins, veneer panels, and wooden tableware. The largest, the Oval Wood Dish Company, was sold in 1964 to

Adirondack Plywood, which has since become an affiliate of the national U.S. Plywood Company and maintains a larger payroll than its predecessor.

But the main industry of Tupper Lake is still Sunmount, the former veterans hospital that my husband wrote of on page 177. When the introduction of chemotherapy reduced the need for institutionalized care for the tuberculous, Sunmount shut down. Ownership has since been transferred to New York State for the operation of a school for retarded children. Now staffed largely by local people, Sunmount is more than ever a boon to Tupper Lake economy.

CONSERVATION DEPARTMENT

The New York State Conservation Department, still staffed by "a magnificent corps of career men, secure in civil service" (page 243), is split by an official dilemma. It has a mandate from the state to administer the forest preserve under the strictest interpretation of "Forever Wild," Article XIV of the constitution; over the years it has developed a policy for multiple use of the preserve, but thus far has been unable to implement much of it because it is inconsistent with the wilderness concept. Within the ranks, as in 1954, dedicated men still believe the preserve's finest future depends upon the precise retention of Article XIV, with decisions rendered by the Attorney General of New York State as need arises to round out policy (also page 243). Others fully as dedicated would like the amendment relaxed in varying degrees to give the department a freer hand (page 239).

Some of the Conservation Department's proposals have met with opposition in the past on the basis that they gave tighter protection to approximately one-third of the preserve as pure wilderness, and opened two-thirds to more intensive recreation and timbering for sale as well as the improvement of deer habitat. In the years since *Adirondack Country* was written, some of the department's rulings (on the use of motorized vehicles within the preserve, the opening and closing of certain roads, and a study initiated in 1965 by former Commissioner Harold G. Wilm) have been withdrawn. The experiment that seemed useful in 1954 of spraying whole areas with DDT from planes (page 31) had to be discontinued as deleterious to wildlife. The department has advocated regional timbered browse areas to increase the deer herd, antlerless seasons, and other extra regulations to keep the population under control. Yet it has never been obliged to restock deer in any region (page 228), and according to one contemporary authority, the highest incidence of illegal killing has occurred in a certain experimental timbered deer yard. Moreover, it has been said that more than fifty per cent of the deer yards in the Adirondacks are on private land and would also require regulation.

For the nonhunter, the resolution of these widely divergent and often heated opinions is best left to the experts. For the hunter, as well as the deer, the latest census in the central Adirondack region seemed to compare favorably with the figures my husband enumerated on page 29: the population in 1959 was calculated at fifty-eight thousand. In recent seasons, about seventeen thousand a year have been killed legally, representing one deer to every eighth hunter.

Perhaps the department's greatest seeming contradiction (mentioned on page 231) is still its administration of the public camp sites. Some people most concerned over the "illegality" of the camps criticize them as competing unfairly with local motels. Others say this is irrelevant; those who choose to camp by a lake are not likely to have either the means or the inclination to vacation elsewhere. In any case, the sites were originally sanctioned by the Attorney General as an emergency measure growing out of the depression of the 1920's, and as my husband pointed out (also on page 231) were deemed consistent with the people's ownership of a recreation area. They have become so firmly rooted and genuinely enjoyed that they must be accepted as permanent features of Adirondack life. The present increased use of the camp sites, as compared with the statistics on page 231, indicate that in the summer of 1966 462,416 persons spent 1,658,511 camper days on forty-two camp sites and separate camping places. Two new campgrounds will be opened in 1967: at Ausable Point, ten miles south of Plattsburgh, and at Moreau Lake in Saratoga County. The present fee for a camping permit covering six persons is $1.50 per night.

PAUL SMITH'S

The standard quip in 1946, when Paul Smith's opened a college (page 135), was: "What does a student need to enter Paul Smith's? Four hundred dollars." This no longer applies. Standards as well as tuition fees have climbed. Under the presidency of Dr. Chester L. Buxton, who assumed the office in 1948, Paul Smith's College has reached an enrollment of almost one thousand, and participates actively in the life of nearby Saranac Lake. Surviving the destruction by fire of several old buildings inherited from the old hotel premises it originally occupied, the college has erected dormitories, study halls, and a library on campus. An adjacent camp as well as a vacated sanatorium have been annexed. A course in liberal arts was added to the curriculum, and in 1961 the Saranac Lake Hotel was bought to be operated as a laboratory of practical experience for students in the department of hotel management. Securely established by 1966, the college sold the Paul Smith's Electric Power and Railroad Company (page 134), which it controlled, to the Niagara Mohawk Company, which now supplies electric power to the Saranac Lake area.

THE NORTHWAY

The final section of the Northway, linking Pottersville to Keeseville and the Canadian border and opening in the spring of 1967, is an expertly engineered facsimile of all others conforming to interstate highway specifications. Admittedly it opens a stretch of magnificent landscape to the motorist who rushes by at thruway speed; one wonders now how deeply it would have penetrated the Wilderness but for the voices raised against it (page 245). The very fact that this highway exists is now used as a testament against the vigilance of "Forever Wilders." But the far more important consideration is that the overwhelming majority wanted it and voted for it. The Northway has materialized despite opposition, even though the objections to it were based on the valid reasoning of the conservationists. Moreover, the project was argued openly during two consecutive terms of the legislature, a procedure now required before any proposed amendment can be brought to the voters. As a result of this informed and aboveboard discussion, all the problems were weighed, and a route was selected that did the least damage to the Forest Preserve.

TAHAWUS

In 1962 one of the most extraordinary processions in Adirondack history passed over the road from Tahawus to Newcomb, thirteen miles away. The complete town (page 235) was moved from the mine site operated by the National Lead Corporation, in order to open its vacated tract to fresh mining operations.

Preparations for the transfer began in June of 1962, when two Syracuse construction companies gouged the new townsite out of the side of a mountain on the outskirts of Newcomb. Foundations were constructed, power lines and water pipes were laid, and six and a half miles of streets were surveyed.

Then the work really began. Tahawus homes were jacked up and hoisted onto giant prime movers: tractors with ninety-foot beams. Houses too large to be moved safely were sawed in half. A school, a church, and a store were trundled over the roads. In stately procession there followed—with furnishings intact—seventy-two single houses, fifteen duplexes, and six apartment buildings (some three-storied) for eight to twelve families. About one hundred families were involved, and they were housed in rotation in an unmovable cement apartment building large enough to accommodate twenty families.

Three young Adirondack men, Wayne, Donald, and Ernest Fleury, who supervised the mammoth exodus, boasted later that every family had been reinstalled by Christmas and all the finishing touches completed by the following July.

If an old Adirondack guide had told the story, no one would have believed him.

TRUDEAU SANATORIUM AND SARANAC LAKE

Faced with a declining patient census due to the successful drug therapy of tuberculosis to which its research had contributed, Trudeau Sanatorium (first mentioned on page 170) closed its world-famed gates in 1954: "a victim of its own success." In the following years, the Saranac Lake Rehabilitation Guild (page 176), also affected by the introduction of "miracle drugs," was forced to drop all of its courses except the training of X-ray technicians for the United States Public Health Service. The continuing downward trend that resulted in the closing of Sunmount also terminated Stoneywold and Gabriels Sanatoriums and all but one of the large state-owned hospital units at Ray Brook.

Each closing was a shock to the economy of Saranac Lake and motivated renewed efforts to draw industry to the area. The modest plant built in 1953 by a civic-minded local corporation (page 177) was taken over by a dress factory that is still in operation. But the hope that this beginning would attract others has not yet materialized.

A sense of relief set in when Trudeau's empty and idle buildings were sold in 1957 to the American Management Association. But that good news was soon dissipated by rumors that the Trudeau Foundation might move to downstate installations. Grim enough, the prospect darkened when Saranac Lake's enforced reliance on the tourist trade was blighted by a succession of snowless winters and summers spent under overcast skies.

After months of deliberation, the trustees of the Trudeau Foundation finally announced their intention to locate the newly formed Trudeau Institute on a high hill overlooking Lower Saranac Lake. Skillfully and with great concern, the first cure cottage, "Little Red" (page 170), and Borglum's statue of Dr. Edward Livingston Trudeau (page 165) were transported across town to the new bases that had been prepared.

The dedication ceremonies on August 1, 1964, generated a wave of optimism that seems to have been justified. An expanding research program has added new doctors and scientists to a community always proud of its distinguished medical men (page 178) and has helped to revive the cosmopolitan atmosphere that once prevailed.

Edward Livingston Trudeau's second son, Dr. Francis B. Trudeau (page 172), carried on his father's work until 1956, when his death passed the Trudeau heritage on to his son, another Dr. Francis B. Trudeau. President of the Trudeau Institute, he is also a practicing physician with his office in the original Trudeau house on Main Street, Saranac Lake.

The purposes of the Trudeau Institute today are to provide space in which scientists working under grants and fellowships may pursue research into the causes, nature, prevention, and treatment of tuberculosis and other respiratory diseases. In the words of a recent brochure: "When, in the pioneering spirit, one dream is fulfilled, another takes its place, and the concept of experiment for the welfare of mankind has been enlarged."

A new Saranac Lake General Hospital (page 178) has risen on the shore of Lake Colby, largely through the generosity of one summer resident, Edmond Guggenheim, and the family of a native of the Adirondacks, the late James Latour. Structural additions to the Saranac Lake Free Library are nearing completion, one of them to provide appropriate housing for the superb collection of Adirondackana owned by the library.

In addition to the Trudeau Institute, the expanded patient care, research, and summer seminars at the Will Rogers Hospital (page 176) and O'Donnell Memorial Research Laboratory give promise of restoring Saranac Lake to its former prestige in the medical world. Further confidence has been stimulated by the announcement that a two-county (Franklin and Essex) North Country College will open in Saranac Lake in the fall of 1968.

And the brooding beauty of the Trudeau bronze, a lasting symbol of faith and hope, now and permanently, it may be assumed, faces the full sweep of an Adirondack lake and the hills beyond.

JOINT LEGISLATIVE COMMITTEE
ON NATURAL RESOURCES

On page 244 William Chapman White commented on the 1953 Report of the Joint Legislative Committee, under the chairmanship of Senator Wheeler Milmoe, indicating it as the type of suggestion that might be forthcoming at some later date. He believed then that if the committee's recommendations were ever adopted, "little of the relative wilderness charm of the [Adirondack] region, its greatest asset, would be left."

By 1966, Assemblyman Louis Wolfe had replaced Senator Milmoe as chairman, as well as his own immediate predecessor, Senator R. Watson Pomeroy. As with all matters touching upon "Forever Wild," the committee's 1966 Report was controversial. Half of the committee, a so-called majority headed by Assemblyman Louis Wolfe, advocated a zoning policy so drastic as to call for legislative amendment. The other half of the committee, named as the minority and headed by Watson Pomeroy, disagreed categorically.

The "majority" advocated zoning the preserve into three areas, with only thirty per cent—the high-peak area—designated as wilderness, but excluding from that protection two beautiful wild mountain ranges close to Saranac Lake and Lake Placid. For the remaining seventy per cent (Zones 2 and 3) the "majority" recommended more intensive recreation, the management of woods and game; the harvesting of timber for profit; and— something William Chapman White could not have dreamed of—"the construction of restaurants at the ends of wilderness trails."

Watson Pomeroy, the chief spokesman for the "minority," was a ten-year member of the committee and for four of those years its chairman. During that period, in consultation with the Conservation Department, Senator Pomeroy had conducted a detailed study of the forest preserve. The findings were made public at three question-and-answer meetings held in the early 1960's at Indian Lake, Saranac Lake, and Utica. At those meetings Senator Pomeroy met not only with the opposition of "Forever Wilders" (to whom the prime uses of the preserve were as a watershed, a natural laboratory, and a haven from the mechanized world) but also from those who believed that the preserve should be administered as an economic resource for the benefit of the Adirondack towns. Both groups, moreover, were suspicious of Senator Pomeroy's proposed "Wilderness Bill" because it concerned only the high-peak area, and advanced no recommendations for the remaining two-thirds of the Adirondack Wilderness.

The study continued, and resulted in recommendations—unanimously agreed upon—which were published in Senator Pomeroy's Minority Report of 1963 and carried over and strengthened in 1966. These urged that Article XIV be continued as fundamental policy and that any future development of public recreational facilities be conducted consistently with the preservation of natural conditions outside of designated Wilderness areas. The report also recommended banning the use of motorized equipment within Wilderness areas, and proposed further study before any enactment of policy on game management. It found the economic harvesting of timber inconsistent "with the Wilderness type recreation which is the attraction of the Preserve to the great number of people who enjoy it."

Many people may be happy to know that R. Watson Pomeroy, representing the 38th District, is a delegate to the constitutional convention and a member of its Committee on Natural Resources and Agriculture.

"FOREVER WILD" AND THE CONSTITUTIONAL CONVENTION

Perhaps the greatest change that has occurred in the Adirondack country since William Chapman White's book was first published has been not in the battle over the Wilderness but in the current attitudes of the contestants. Debates in the past, ridden with invective (page 239), have raged over single issues— a power dam, another ski run, a six-lane highway. The present conflict, at least in its preliminary stage, is calmer, more legalistic, and aimed at many objectives and the very structure of Article XIV itself. Shall it be retained precisely, modified to protect the high-peak area only, or altogether written out of the new constitution? Shall it be a broad statement of the principles contained in Sections 1 and 4, with administrative details incorporated in a separate document? Shall the guardianship of all, or any part, of the Wilderness be placed within the Conservation Department (page 242) or given over to the legislature (page 244)?

In the months ahead strong pressures will be exerted on the delegates. The antagonists may be expected to mobilize, as they have in the past (pages 222–3). On one side will be the pulp and paper industries, lumber and sawmill operators, manufacturers of motorized equipment (including the fast-selling snowmobile), schools of forestry, the Adirondack Park Association, some members of the Joint Legislative Committee, and perhaps even the Conservation Department seeking a freer hand in forest management. On the other side will be protectionist groups—the New York State Conservation Council, the Conservation Forum, the Adirondack Mountain Club, and others. Many have joined a common front with the Constitutional Council for the Forest Preserve to advocate the verbatim retention of Sections 1 and 4 of Article XIV. These are respectively the amendment itself and the legal provision for restraint of violations.

The arguments employed by both sides need not be discussed here; they have been thoughtfully weighed in the preceding pages of William Chapman White's book. Between the two camps, those unallied with either faction may vote, as they have in the past, to determine the outcome. As my husband wrote, "It is their woods. It should remain so."

R. M. W.
Saranac Lake, New York

May 1, 1967

Postscript

Turbulent years have passed since the convening of the 1967 New York State Constitutional Convention augured a threat (p. 323) to the retention of Article XIV, "Forever Wild." During these years, as my husband predicted, the age-old battle has spread from the state-owned Forest Preserve to the remaining privately owned acres within the Adirondack Park.

On July 29, 1967, as the delegates seated in Albany were mulling over recommendations to weaken the protection of Article XIV, they were shocked out of their contemplation by a news release detailing a plan advanced by Laurance Rockefeller. He proposed the transformation of 1.72 million acres of state-owned Preserve and 600,000 acres of privately owned land into a national park. Private tracts could be acquired by gift, purchase, or, if need be, condemnation.

The explosion of Laurance Rockefeller's bombshell brought about a situation that no student of Adirondack history would have thought possible: the bringing together of every conflicting opinion about "Forever Wild." With the exception of a perennial North Country political bloc, a united front arose against this proposed takeover by the Federal Government.

On August 1, the publication date of the Rockefeller National Park Plan, the Convention voted by a resounding 152–18 to retain "Forever Wild." An amendment that would have increased recreational facilities was voted down; phrasing was simplified without weakening the content.

Although the idea of a national park was rejected summarily, it nevertheless triggered a steadily growing consciousness of other explosions—population and pollution, the snowmobile, potential land-grabbing by large-scale developers—and the urgency of doing something about them.

To lay the groundwork, Governor Nelson Rockefeller appointed a Temporary Study Commission, chaired by Harold K. Hochschild (pp. 229, 312). In its preliminary report, "The Future of the Adirondacks," the Commission dealt with recommendations for the Preserve and included pioneering variations on an even touchier theme: the management of private land use within the Park.

This report led to the passage, on June 7, 1971, of the Adirondack Park Agency Bill. Under the chairmanship of Richard W. Lawrence, Jr. of Elizabethtown, the nine-member Agency created by this law was empowered to draw up, in one year, a plan recommending a diversity of uses for state-owned land; the plan would not be subject to legislative review.

The Agency was also instructed to produce, in two years, a plan for private land use, subject to passage by the Legislature and approval by the Governor. The Agency also was given, for the span of those two years, veto power over private land development in towns where subdivision and zoning regulations had not been in force prior to July 1, 1972.

Considering the amount of territory covered, and, moreover, the economies ordained by inadequate funding, the Agency's accomplishment in publishing "The Adirondack State Land Master Plan"—on June 1, 1972—was phenomenal. Phenomenal, too, was the absence of audible protests from preservationists, traditionally opposed (see p. 241) to zoning of any kind within the Preserve.

The Agency's plan designated five zones within the Preserve ranging from "Wilderness" through four other categories permitting varying extents of recreational facilities, all to be executed in a rustic style suited to the scenic beauty of the respective regions and within the constraints of Article XIV.

It may be assumed that the comparative silence of the preservationists resulted from their awareness of the critical need to protect the most ecologically sensitive areas of the Preserve from mounting pressures of campers, hikers, tourists, and snowmobile enthusiasts. And so, despite its paradoxical aspect, the plan, covering 2.27 million acres of state-owned land, was endorsed by the Governor and made state policy.

Nearly a year later, in May 1973, the Agency published its final recommendations, in "The Private Land Use and Development Plan." In this report it really trod on sacred ground by insisting on a new approach to the use of privately owned land within the Adirondack Park. It is not possible to outline this plan here in any detail, except to say that it delineated, in contrasting colors on a map of the Blue Line (pp. xii–xiii, 9–10), eleven categories, including those previously designated as Forest Preserve and six additional gradations applied to privately owned land. It indicated varying limits on buildings and, hence, population densities in the private section.*

The preservationists were pleased, but remained wary of loopholes; the opposition North Country bloc was outraged. Spearheaded by Assemblyman Glenn Harris (R.–Canada Lake, whose boast, "I will fight this legislation to the bitter end,"

* Agency publications may be consulted at Adirondack Park Agency, Ray Brook, New York, the William Chapman White Memorial Adirondack Room of the Saranac Lake Free Library, and other state and regional libraries.

was homing-pigeoned to his constituency); supported by the editor and publisher of the only daily newspaper in the Adirondacks; echoed in private meetings and sidewalk debates, the cries of "elitism," "invasion of property rights," "excessive government regulation," "impeachment" (for the Governor), and "abolishment" (of the APA) reverberated throughout the North Country.

Nonetheless, in spite of the furor created by public hearings, injunctions, and legislative delaying tactics, the APA's Private Land Use and Development Bill, providing control over all "environmentally significant projects," had so much to recommend it that it was passed by the Legislature. Modified by compromises the state had traded for the acquiescence of North Country politicians, it was signed into law by the Governor on May 23, 1973, to take effect August 1. In ceremonies appropriate to the signing of such a significant document, Governor Rockefeller proclaimed: "The Adirondacks are preserved forever."

Alert North Country observers, however, were not convinced that prospects were quite that rosy. It was undeniably a restrictive and ecologically aware plan, one setting a bold precedent in conservation history, that had been written into the law of New York State; but thus far it was only a plan.

Since then, its principles have been implemented by various rules and regulations; but conflicting viewpoints and ambiguities still exist on vital issues, and the typical Adirondacker—like the traditional Adirondack guide—is not readily amenable to "Down Staters" telling him what he may or may not do with his land. Others find it convenient to distort issues remaining to be resolved by the APA in consultation with local governments, on the basis of worldwide economic and political uncertainties that appear to have reduced to relative insignificance any concern over the ecology of any given region.

Meanwhile, the Department of Environmental Conservation holds its mandate to administer the state-owned land within the Forest Preserve, as well as to deal with certain pollution and health problems in the private sector. At the same time, it endeavors to educate a new generation in the proper use of and respect for the woods—a formidable assignment.

Coloring these complexities with a less than roseate glow looms the uncomfortable knowledge that the APA is an appointive body, the character of its membership subject to the discretion and integrity of successive Governors. The future still demands vigilance on the part of those conservationist groups (pp. 241, 325) which have defended the Adirondacks in the past.* Even now, in and around this mountain village, threats are heard of impending lawsuits seeking to prove that APA regulation of private land use is unconstitutional. The plaintiffs and their supporters ignore the fact that many of the economic and social ills besetting the Adirondacks are nationwide, rather than local, in character. They overlook the basic reality that the unique quality which draws residents, tourists, and health and research institutions, to the economic benefit of the Adirondack Country, is its heritage of unsurpassed beauty; if the much-to-be-desired growth of the region's economy is not interlinked with an imperative protection of its ecology, then both are doomed.

R. M. W.
Saranac Lake, New York

November 1974

---

* Preservationist materials may be obtained from the organizations mentioned in the foregoing pages.

◄§ Sources and Acknowledgments

No one can write on Adirondack history to 1920 without acknowledging a debt to Alfred L. Donaldson and his *A History of the Adirondacks*. I have not only used his book as a guide but I have been able to go back to many of his original sources. Thanks to his generosity they are preserved in the Saranac Lake Free Library and are listed in his bibliography. To them the Library has added, since his death, the Munson collection of Adirondackana and a superb collection of old maps, making the finest collection of Adirondack materials extant. I have made the fullest use of everything in that collection, particularly the many rare pamphlets and newspaper clippings.

I have also used the complete file of *Forest and Stream* from its first issue in 1873; the many publications of the New York State Department of Conservation, particularly the magazine *Conservationist;* issues of the excellent regional magazines *North Country Life* and the *Living Wilderness;* the *Ad-i-ron-dac,* the bulletin of the Adirondack Mountain Club; Harold K. Hochschild's superb volume *Township 34,* on the Blue Mountain Lake area; and Mildred P. Stokes Hooker's memoirs of Upper Saint Regis Lake.

I have been fortunate in being permitted by John B. Johnson, publisher of the *Watertown Times,* to use without limit the tremendous amount of North Country material in the files and morgue of his paper and particularly in the diaries of his father, the late Harold B. Johnson. I am indebted to Harry F. Landon, editor of that paper, for many suggestions on source materials and to J. Reese Price, curator of the Jefferson County Historical Society, and Mrs. D. F. White of Philadelphia, Pennsylvania, for help with the Bonaparte-Benton story.

Many individuals have shared generously their knowledge in specific fields, including Norman Fee and T. E. Layng of the Dominion Archives at Ottawa, Canada; Dr. William A. Ritchie, New York State archaeologist; Dr. John G. Broughton, New York State geologist; Dr. J. J. Prucha, senior geologist; Al Davis, state surveyor; P. W. Fosburgh, editor of *Conservationist;* Justin T. Mahoney, director of the Division of Fish and Game of the New York State Department of Conservation; Miss Marjorie G. Smith, librarian of the Trudeau Foundation; William E. Petty, district forester; Dr. Gordon M. Meade, executive director of the Trudeau-Saranac Institute; Mrs. J. Halsey Gulick of South Casco, Maine; Thomas Hart Benton of Kansas City, Missouri; and George Marshall of New York City.

Much that is in this book has come from the memories of guides, campers, physicians, and just plain Adirondack people. Collectively, they know more about the Adirondack country than any one man could ever learn from printed sources. The breadth of their knowledge is matched only by their generosity in sharing it.

I am deeply indebted to Mrs. Ruth D. Worthington, librarian of the Saranac Lake Free Library, whose selfless and clockless generosity, too often taken for granted in librarians, helped to track down many an elusive page or fact.

I wish to thank the publishers of the *New York Herald Tribune,* the *New York Times* and the *Saturday Evening Post* for permission to use material that has appeared earlier in their columns.

W. C. W.

Index

INDEX

iv

A NOTE ABOUT THE AUTHOR

WILLIAM CHAPMAN WHITE was perhaps best known as a columnist for *The New York Times* and the *New York Herald Tribune.* A collection of his columns for these papers, *Just About Everything in the Adirondacks* was published in 1960; and quotations from his work accompany the color plates by Eliot Porter in *Forever Wild: The Adirondacks* (1966). Mr. White, who was the author of numerous books, was born in Reading, Pennsylvania, in 1903, educated at Princeton, the University of Pennsylvania, and as a Penfield scholar at the University of Moscow. He was a foreign correspondent in the 1930's, served with the Office of War Information, and after the war made his home in New York City and Saranac Lake in the Adirondacks. Mr. White died in 1955, shortly after the first publication of *Adirondack Country.*